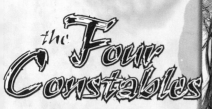

# the Four Constables

**THE FOUR CONSTABLES ARE MEMORABLE NOT ONLY FOR THEIR LAUDABLE STRUGGLE AGAINST EVIL, BUT FOR THE STRONG FRIENDSHIP AND CAMARADERIE THEY SHARED AS WELL.**

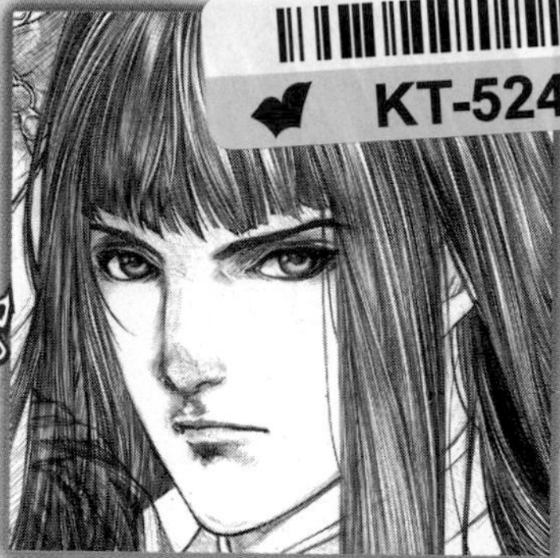

"EMOTIONLESS"
YAYU SHENG

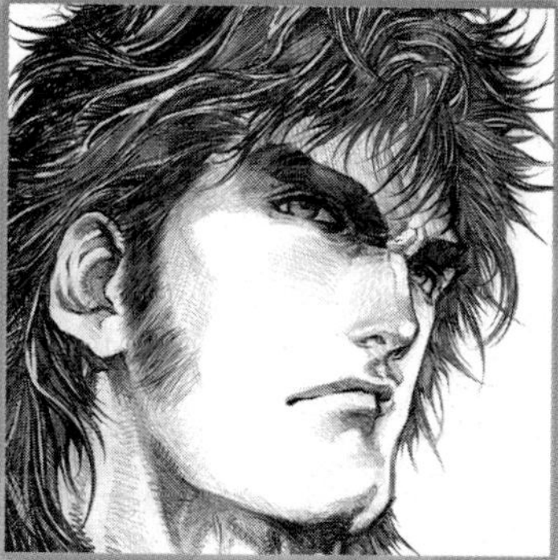

"IRON HANDS"
YUXIA TIE

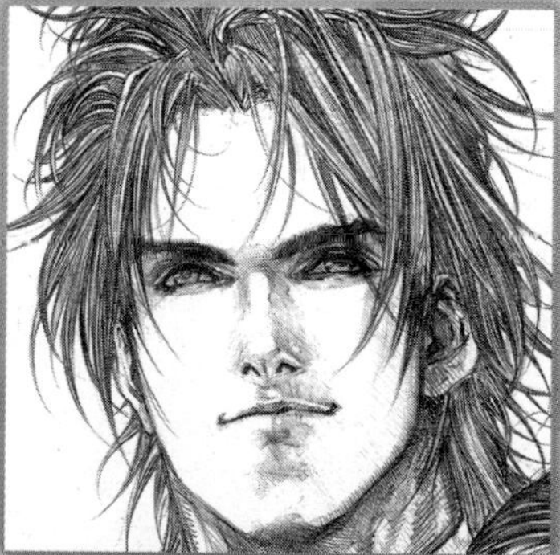

"LIFE SNATCHER"
LIESHAN CUI

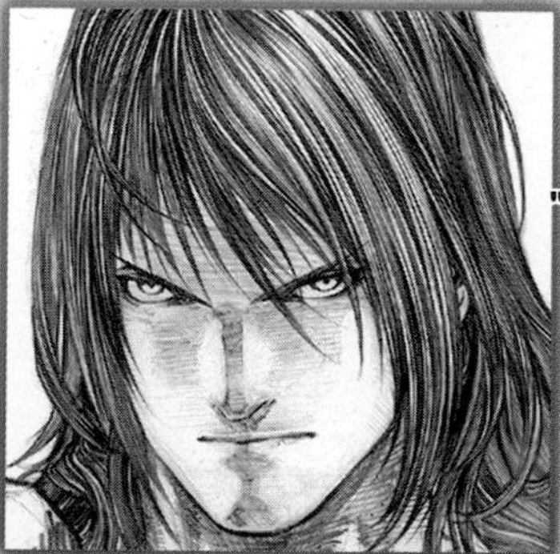

"COLD BLOODED"
LINGQI LEN

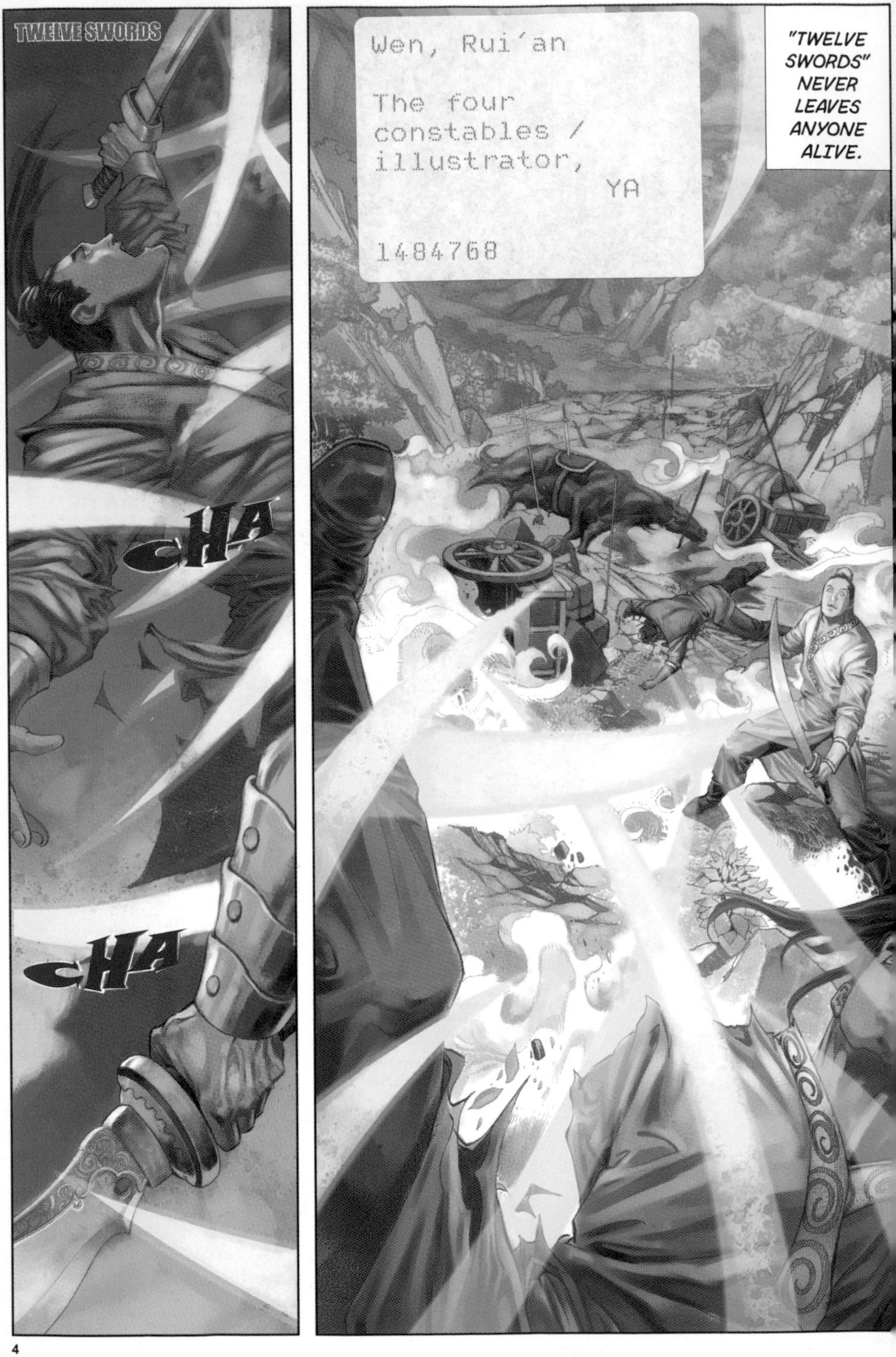
CHA
CHA
"TWELVE SWORDS" NEVER LEAVES ANYONE ALIVE.

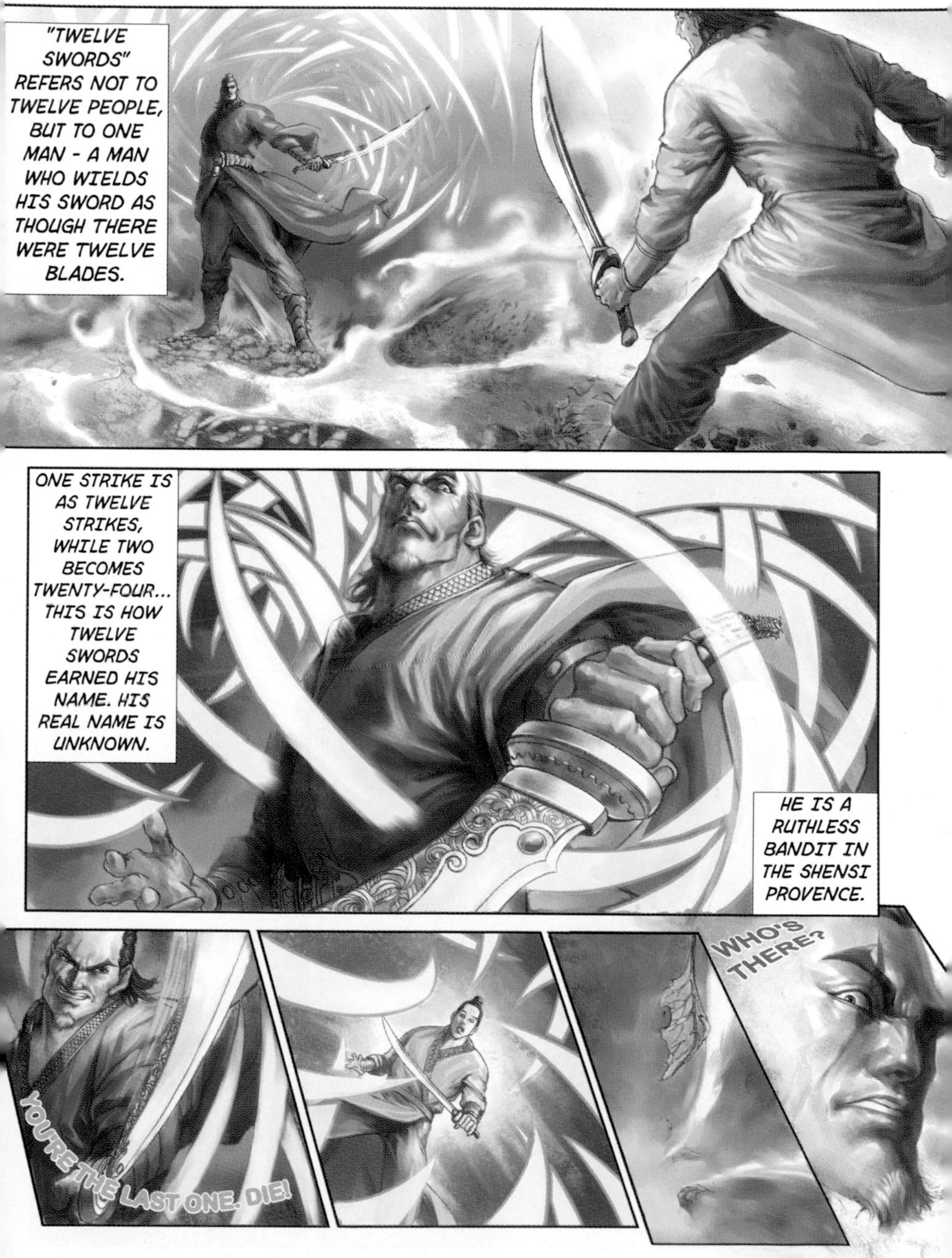
"TWELVE SWORDS" REFERS NOT TO TWELVE PEOPLE, BUT TO ONE MAN - A MAN WHO WIELDS HIS SWORD AS THOUGH THERE WERE TWELVE BLADES.
ONE STRIKE IS AS TWELVE STRIKES, WHILE TWO BECOMES TWENTY-FOUR... THIS IS HOW TWELVE SWORDS EARNED HIS NAME. HIS REAL NAME IS UNKNOWN.
HE IS A RUTHLESS BANDIT IN THE SHENSI PROVENCE.
YOU'RE THE LAST ONE. DIE!
WHO'S THERE?

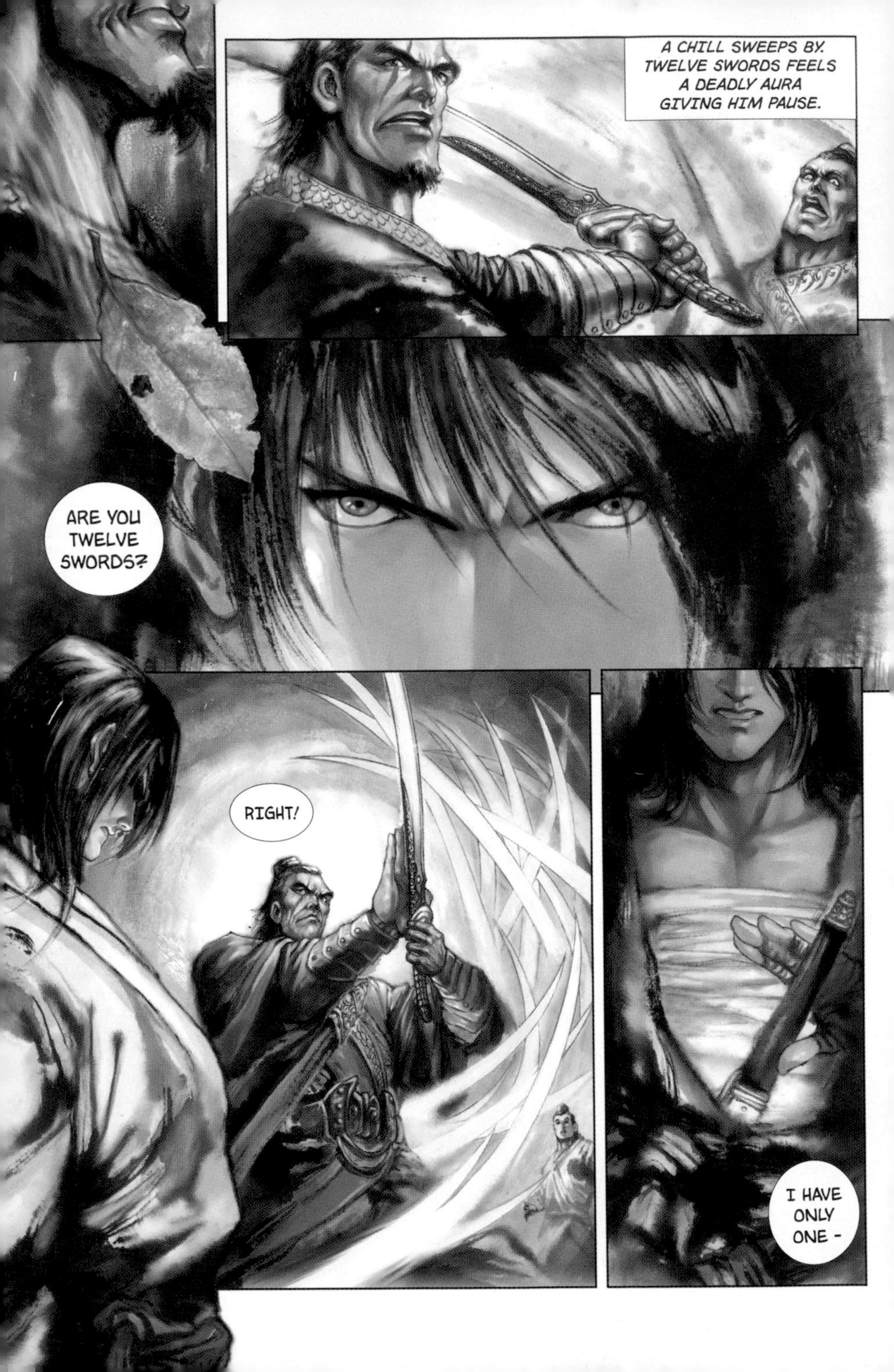
A CHILL SWEEPS BY. TWELVE SWORDS FEELS A DEADLY AURA GIVING HIM PAUSE.
ARE YOU TWELVE SWORDS?
RIGHT!
I HAVE ONLY ONE -

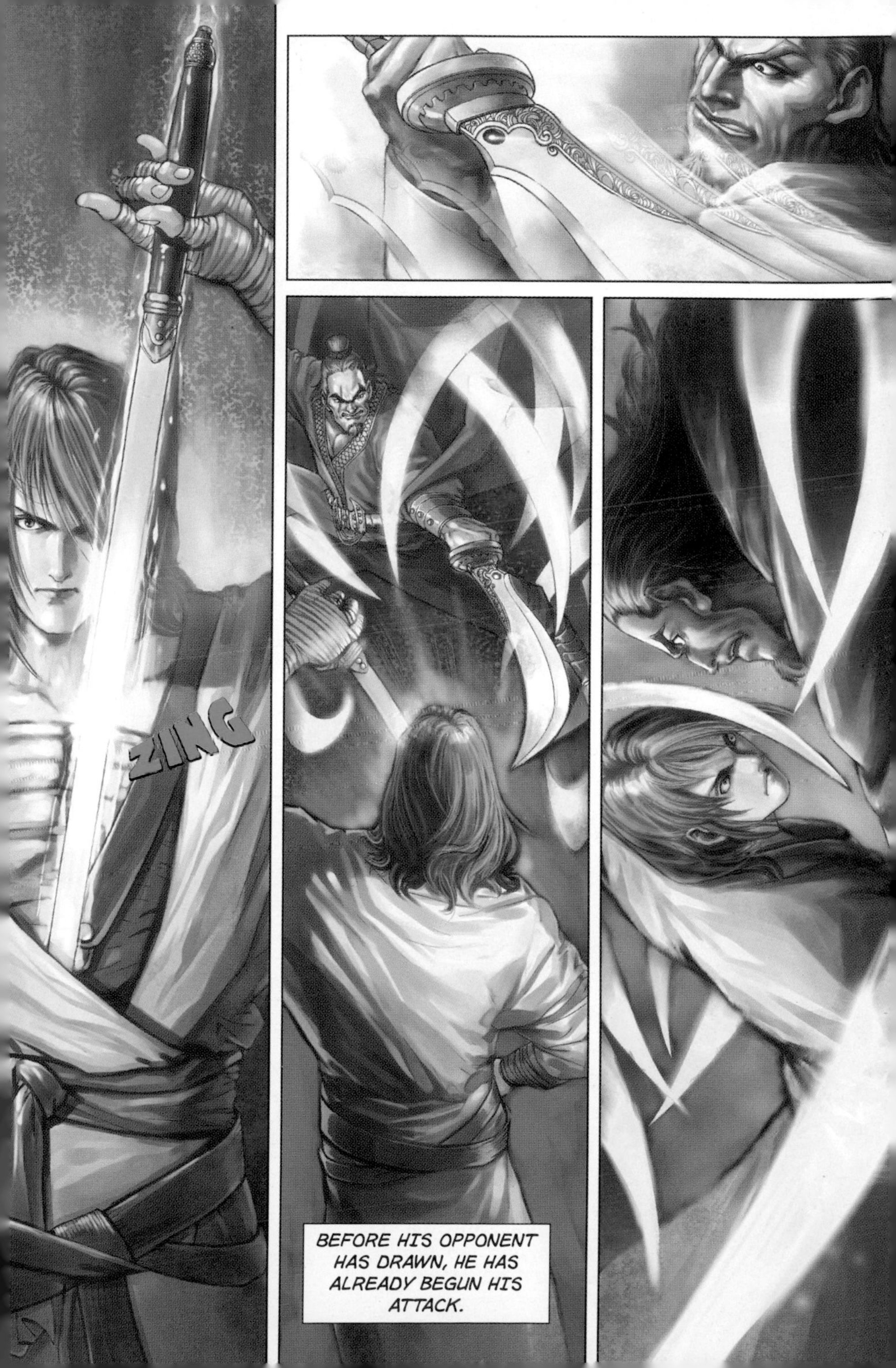
ZING
BEFORE HIS OPPONENT HAS DRAWN, HE HAS ALREADY BEGUN HIS ATTACK.

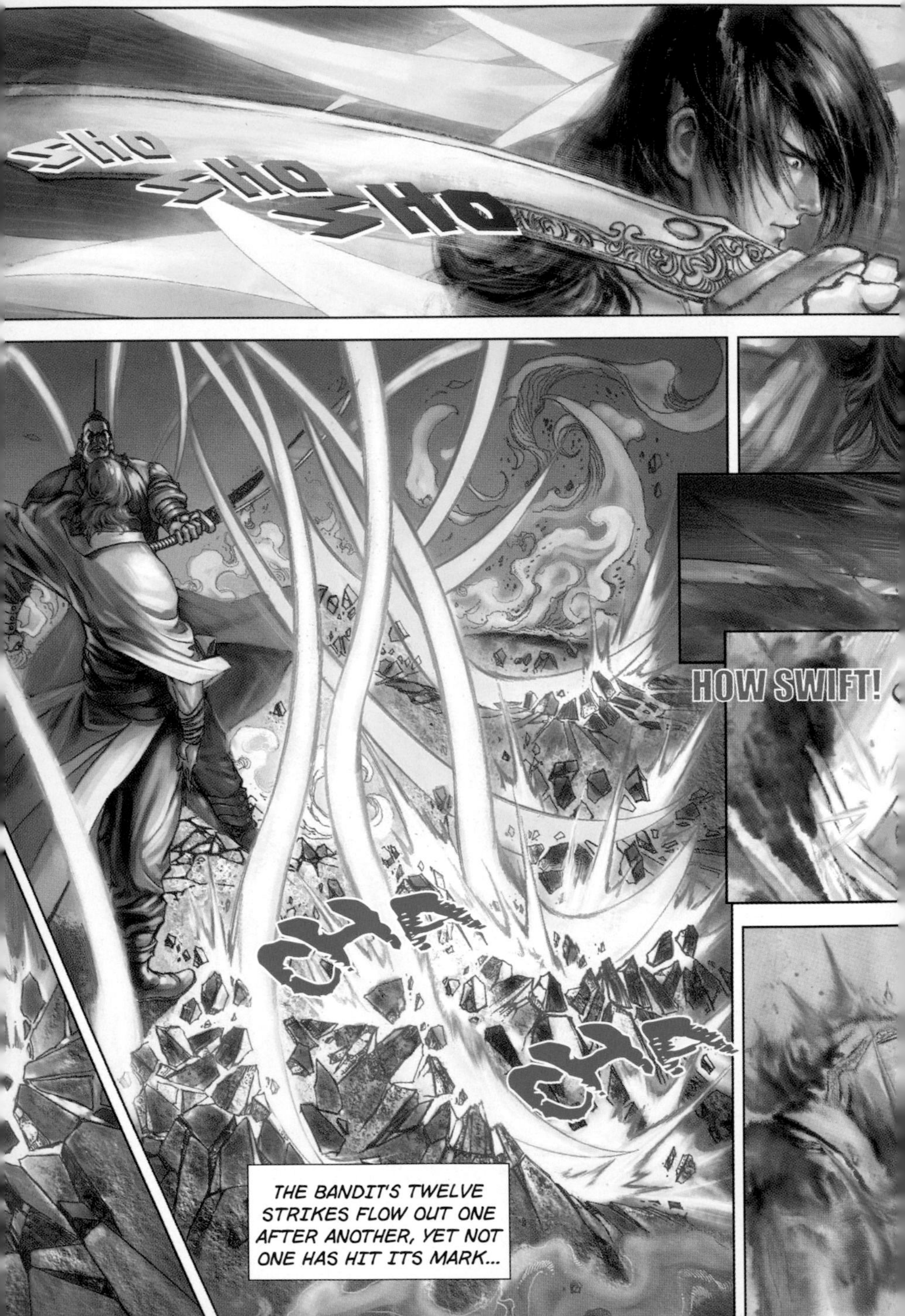
SHO SHO SHO
HOW SWIFT!
THE BANDIT'S TWELVE STRIKES FLOW OUT ONE AFTER ANOTHER, YET NOT ONE HAS HIT ITS MARK...

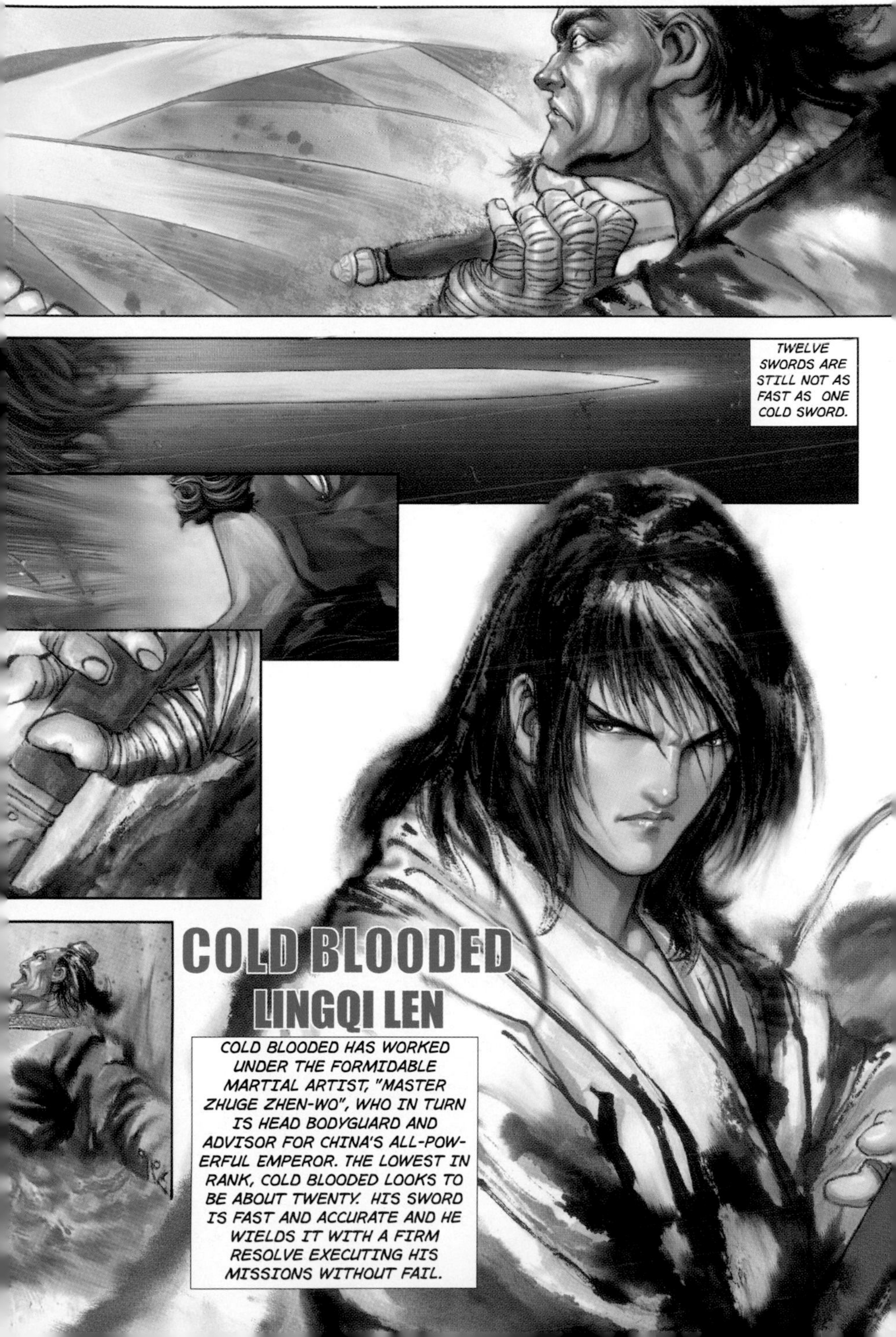
TWELVE SWORDS ARE STILL NOT AS FAST AS ONE COLD SWORD.
COLD BLOODED
LINGQI LEN
COLD BLOODED HAS WORKED UNDER THE FORMIDABLE MARTIAL ARTIST, "MASTER ZHUGE ZHEN-WO", WHO IN TURN IS HEAD BODYGUARD AND ADVISOR FOR CHINA'S ALL-POWERFUL EMPEROR. THE LOWEST IN RANK, COLD BLOODED LOOKS TO BE ABOUT TWENTY. HIS SWORD IS FAST AND ACCURATE AND HE WIELDS IT WITH A FIRM RESOLVE EXECUTING HIS MISSIONS WITHOUT FAIL.

LIFE SNATCHER - SNATCHER OF LIVES, ESPECIALLY THOSE DESERVING OF DEATH.

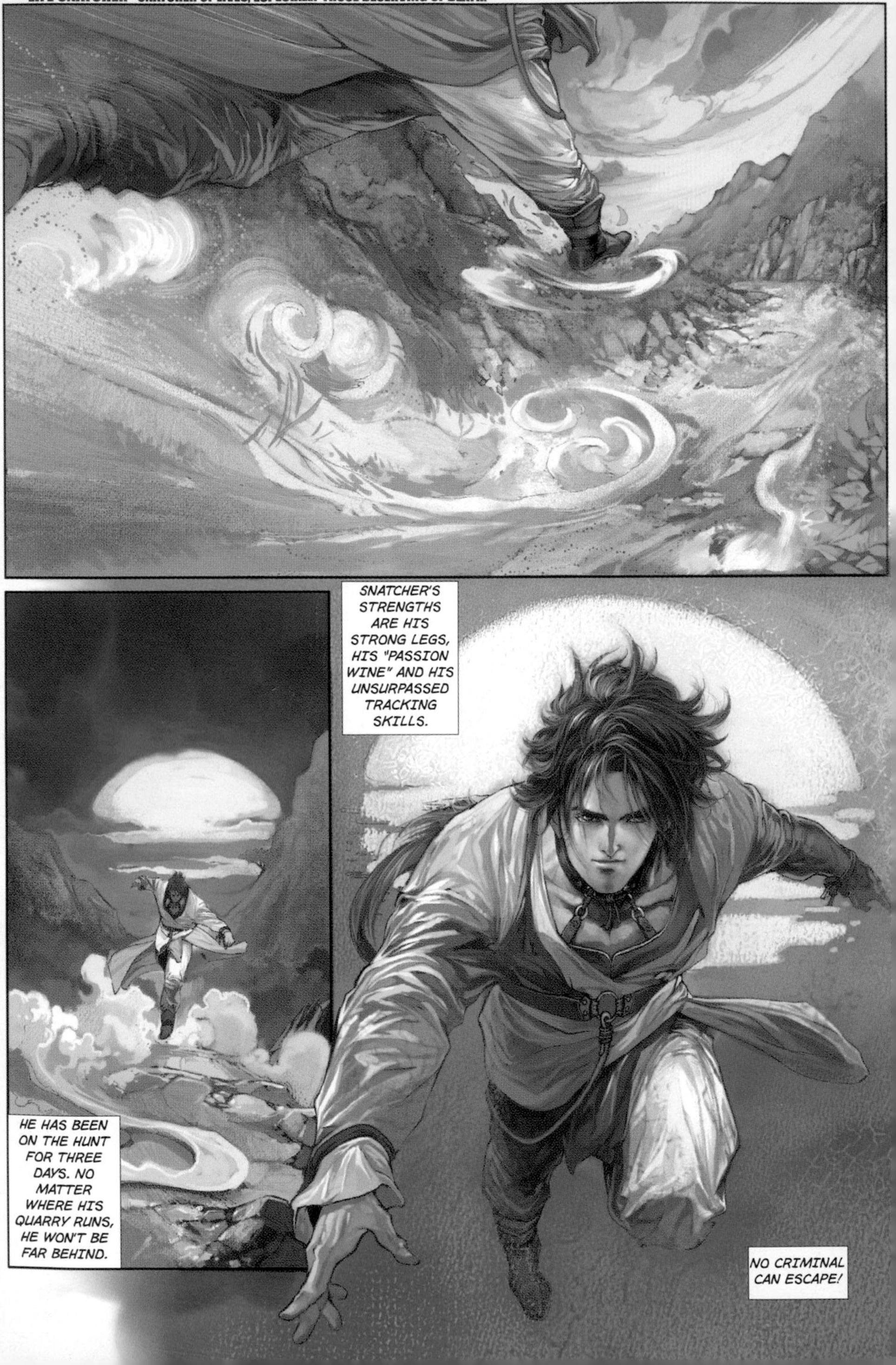

SNATCHER'S STRENGTHS ARE HIS STRONG LEGS, HIS "PASSION WINE" AND HIS UNSURPASSED TRACKING SKILLS.
HE HAS BEEN ON THE HUNT FOR THREE DAYS. NO MATTER WHERE HIS QUARRY RUNS, HE WON'T BE FAR BEHIND.
NO CRIMINAL CAN ESCAPE!

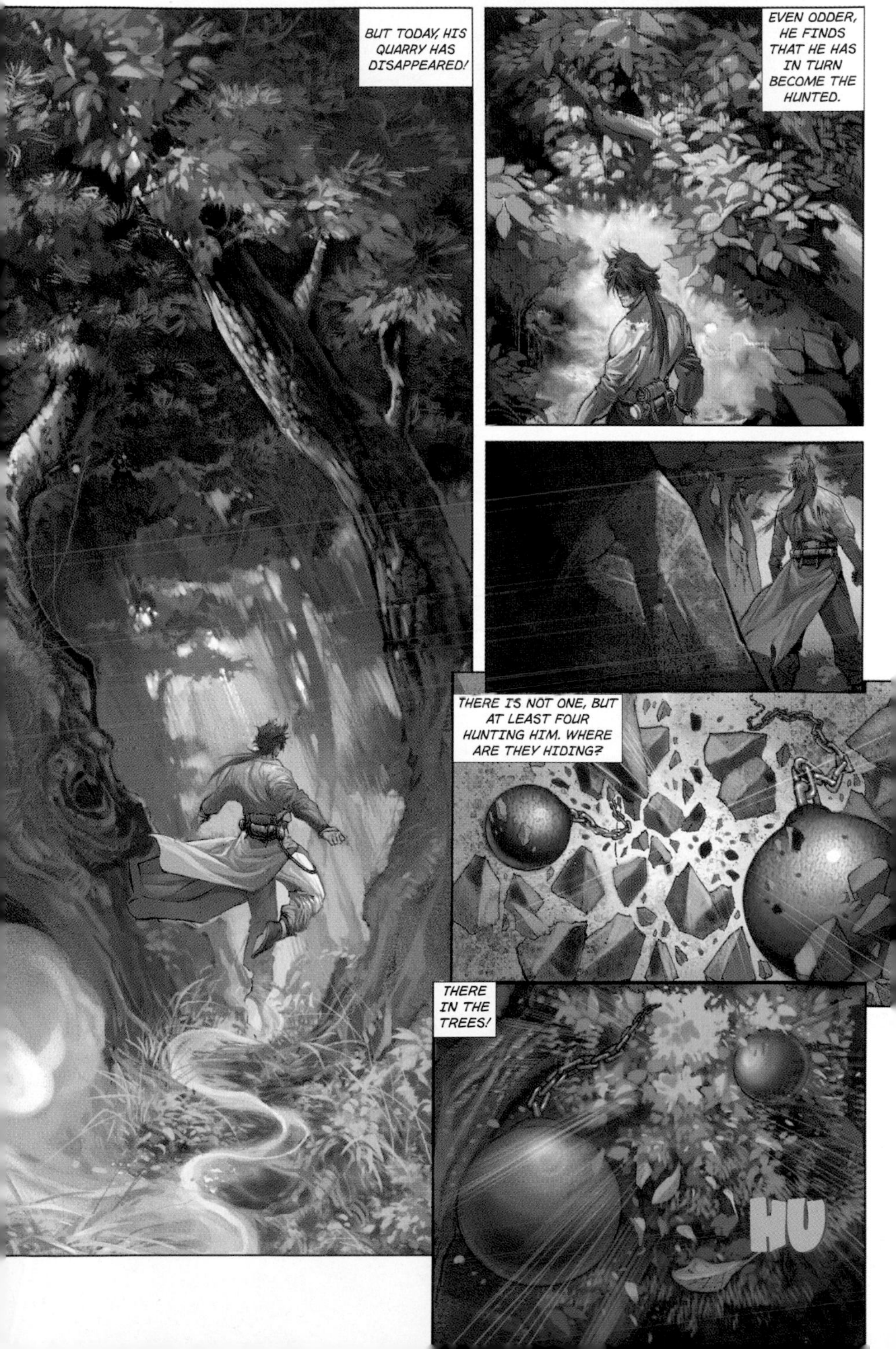
BUT TODAY, HIS QUARRY HAS DISAPPEARED!
EVEN ODDER, HE FINDS THAT HE HAS IN TURN BECOME THE HUNTED.
THERE IS NOT ONE, BUT AT LEAST FOUR HUNTING HIM. WHERE ARE THEY HIDING?
THERE IN THE TREES!
HU

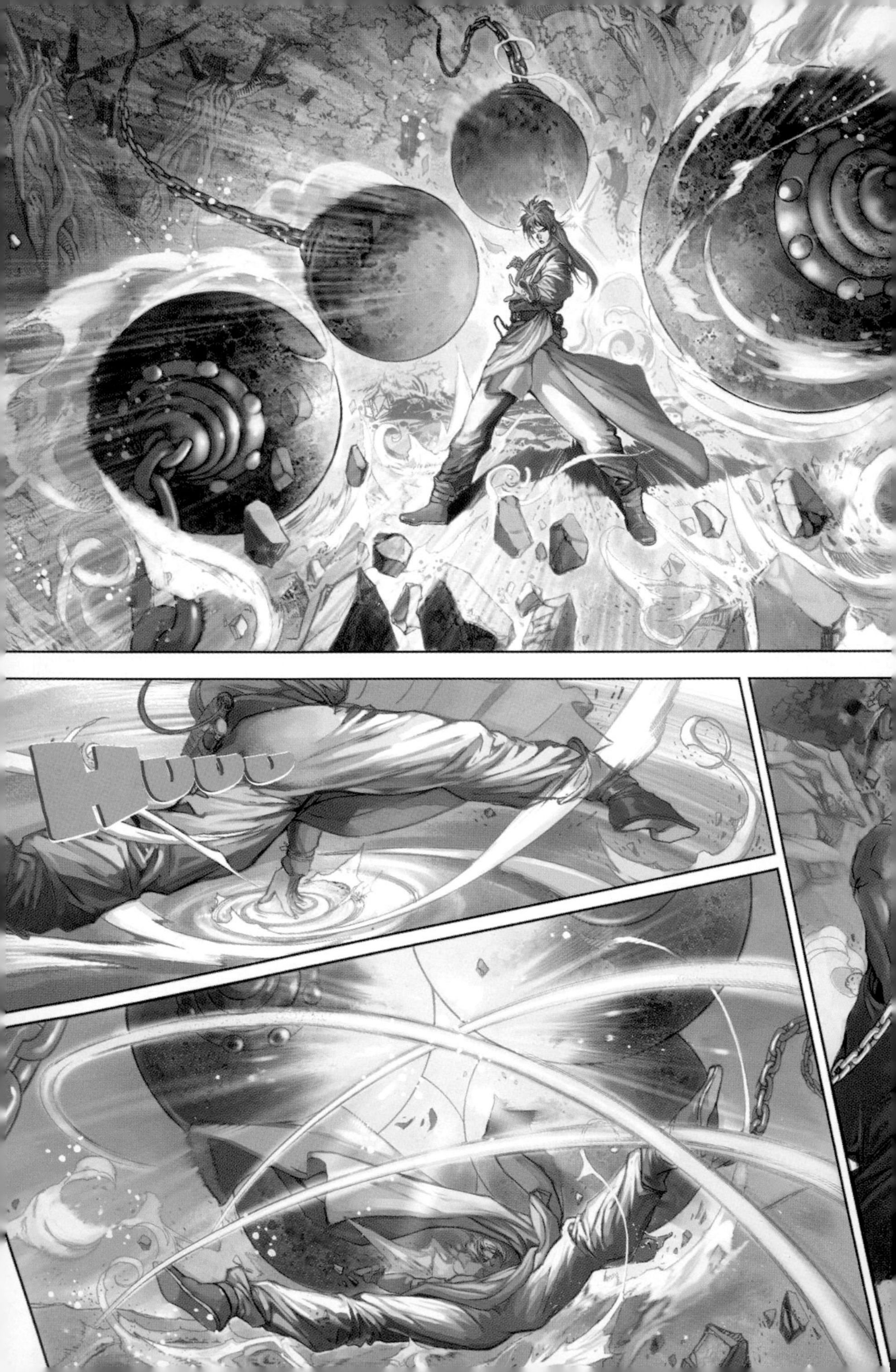
HUUU

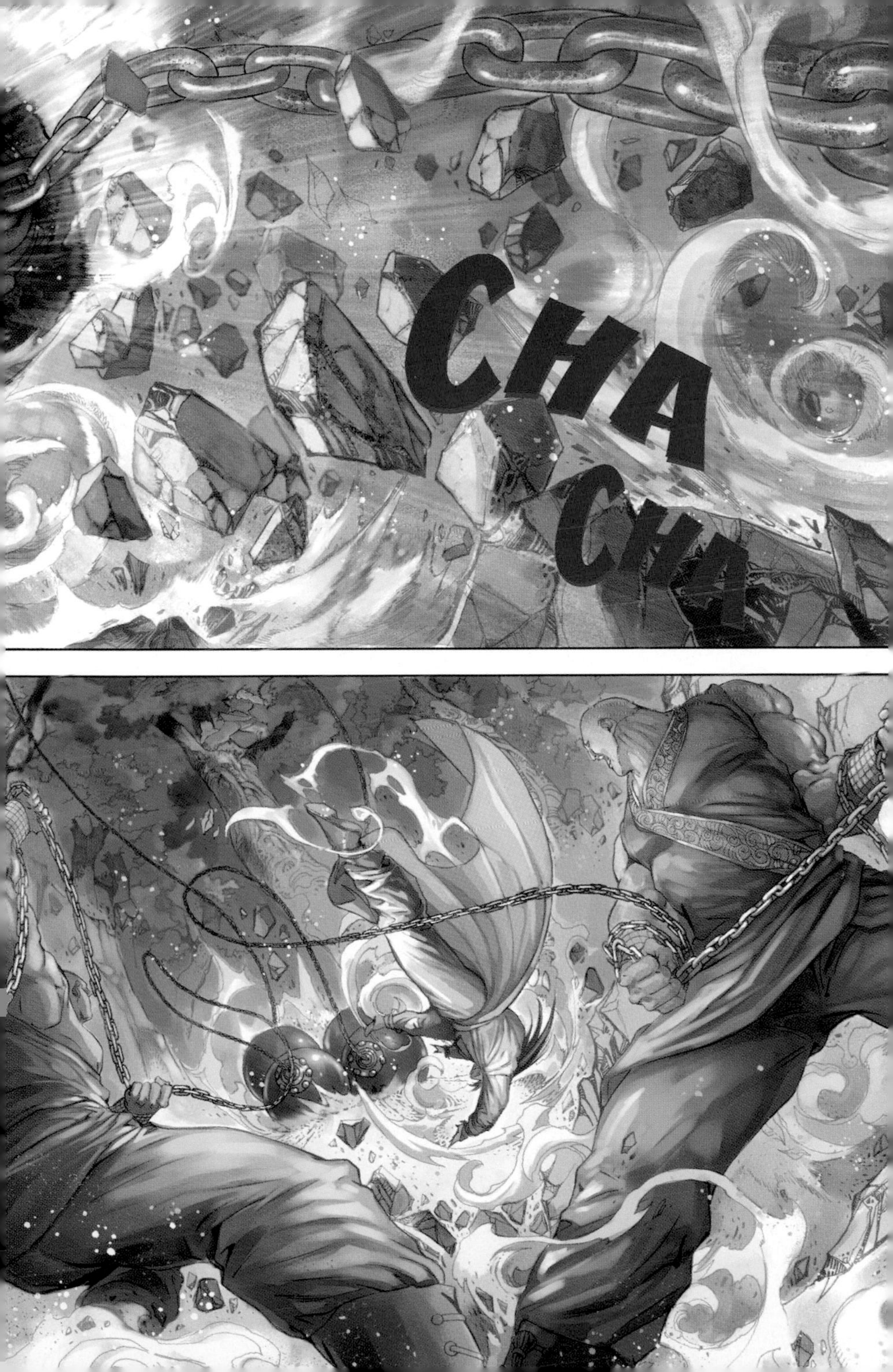
CHA
CHA

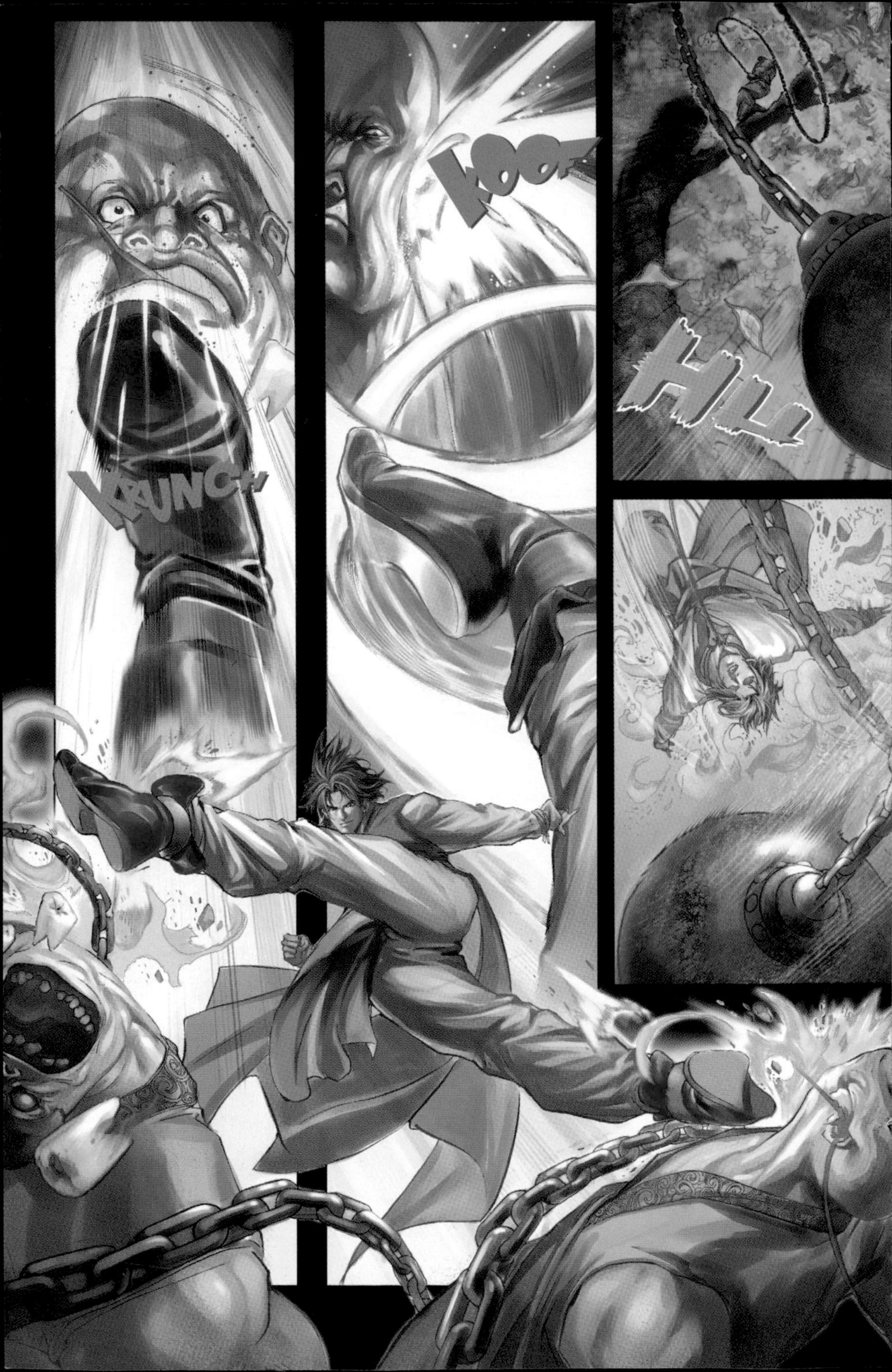
KRUNCH
KOOF
HU

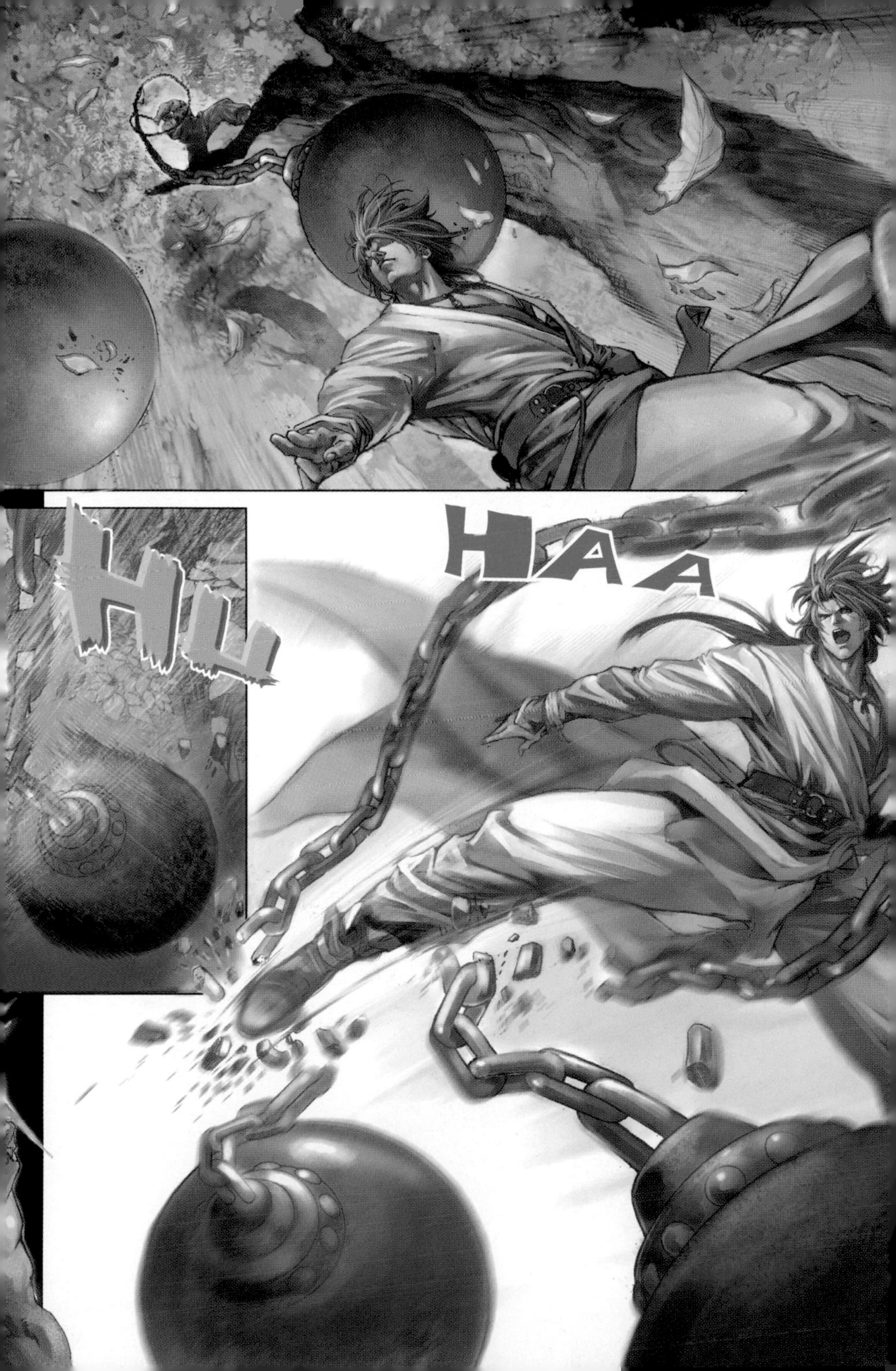
HU
HAA

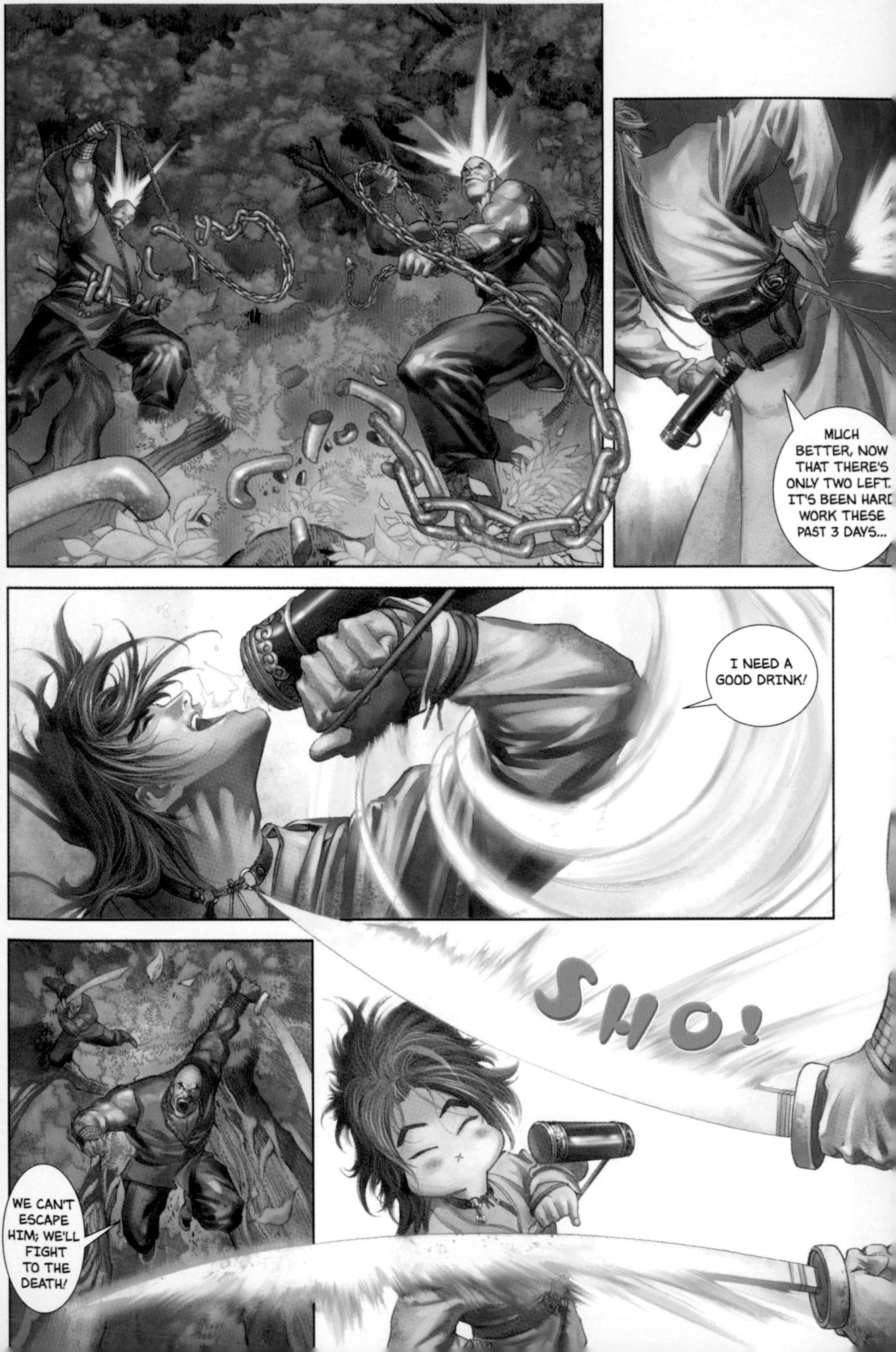
MUCH BETTER, NOW THAT THERE'S ONLY TWO LEFT. IT'S BEEN HARD WORK THESE PAST 3 DAYS...
I NEED A GOOD DRINK!
SHO!
WE CAN'T ESCAPE HIM; WE'LL FIGHT TO THE DEATH!

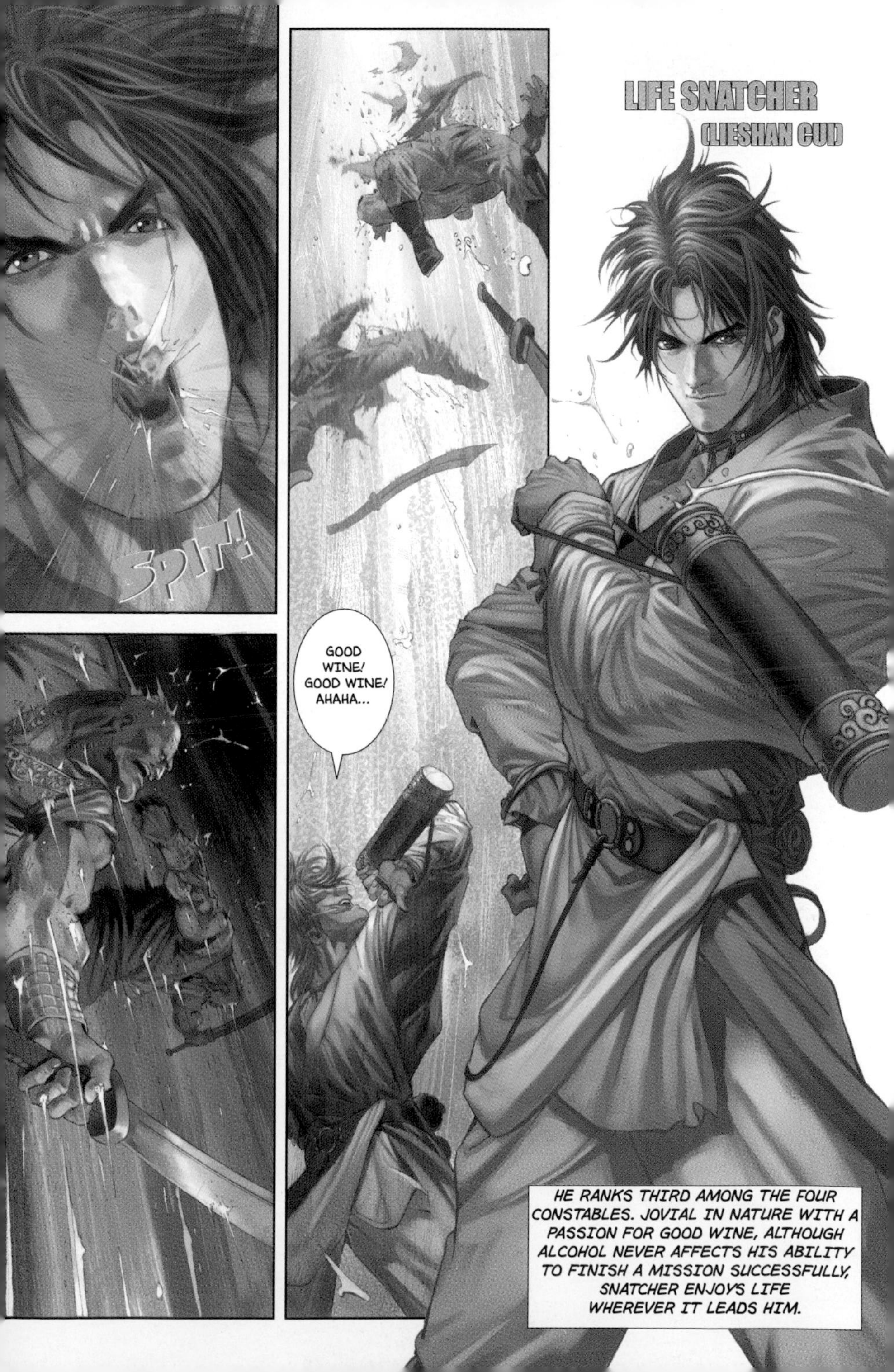

SPIT!
LIFE SNATCHER
(LIESHAN CUI)
GOOD WINE! GOOD WINE! AHAHA...
HE RANKS THIRD AMONG THE FOUR CONSTABLES. JOVIAL IN NATURE WITH A PASSION FOR GOOD WINE, ALTHOUGH ALCOHOL NEVER AFFECTS HIS ABILITY TO FINISH A MISSION SUCCESSFULLY, SNATCHER ENJOYS LIFE WHEREVER IT LEADS HIM.

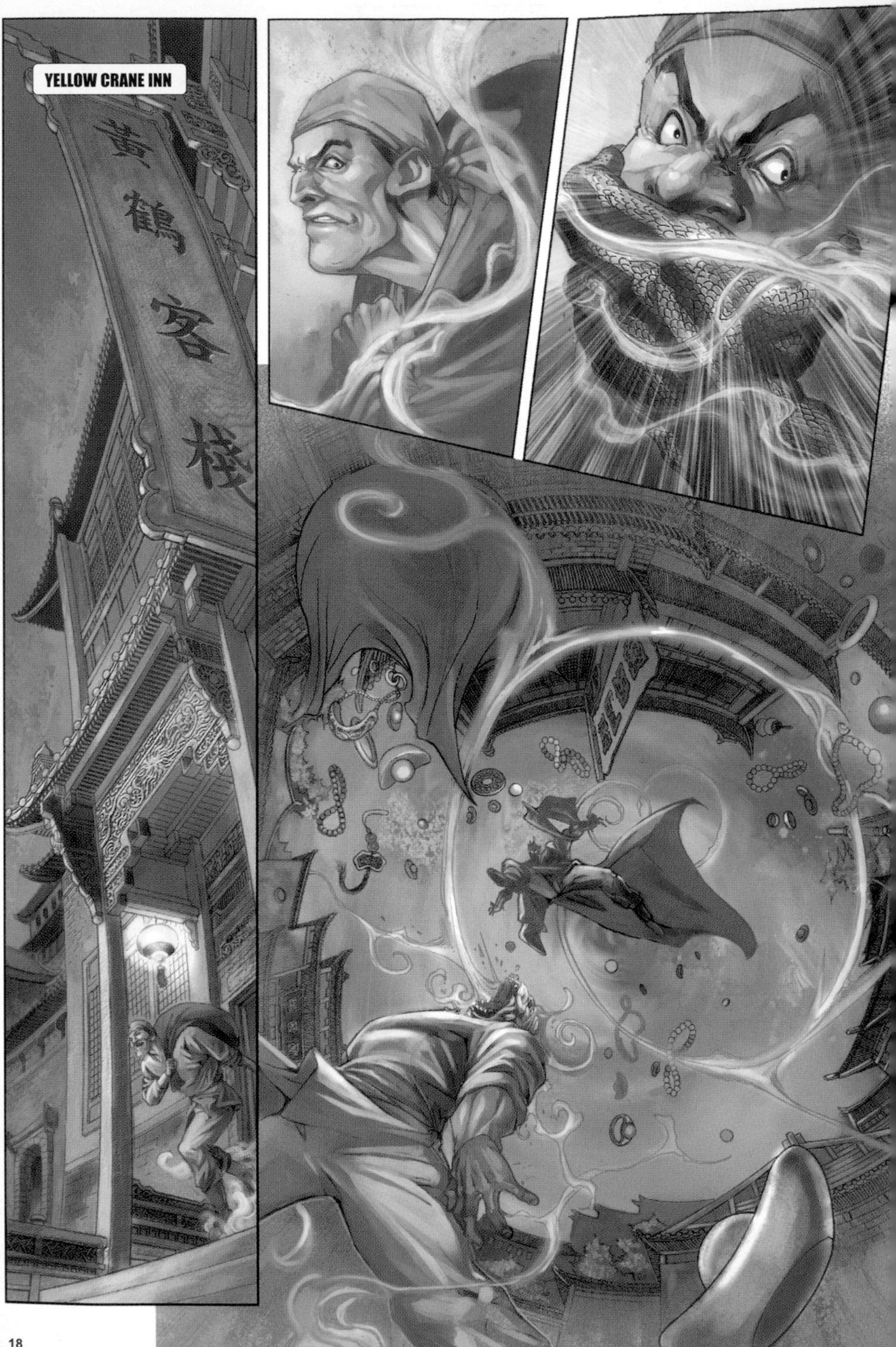
YELLOW CRANE INN
黃鶴客棧

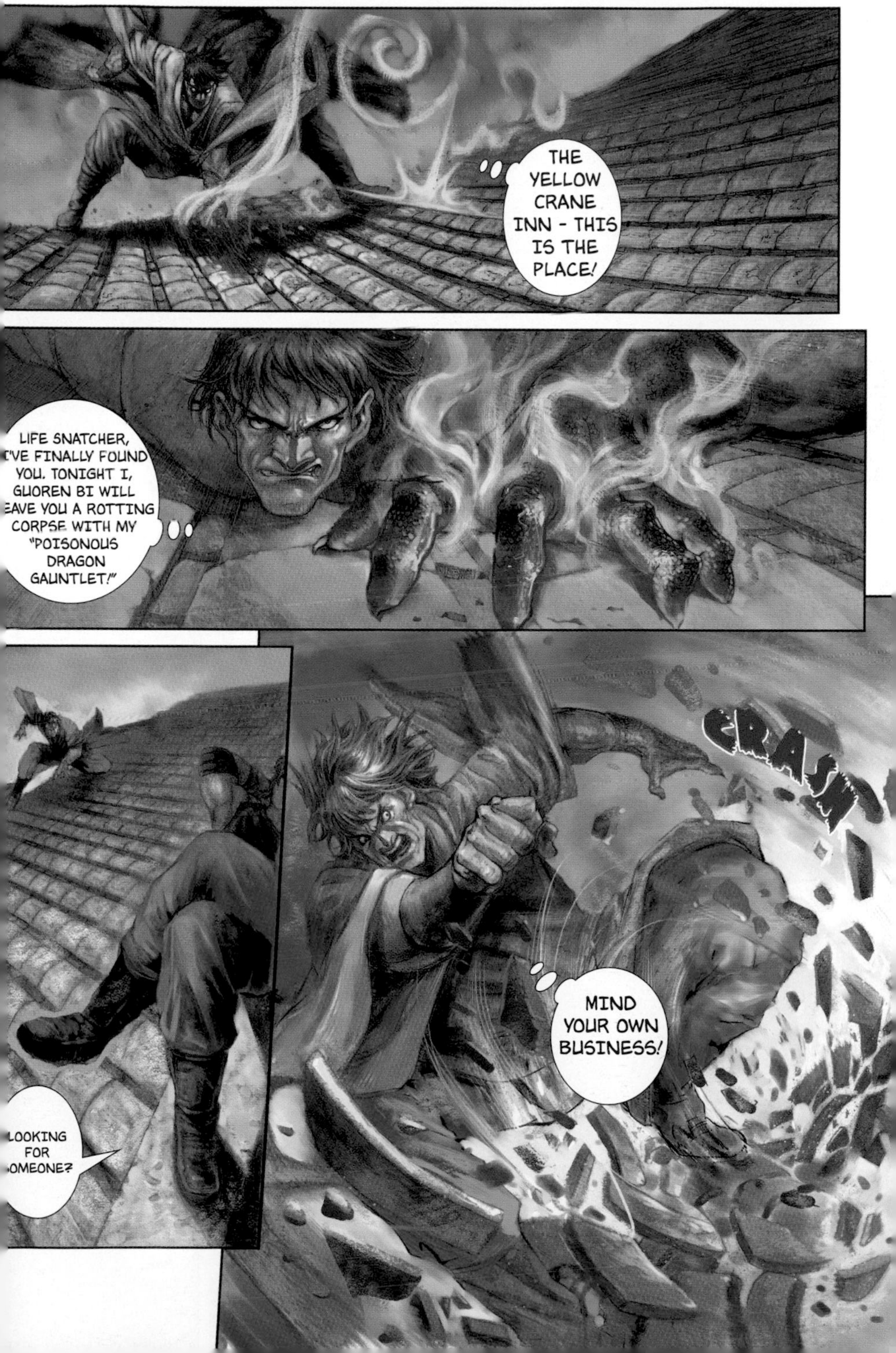
THE YELLOW CRANE INN - THIS IS THE PLACE!
LIFE SNATCHER, I'VE FINALLY FOUND YOU. TONIGHT I, GUOREN BI WILL LEAVE YOU A ROTTING CORPSE WITH MY "POISONOUS DRAGON GAUNTLET!"
CRASH
MIND YOUR OWN BUSINESS!
LOOKING FOR SOMEONE?

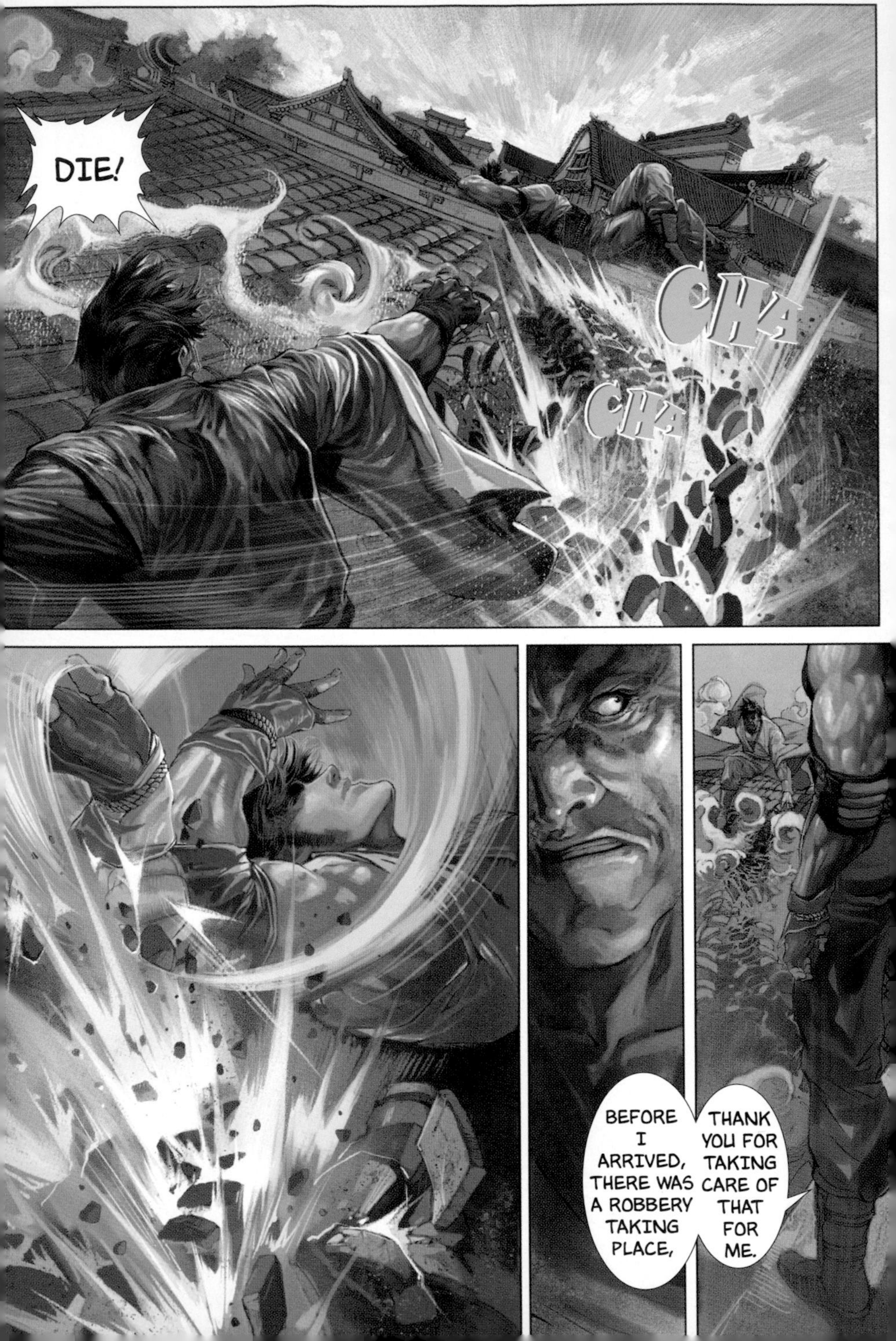
DIE!
CHA
CHA
BEFORE I ARRIVED, THERE WAS A ROBBERY TAKING PLACE,
THANK YOU FOR TAKING CARE OF THAT FOR ME.

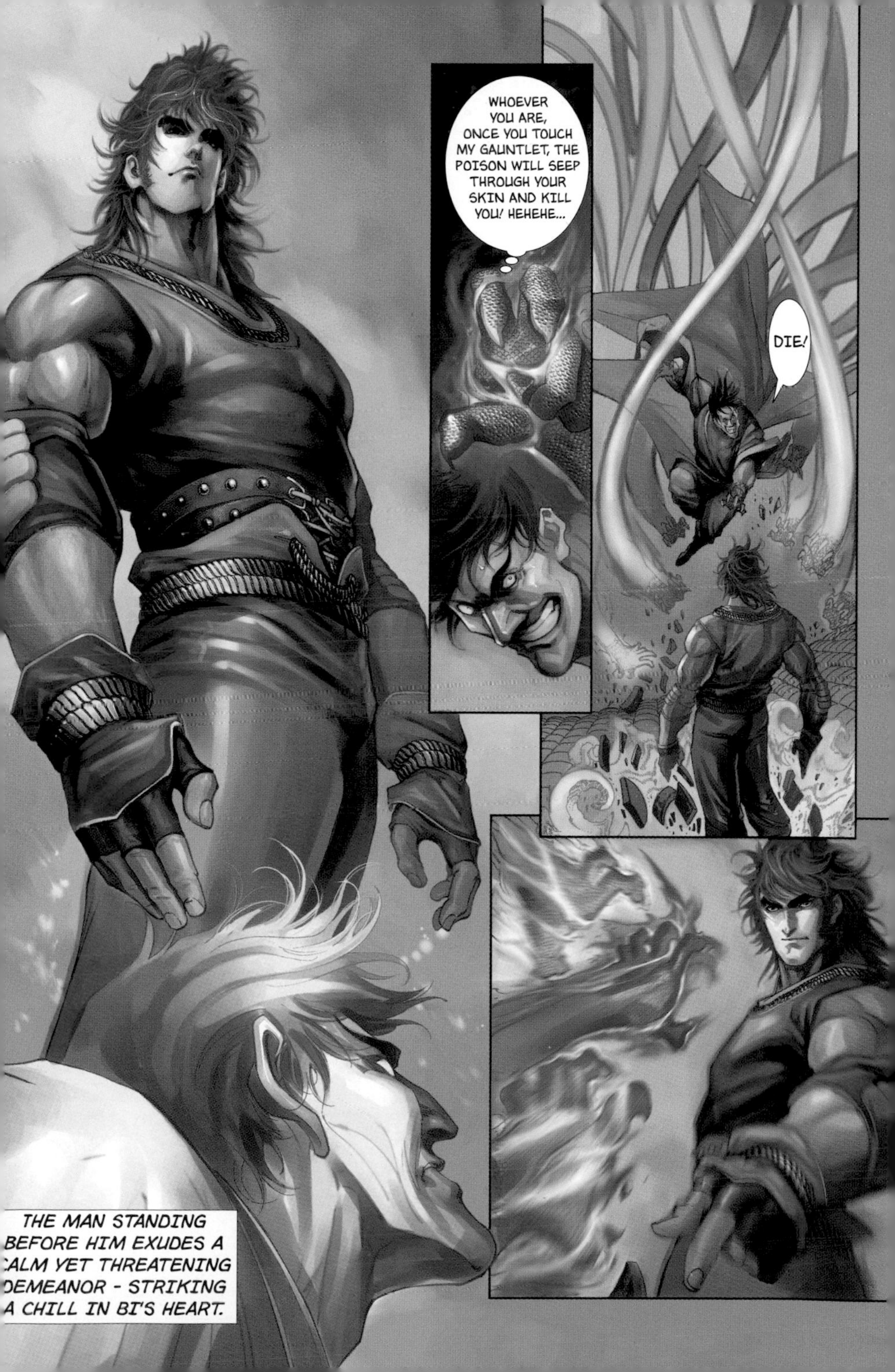
WHOEVER YOU ARE, ONCE YOU TOUCH MY GAUNTLET, THE POISON WILL SEEP THROUGH YOUR SKIN AND KILL YOU! HEHEHE...
DIE!
THE MAN STANDING BEFORE HIM EXUDES A CALM YET THREATENING DEMEANOR - STRIKING A CHILL IN BI'S HEART.

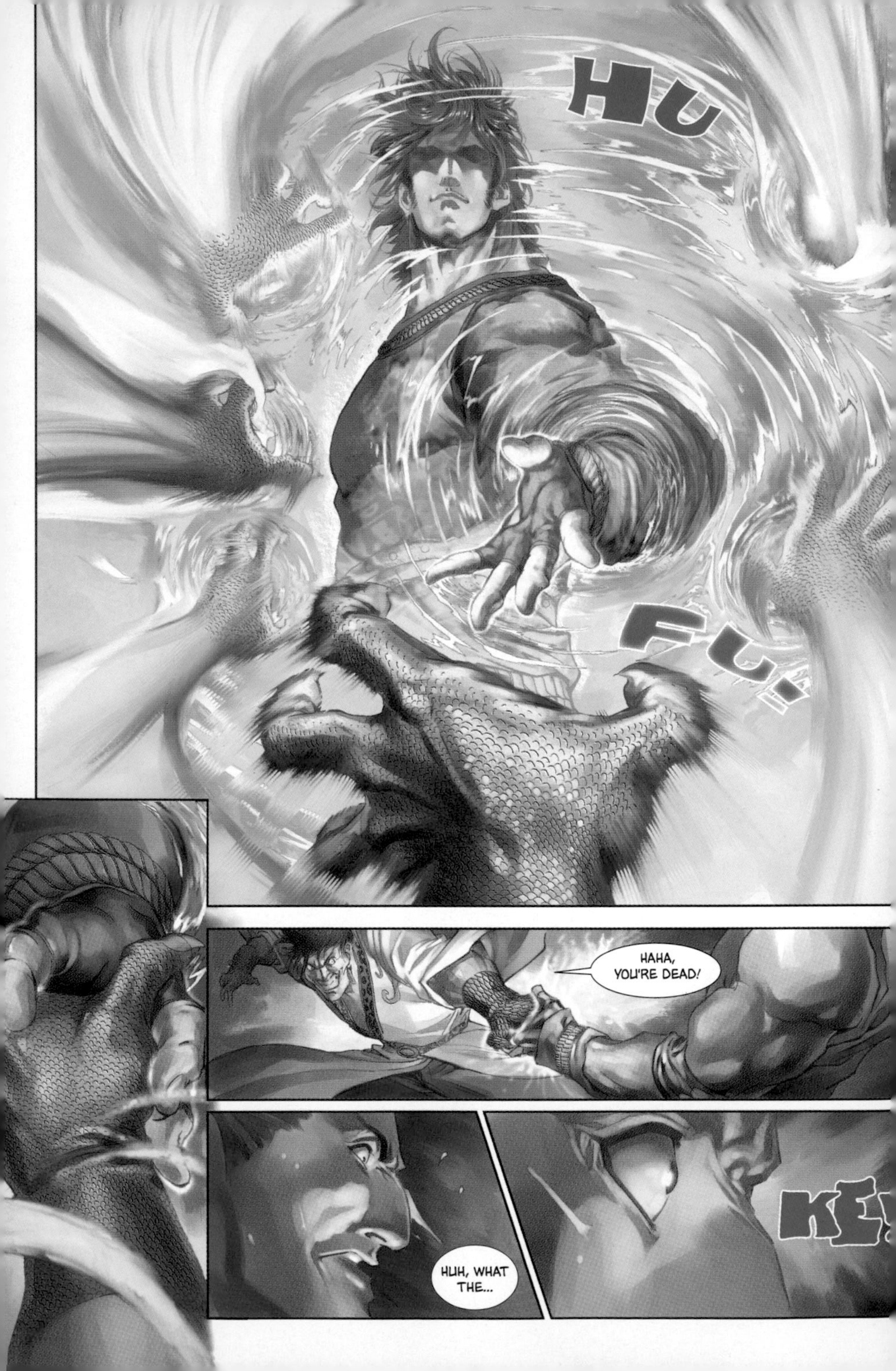
HU
FU!
HAHA, YOU'RE DEAD!
HUH, WHAT THE...
KE!

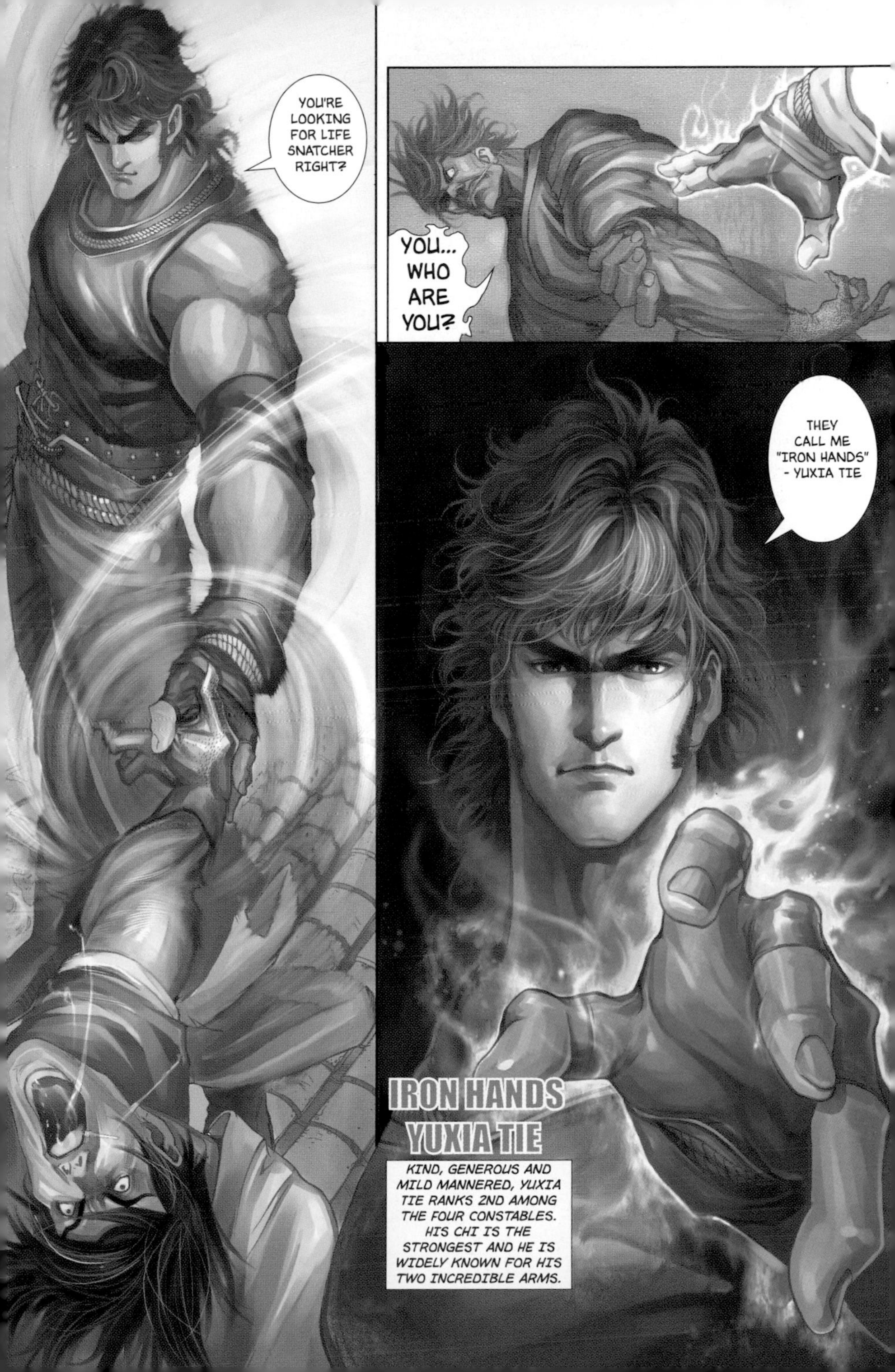
YOU'RE LOOKING FOR LIFE SNATCHER RIGHT?
YOU... WHO ARE YOU?
THEY CALL ME "IRON HANDS" - YUXIA TIE
IRON HANDS YUXIA TIE
KIND, GENEROUS AND MILD MANNERED, YUXIA TIE RANKS 2ND AMONG THE FOUR CONSTABLES. HIS CHI IS THE STRONGEST AND HE IS WIDELY KNOWN FOR HIS TWO INCREDIBLE ARMS.

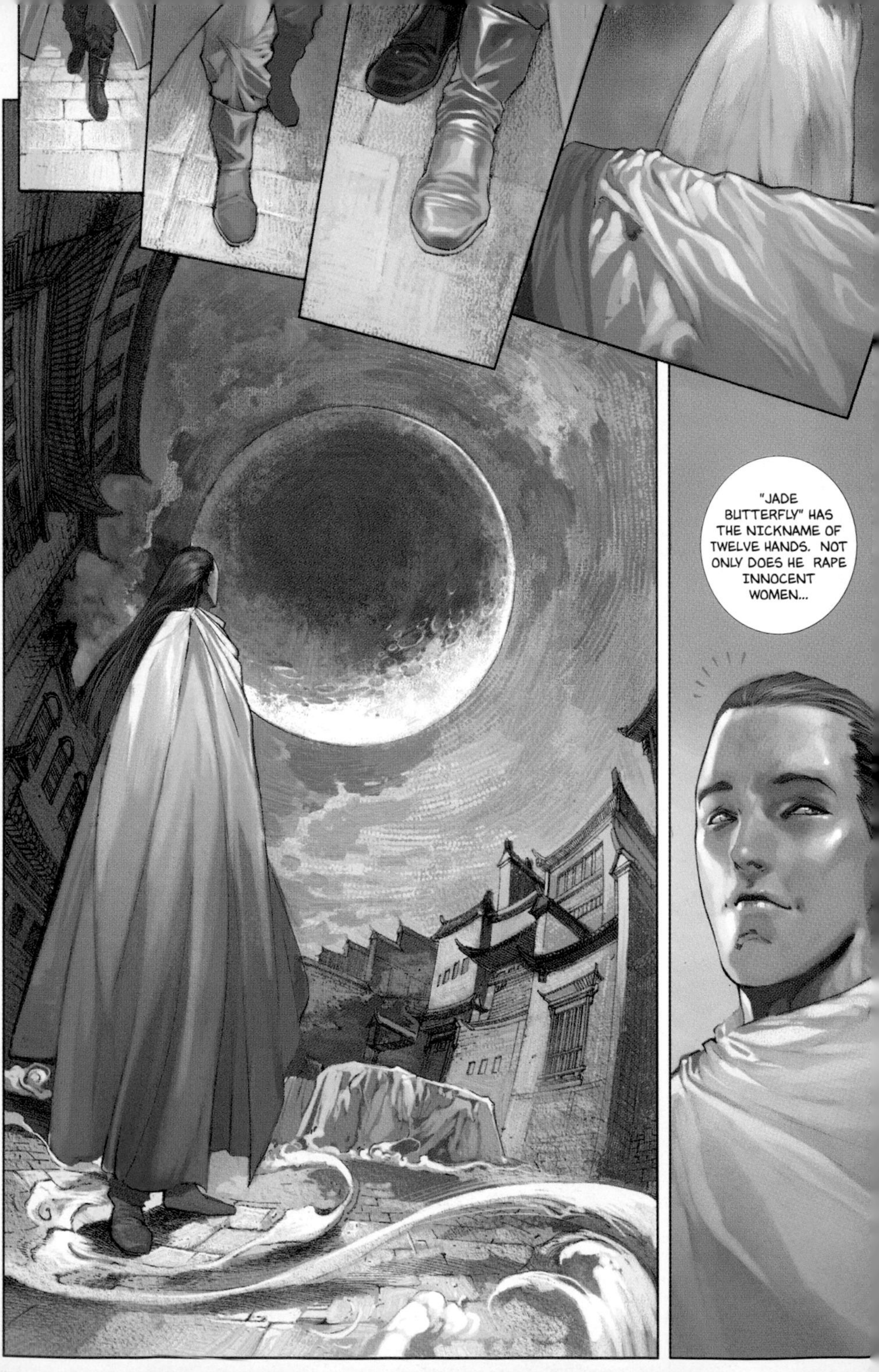
"JADE BUTTERFLY" HAS THE NICKNAME OF TWELVE HANDS. NOT ONLY DOES HE RAPE INNOCENT WOMEN...

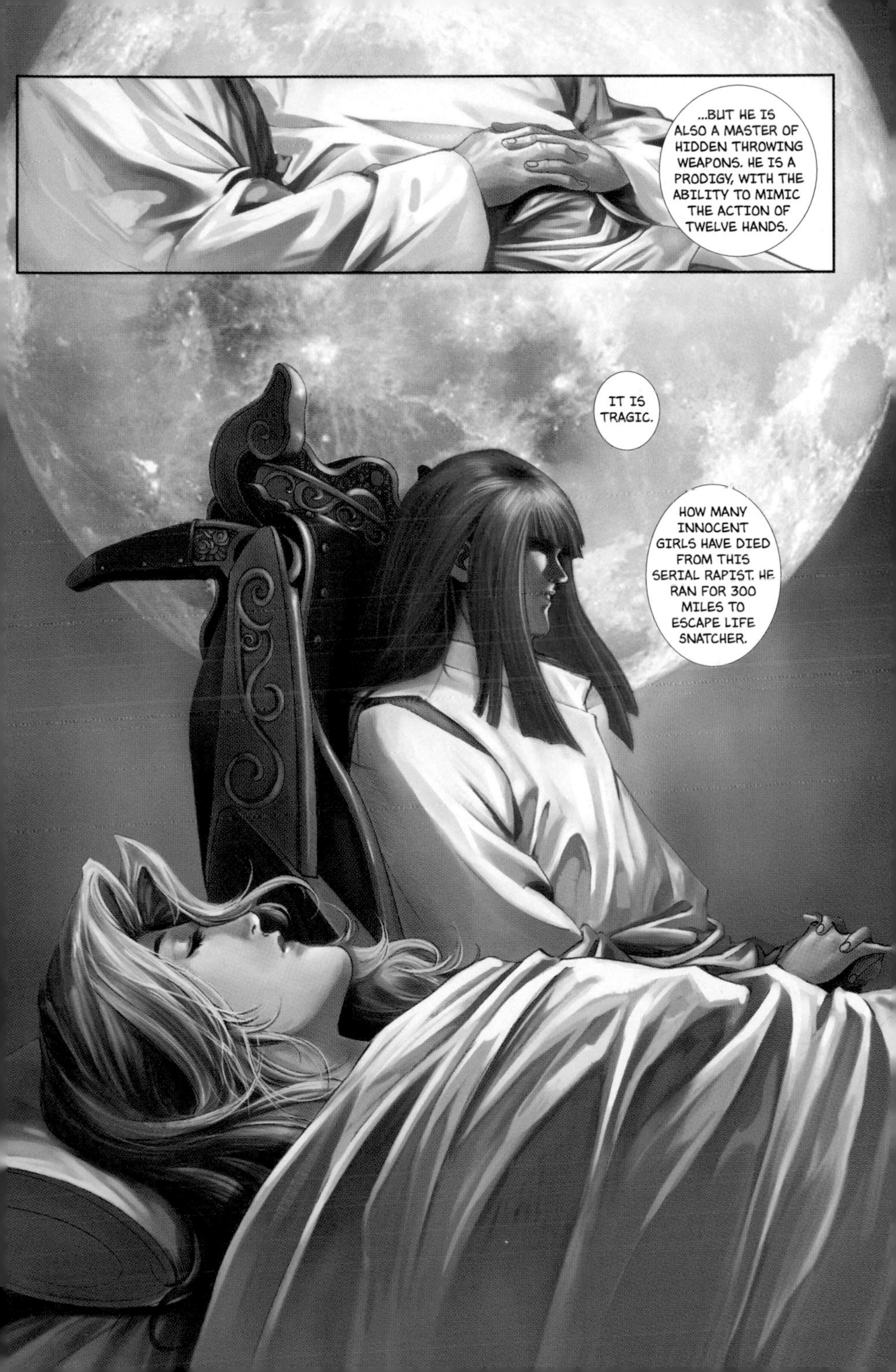
...BUT HE IS ALSO A MASTER OF HIDDEN THROWING WEAPONS. HE IS A PRODIGY, WITH THE ABILITY TO MIMIC THE ACTION OF TWELVE HANDS.
IT IS TRAGIC.
HOW MANY INNOCENT GIRLS HAVE DIED FROM THIS SERIAL RAPIST. HE RAN FOR 300 MILES TO ESCAPE LIFE SNATCHER.

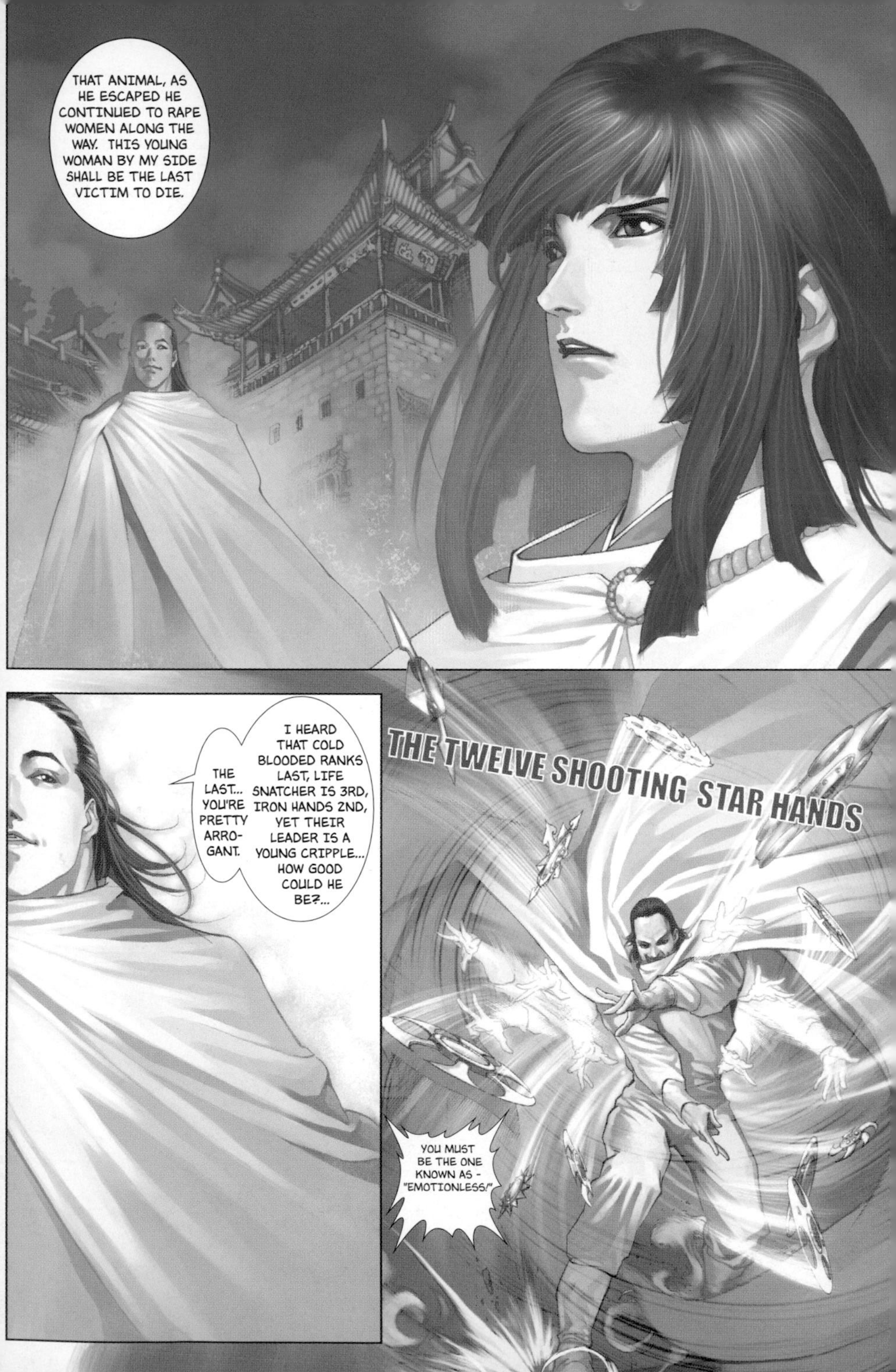
THAT ANIMAL, AS HE ESCAPED HE CONTINUED TO RAPE WOMEN ALONG THE WAY. THIS YOUNG WOMAN BY MY SIDE SHALL BE THE LAST VICTIM TO DIE.
THE LAST... YOU'RE PRETTY ARRO-GANT.
I HEARD THAT COLD BLOODED RANKS LAST, LIFE SNATCHER IS 3RD, IRON HANDS 2ND, YET THEIR LEADER IS A YOUNG CRIPPLE... HOW GOOD COULD HE BE?...
THE TWELVE SHOOTING STAR HANDS
YOU MUST BE THE ONE KNOWN AS - "EMOTIONLESS!"

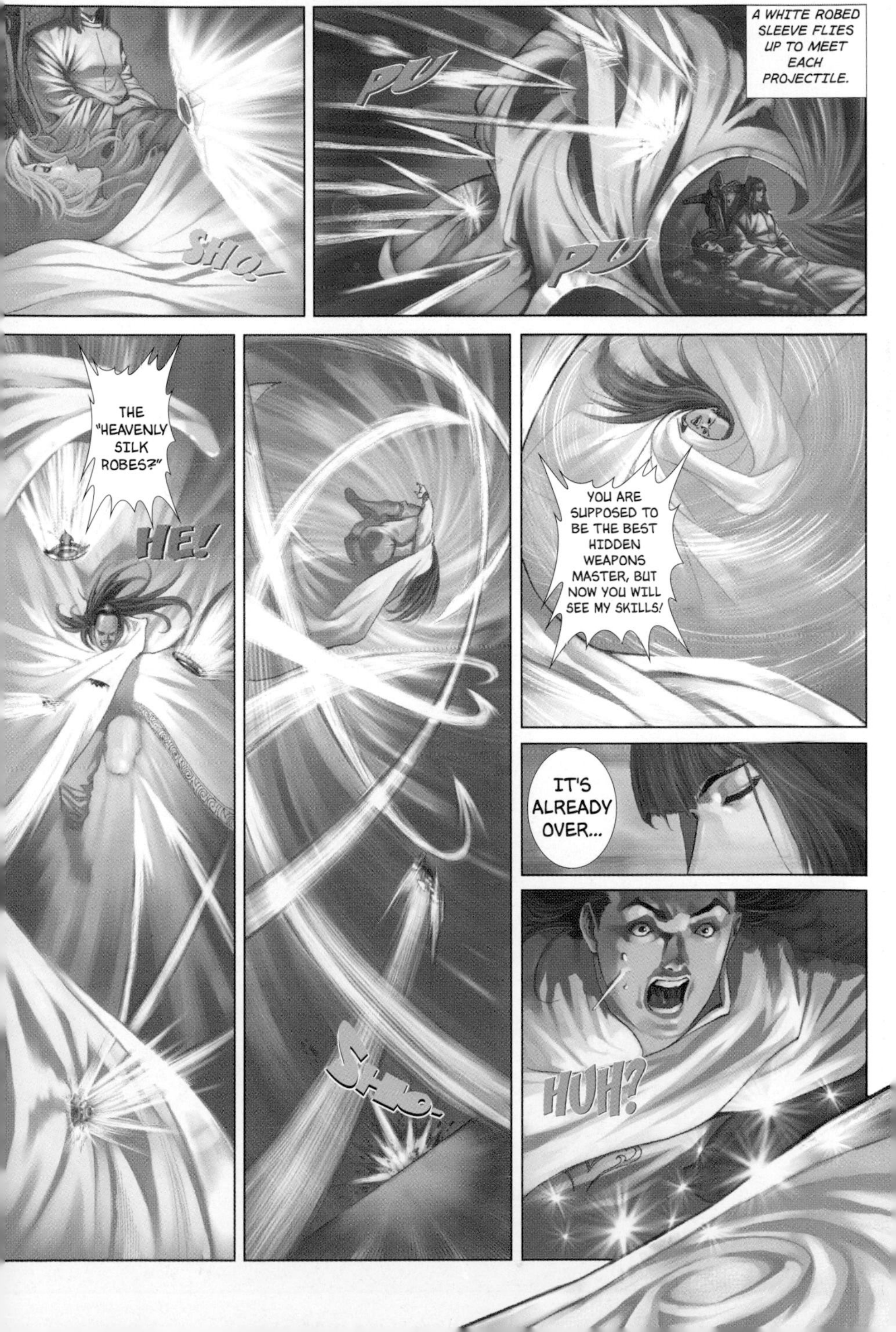
SHIO!
A WHITE ROBED SLEEVE FLIES UP TO MEET EACH PROJECTILE.
PU
PU
THE "HEAVENLY SILK ROBES?"
HE!
SHIO-
YOU ARE SUPPOSED TO BE THE BEST HIDDEN WEAPONS MASTER, BUT NOW YOU WILL SEE MY SKILLS!
IT'S ALREADY OVER...
HUH?

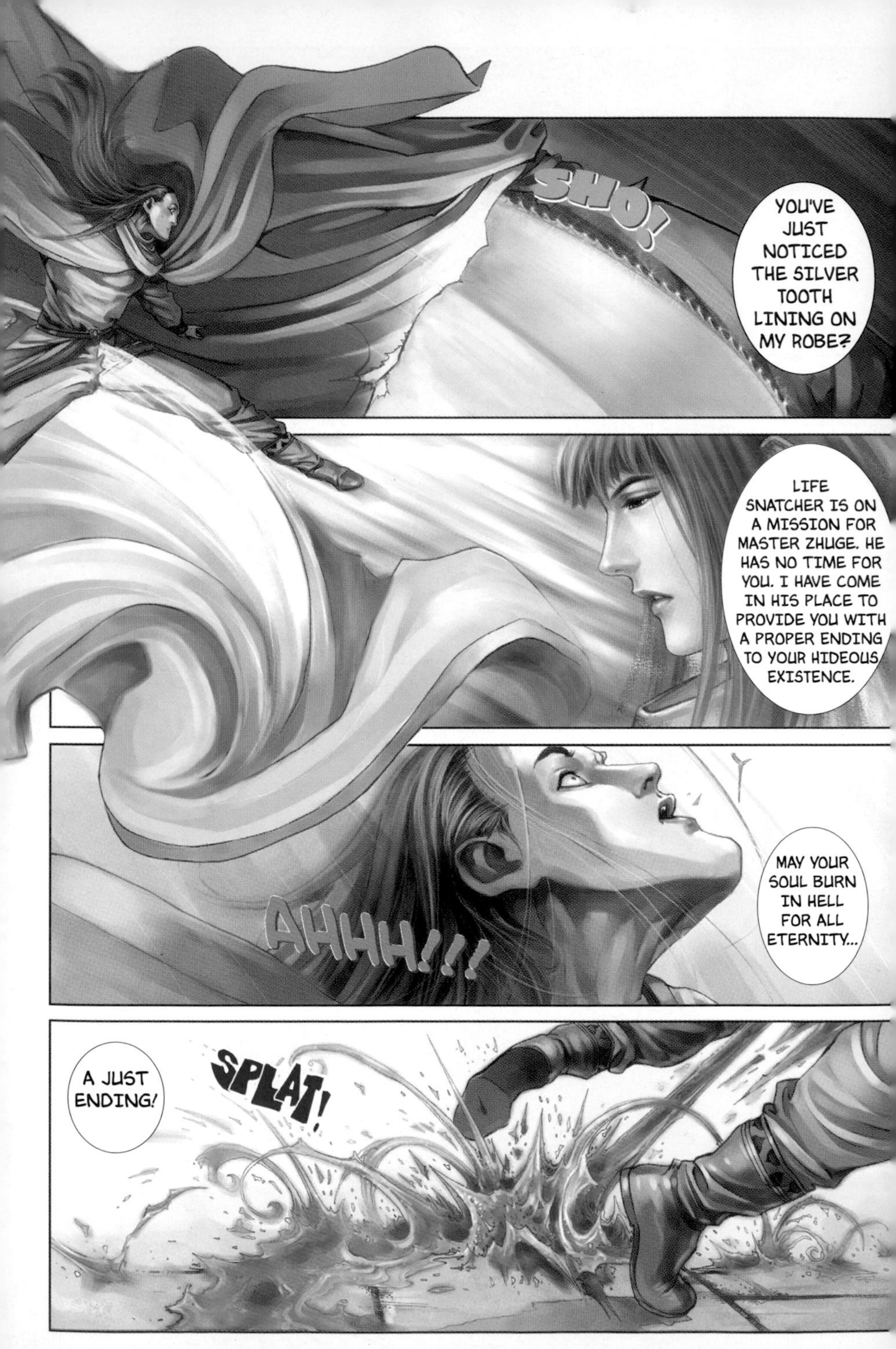
SHO!
YOU'VE JUST NOTICED THE SILVER TOOTH LINING ON MY ROBE?
LIFE SNATCHER IS ON A MISSION FOR MASTER ZHUGE. HE HAS NO TIME FOR YOU. I HAVE COME IN HIS PLACE TO PROVIDE YOU WITH A PROPER ENDING TO YOUR HIDEOUS EXISTENCE.
AHHH!!!
MAY YOUR SOUL BURN IN HELL FOR ALL ETERNITY...
A JUST ENDING!
SPLAT!

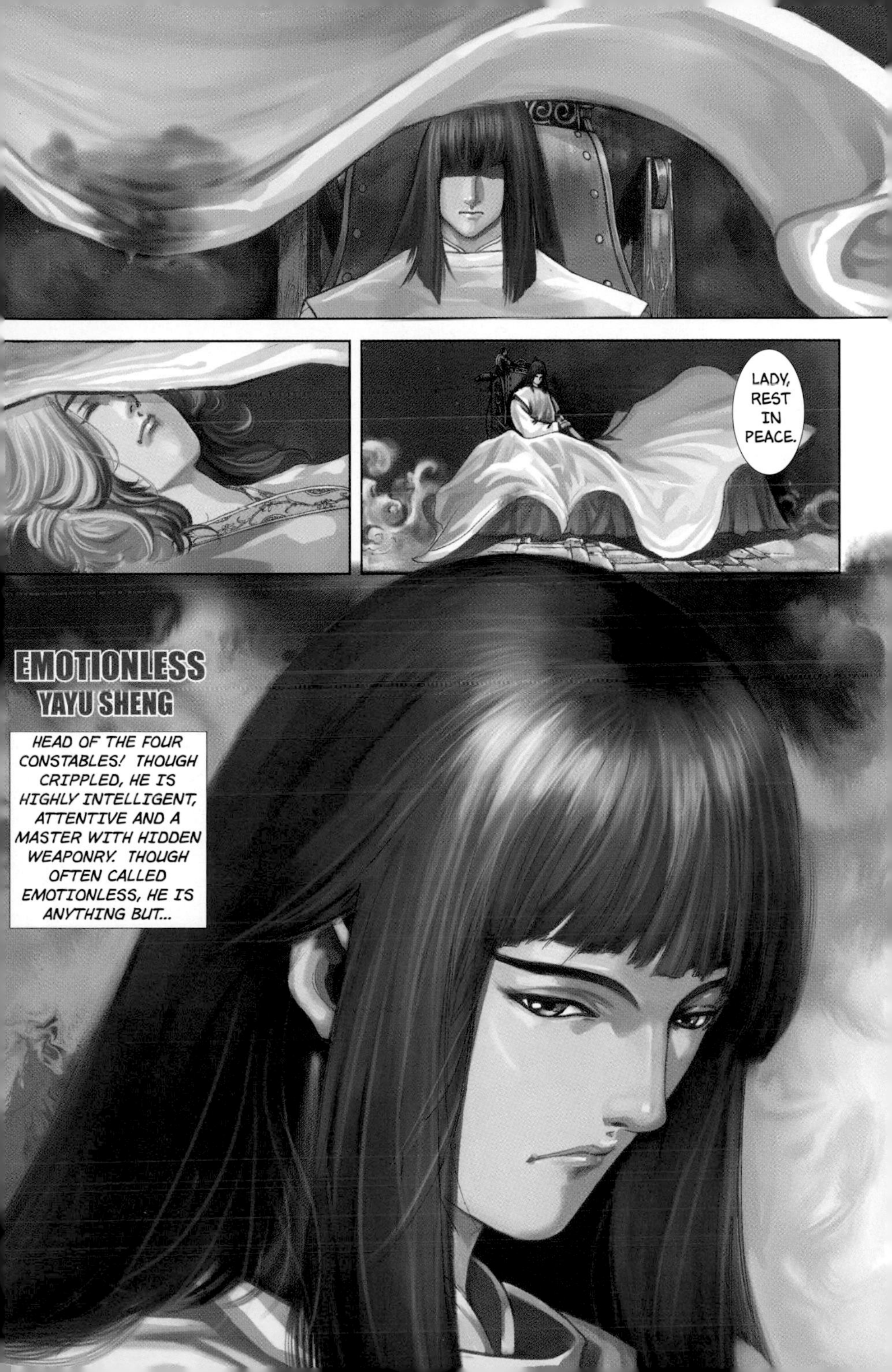
LADY, REST IN PEACE.
EMOTIONLESS
YAYU SHENG
HEAD OF THE FOUR CONSTABLES! THOUGH CRIPPLED, HE IS HIGHLY INTELLIGENT, ATTENTIVE AND A MASTER WITH HIDDEN WEAPONRY. THOUGH OFTEN CALLED EMOTIONLESS, HE IS ANYTHING BUT...

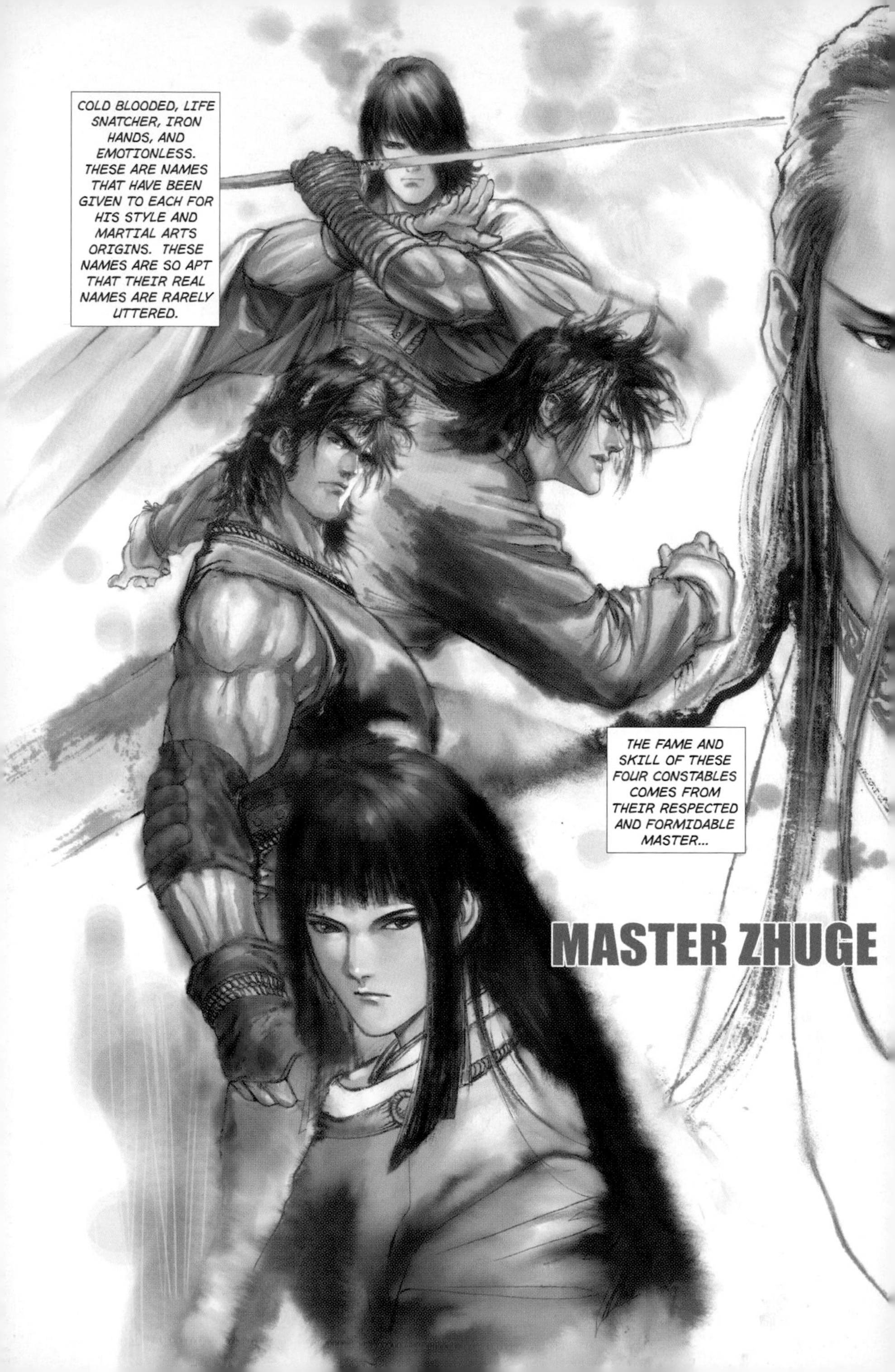
COLD BLOODED, LIFE SNATCHER, IRON HANDS, AND EMOTIONLESS. THESE ARE NAMES THAT HAVE BEEN GIVEN TO EACH FOR HIS STYLE AND MARTIAL ARTS ORIGINS. THESE NAMES ARE SO APT THAT THEIR REAL NAMES ARE RARELY UTTERED.
THE FAME AND SKILL OF THESE FOUR CONSTABLES COMES FROM THEIR RESPECTED AND FORMIDABLE MASTER...
MASTER ZHUGE

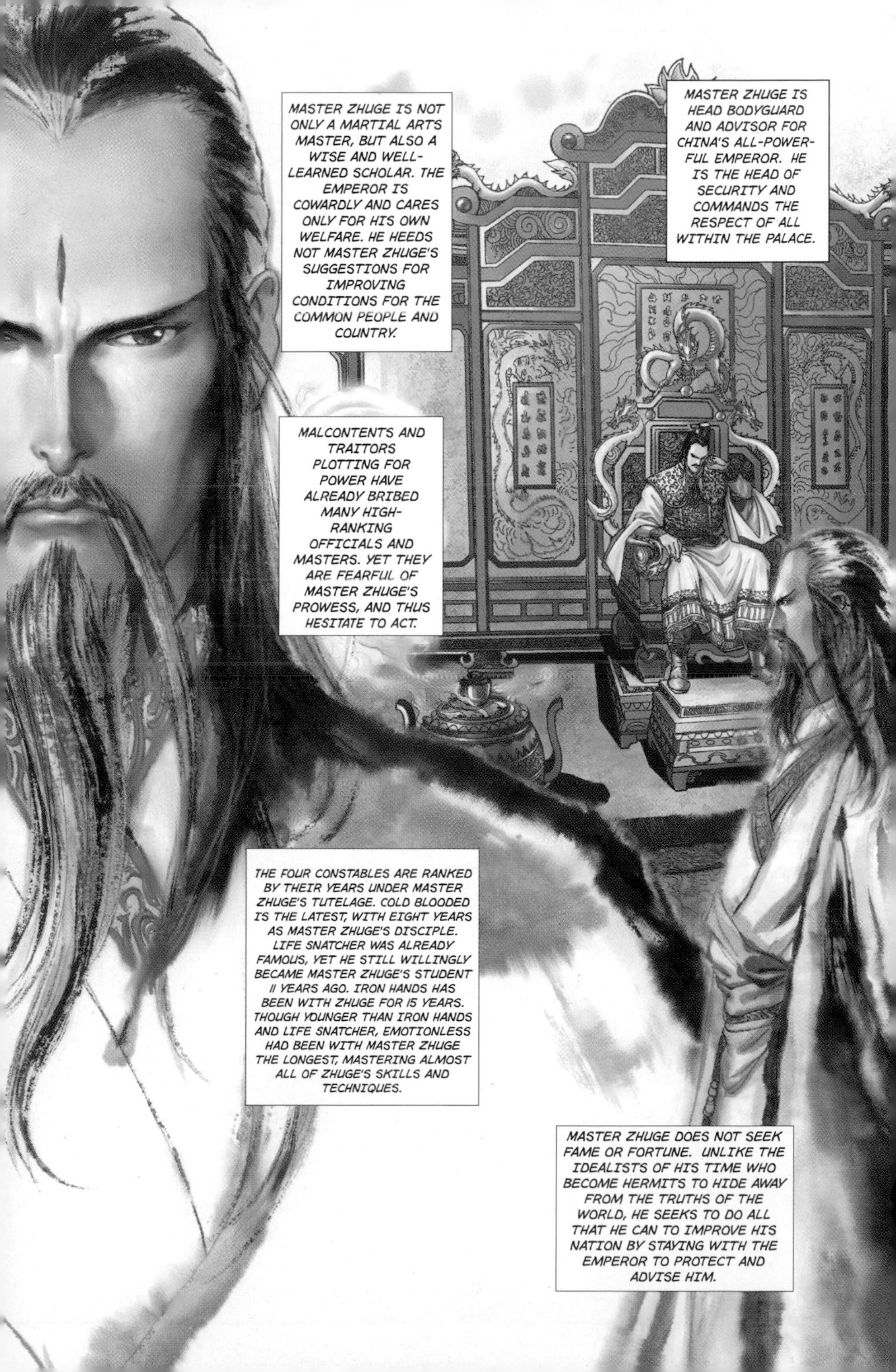
MASTER ZHUGE IS NOT ONLY A MARTIAL ARTS MASTER, BUT ALSO A WISE AND WELL-LEARNED SCHOLAR. THE EMPEROR IS COWARDLY AND CARES ONLY FOR HIS OWN WELFARE. HE HEEDS NOT MASTER ZHUGE'S SUGGESTIONS FOR IMPROVING CONDITIONS FOR THE COMMON PEOPLE AND COUNTRY.
MASTER ZHUGE IS HEAD BODYGUARD AND ADVISOR FOR CHINA'S ALL-POWERFUL EMPEROR. HE IS THE HEAD OF SECURITY AND COMMANDS THE RESPECT OF ALL WITHIN THE PALACE.
MALCONTENTS AND TRAITORS PLOTTING FOR POWER HAVE ALREADY BRIBED MANY HIGH-RANKING OFFICIALS AND MASTERS. YET THEY ARE FEARFUL OF MASTER ZHUGE'S PROWESS, AND THUS HESITATE TO ACT.
THE FOUR CONSTABLES ARE RANKED BY THEIR YEARS UNDER MASTER ZHUGE'S TUTELAGE. COLD BLOODED IS THE LATEST, WITH EIGHT YEARS AS MASTER ZHUGE'S DISCIPLE. LIFE SNATCHER WAS ALREADY FAMOUS, YET HE STILL WILLINGLY BECAME MASTER ZHUGE'S STUDENT 11 YEARS AGO. IRON HANDS HAS BEEN WITH ZHUGE FOR 15 YEARS. THOUGH YOUNGER THAN IRON HANDS AND LIFE SNATCHER, EMOTIONLESS HAD BEEN WITH MASTER ZHUGE THE LONGEST, MASTERING ALMOST ALL OF ZHUGE'S SKILLS AND TECHNIQUES.
MASTER ZHUGE DOES NOT SEEK FAME OR FORTUNE. UNLIKE THE IDEALISTS OF HIS TIME WHO BECOME HERMITS TO HIDE AWAY FROM THE TRUTHS OF THE WORLD, HE SEEKS TO DO ALL THAT HE CAN TO IMPROVE HIS NATION BY STAYING WITH THE EMPEROR TO PROTECT AND ADVISE HIM.

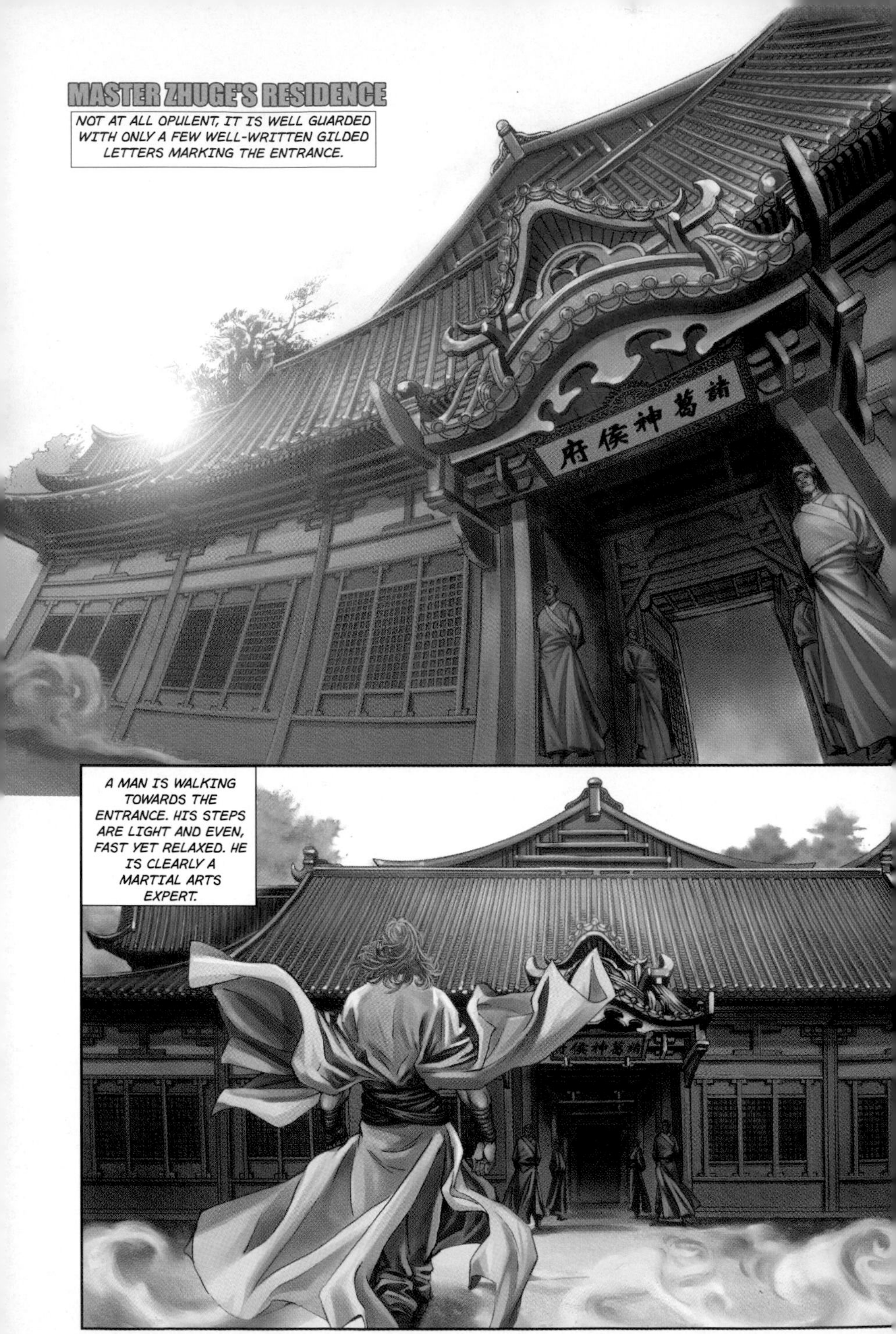
MASTER ZHUGE'S RESIDENCE
NOT AT ALL OPULENT, IT IS WELL GUARDED WITH ONLY A FEW WELL-WRITTEN GILDED LETTERS MARKING THE ENTRANCE.
諸葛神侯府
A MAN IS WALKING TOWARDS THE ENTRANCE. HIS STEPS ARE LIGHT AND EVEN, FAST YET RELAXED. HE IS CLEARLY A MARTIAL ARTS EXPERT.

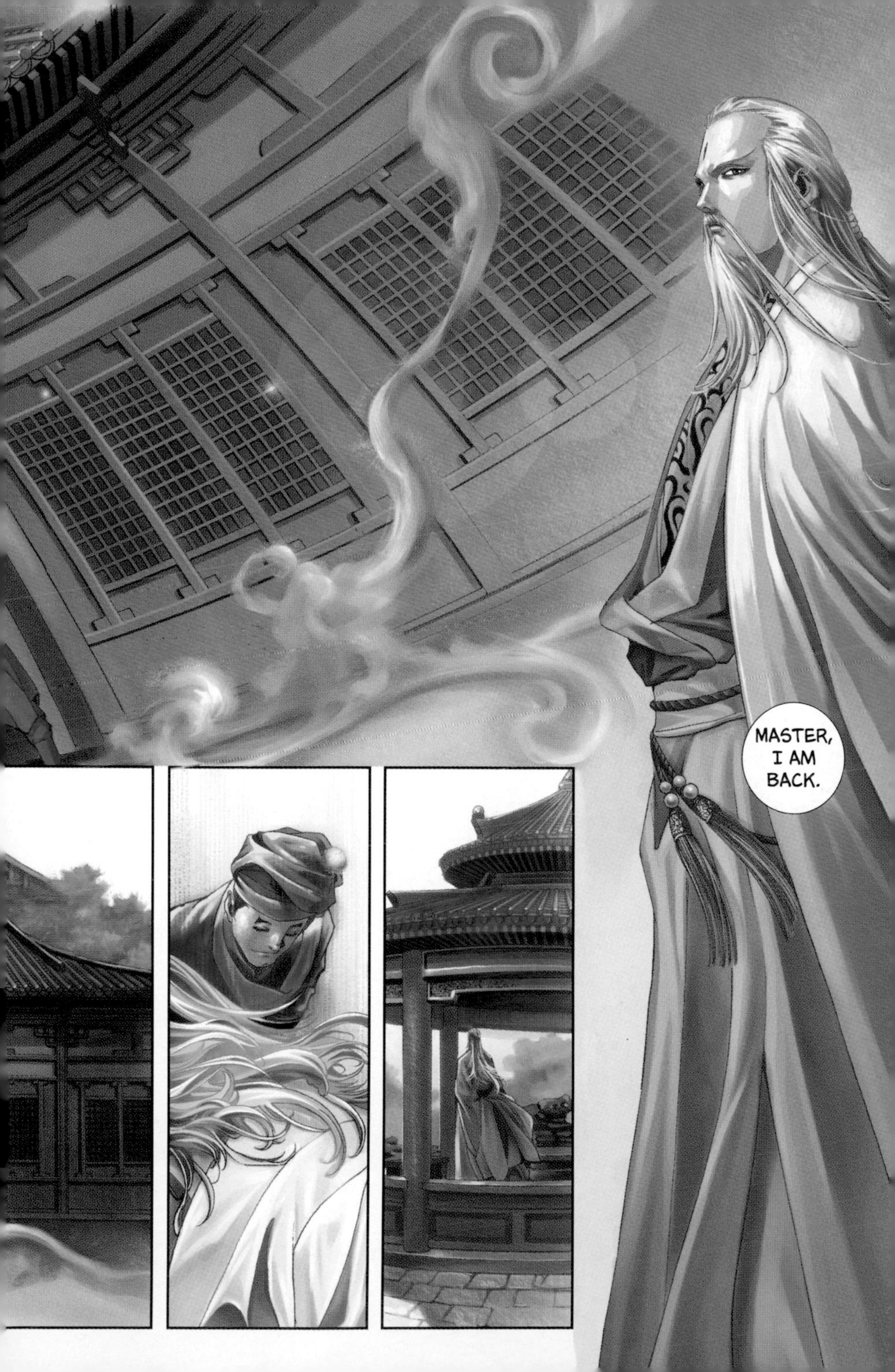
MASTER, I AM BACK.

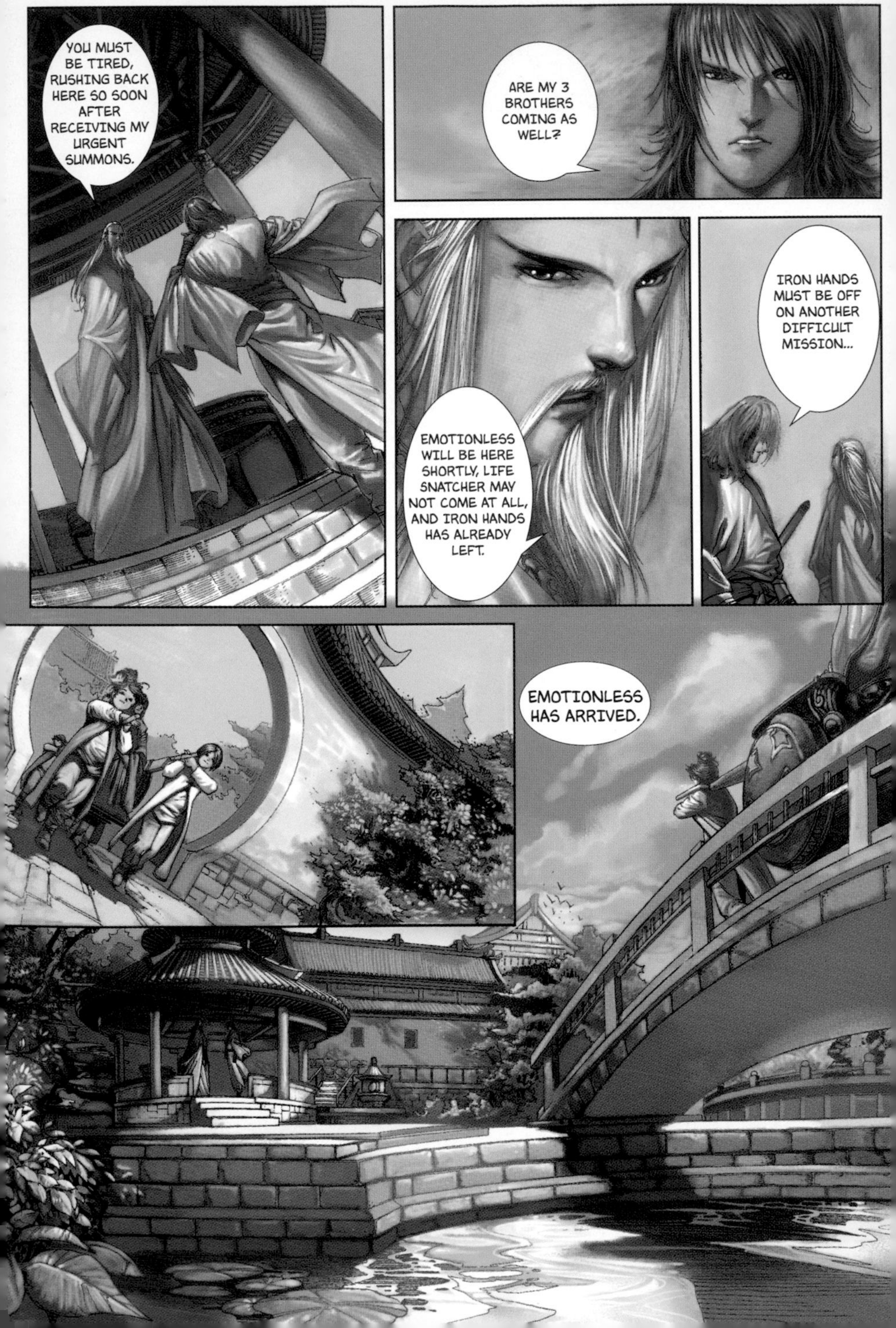
YOU MUST BE TIRED, RUSHING BACK HERE SO SOON AFTER RECEIVING MY URGENT SUMMONS.
ARE MY 3 BROTHERS COMING AS WELL?
EMOTIONLESS WILL BE HERE SHORTLY, LIFE SNATCHER MAY NOT COME AT ALL, AND IRON HANDS HAS ALREADY LEFT.
IRON HANDS MUST BE OFF ON ANOTHER DIFFICULT MISSION...
EMOTIONLESS HAS ARRIVED.

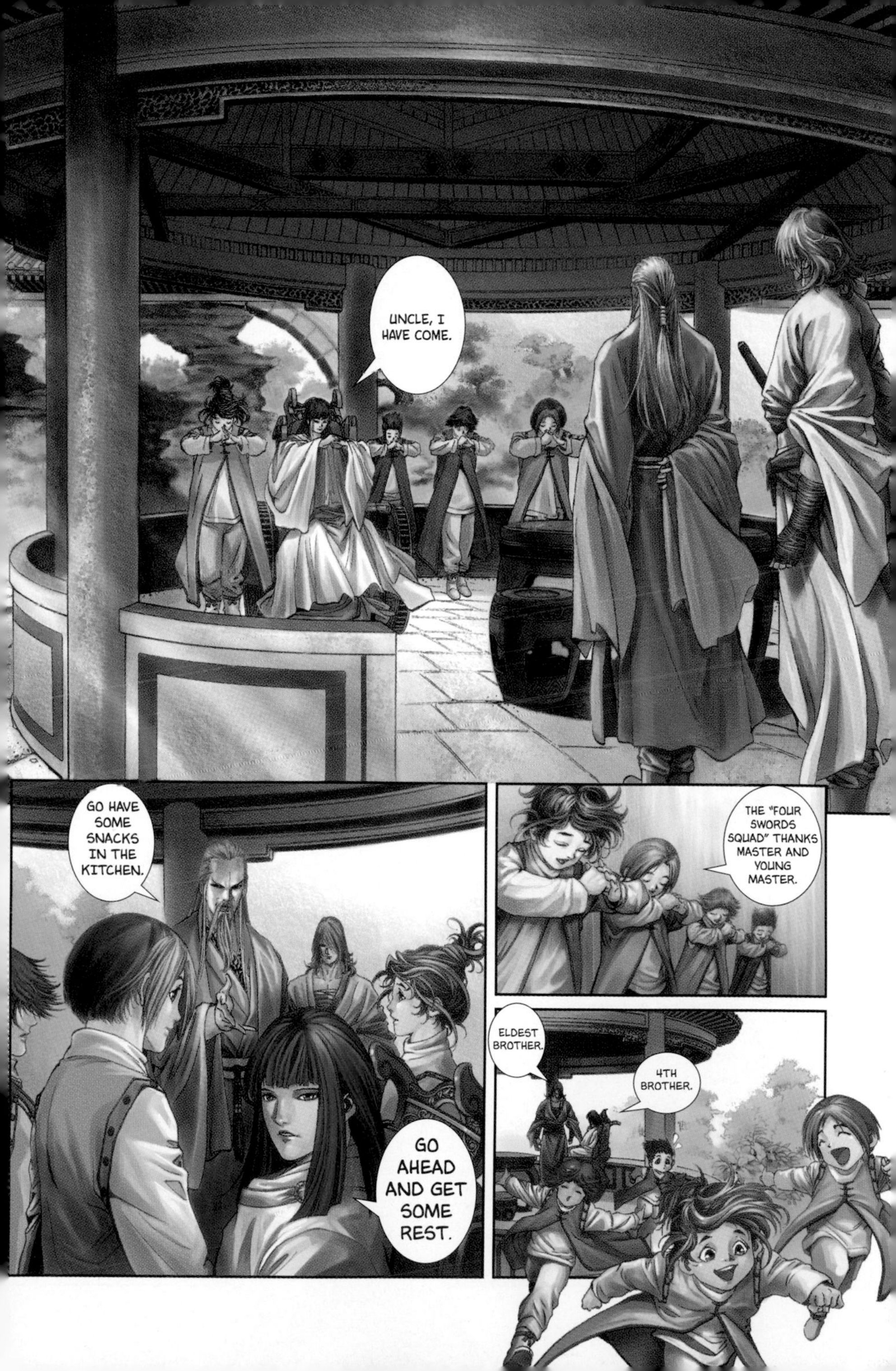
UNCLE, I HAVE COME.
GO HAVE SOME SNACKS IN THE KITCHEN.
GO AHEAD AND GET SOME REST.
THE "FOUR SWORDS SQUAD" THANKS MASTER AND YOUNG MASTER.
ELDEST BROTHER.
4TH BROTHER.

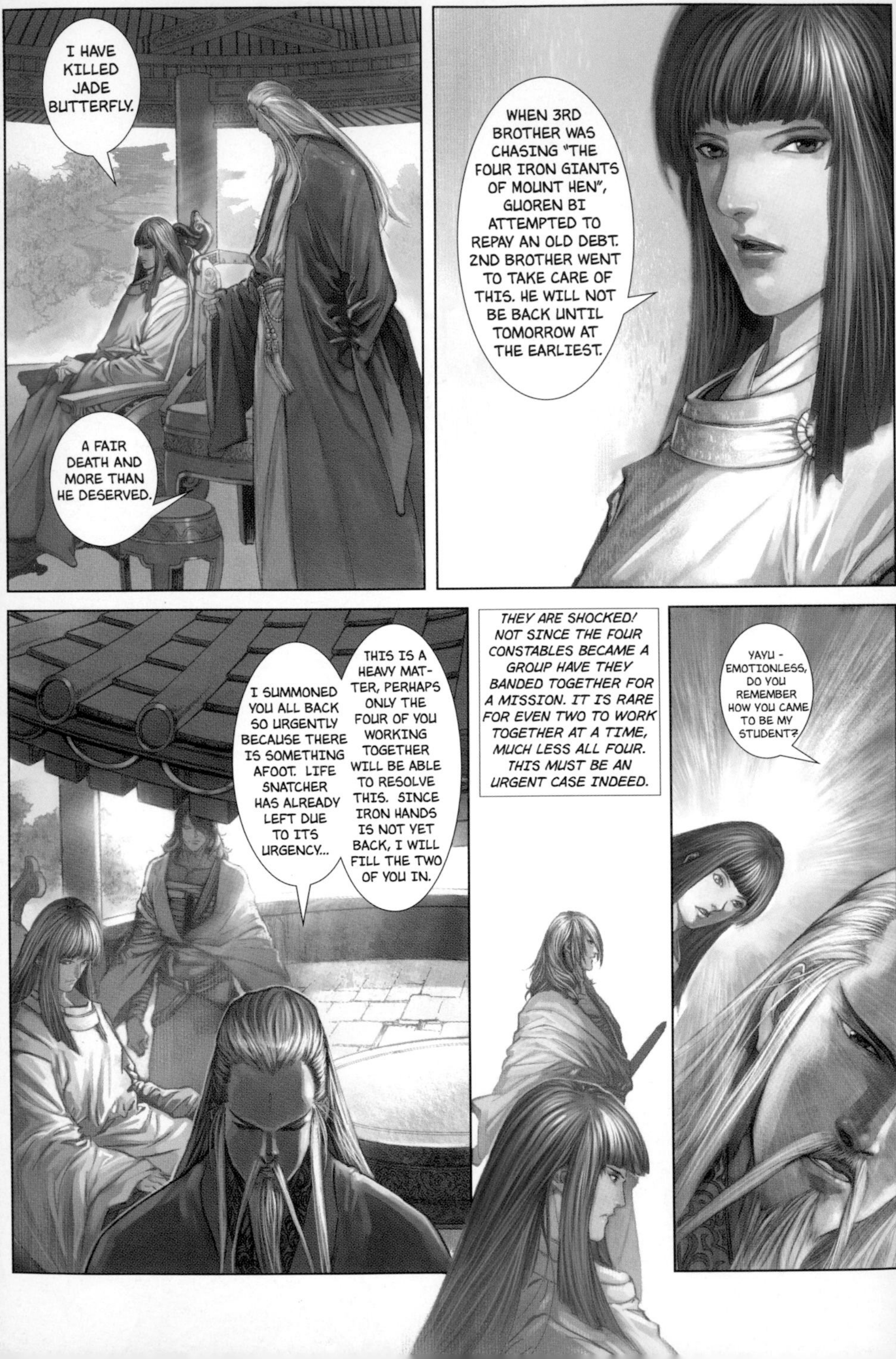
I HAVE KILLED JADE BUTTERFLY.
A FAIR DEATH AND MORE THAN HE DESERVED.
WHEN 3RD BROTHER WAS CHASING "THE FOUR IRON GIANTS OF MOUNT HEN", GUOREN BI ATTEMPTED TO REPAY AN OLD DEBT. 2ND BROTHER WENT TO TAKE CARE OF THIS. HE WILL NOT BE BACK UNTIL TOMORROW AT THE EARLIEST.
I SUMMONED YOU ALL BACK SO URGENTLY BECAUSE THERE IS SOMETHING AFOOT. LIFE SNATCHER HAS ALREADY LEFT DUE TO ITS URGENCY...
THIS IS A HEAVY MATTER, PERHAPS ONLY THE FOUR OF YOU WORKING TOGETHER WILL BE ABLE TO RESOLVE THIS. SINCE IRON HANDS IS NOT YET BACK, I WILL FILL THE TWO OF YOU IN.
THEY ARE SHOCKED! NOT SINCE THE FOUR CONSTABLES BECAME A GROUP HAVE THEY BANDED TOGETHER FOR A MISSION. IT IS RARE FOR EVEN TWO TO WORK TOGETHER AT A TIME, MUCH LESS ALL FOUR. THIS MUST BE AN URGENT CASE INDEED.
YAYU - EMOTIONLESS, DO YOU REMEMBER HOW YOU CAME TO BE MY STUDENT?

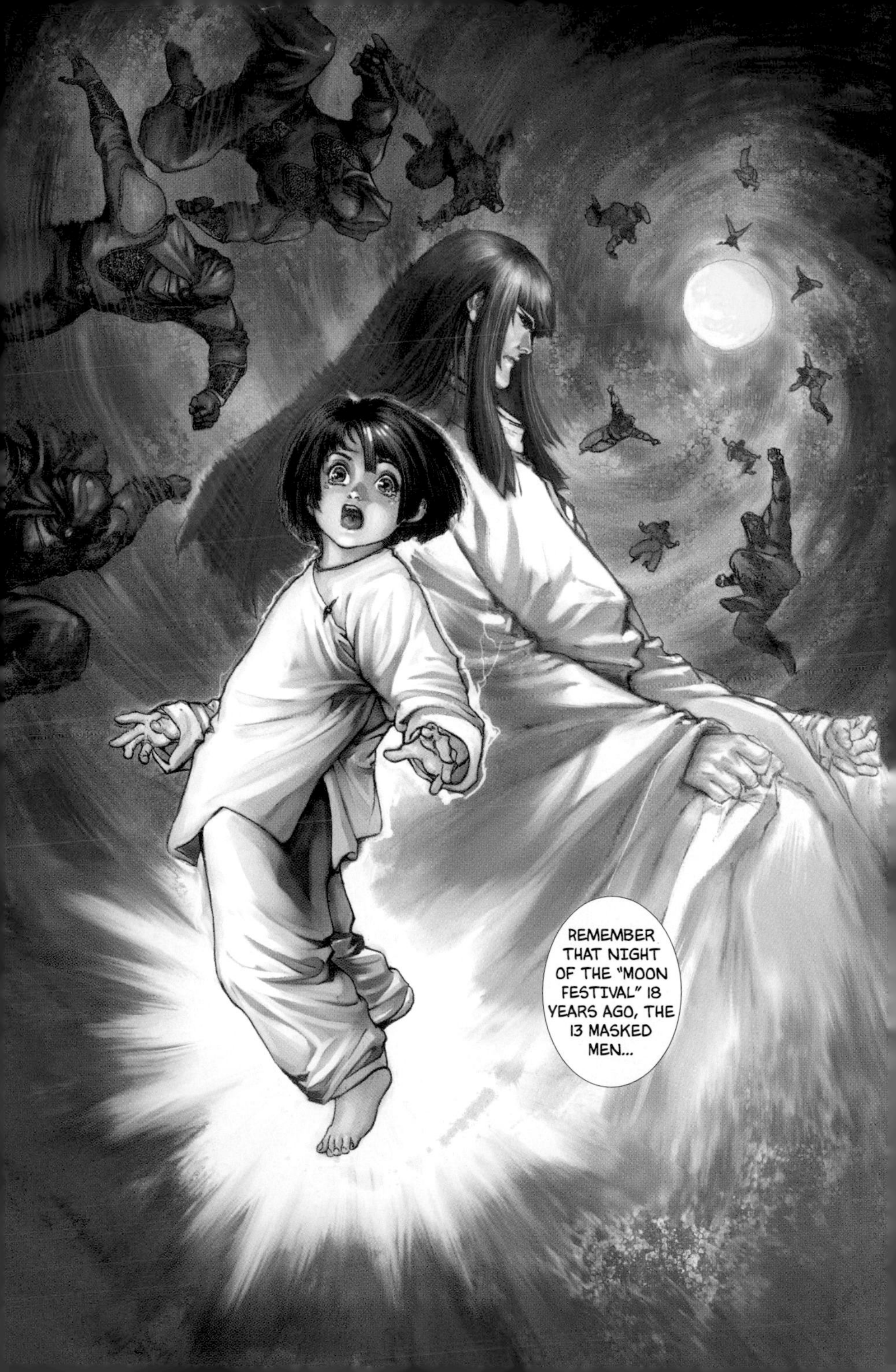
REMEMBER THAT NIGHT OF THE "MOON FESTIVAL" 18 YEARS AGO, THE 13 MASKED MEN...

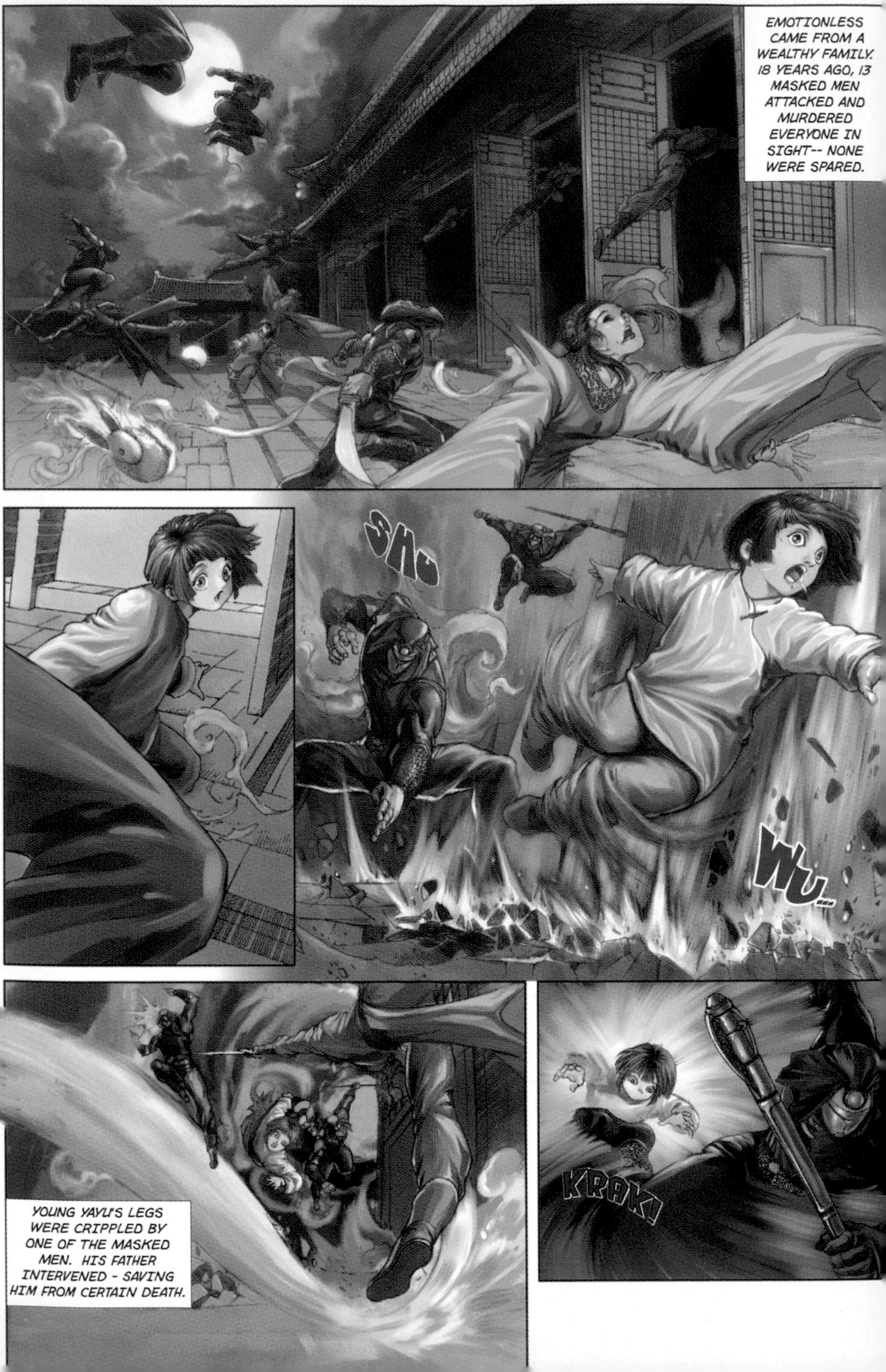
EMOTIONLESS CAME FROM A WEALTHY FAMILY. 18 YEARS AGO, 13 MASKED MEN ATTACKED AND MURDERED EVERYONE IN SIGHT-- NONE WERE SPARED.
SHU
WU..
YOUNG YAYU'S LEGS WERE CRIPPLED BY ONE OF THE MASKED MEN. HIS FATHER INTERVENED - SAVING HIM FROM CERTAIN DEATH.
KRAK!

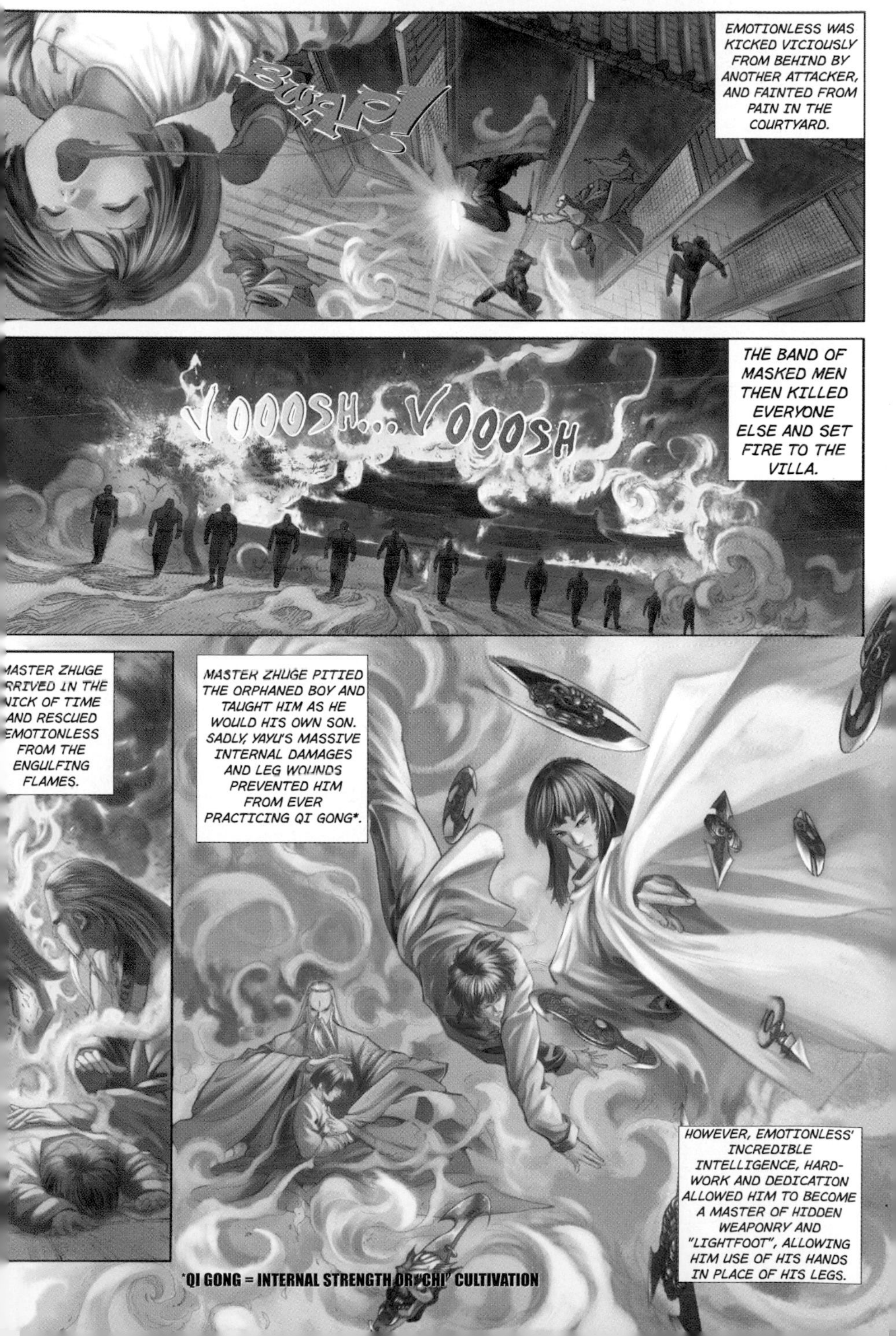
EMOTIONLESS WAS KICKED VICIOUSLY FROM BEHIND BY ANOTHER ATTACKER, AND FAINTED FROM PAIN IN THE COURTYARD.
BWAP!
THE BAND OF MASKED MEN THEN KILLED EVERYONE ELSE AND SET FIRE TO THE VILLA.
VOOOSH...VOOOSH
MASTER ZHUGE RRIVED IN THE NICK OF TIME AND RESCUED EMOTIONLESS FROM THE ENGULFING FLAMES.
MASTER ZHUGE PITIED THE ORPHANED BOY AND TAUGHT HIM AS HE WOULD HIS OWN SON. SADLY, YAYU'S MASSIVE INTERNAL DAMAGES AND LEG WOUNDS PREVENTED HIM FROM EVER PRACTICING QI GONG*.
HOWEVER, EMOTIONLESS' INCREDIBLE INTELLIGENCE, HARD-WORK AND DEDICATION ALLOWED HIM TO BECOME A MASTER OF HIDDEN WEAPONRY AND "LIGHTFOOT", ALLOWING HIM USE OF HIS HANDS IN PLACE OF HIS LEGS.
*QI GONG = INTERNAL STRENGTH OR "CHI" CULTIVATION

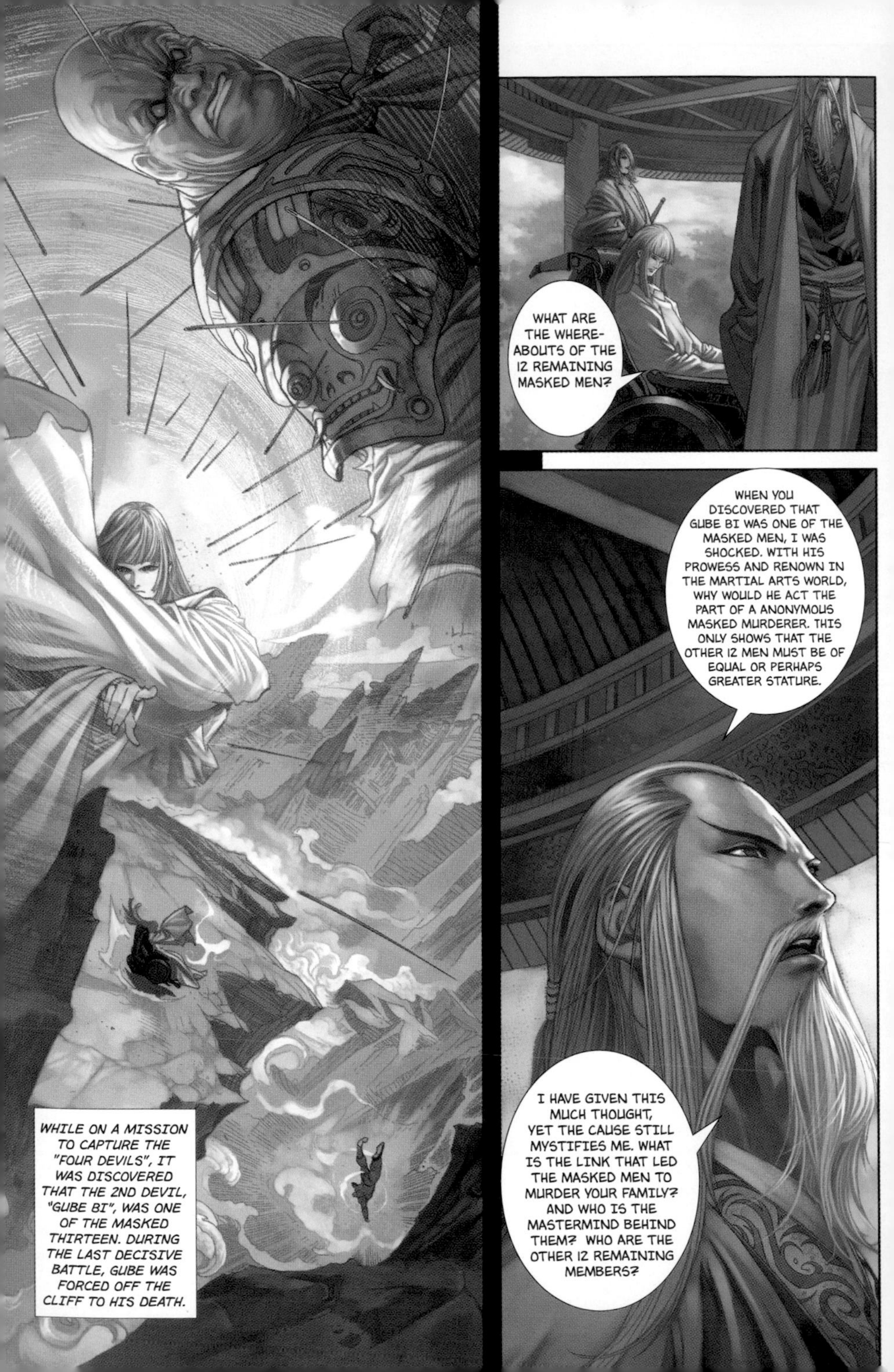
WHILE ON A MISSION TO CAPTURE THE "FOUR DEVILS", IT WAS DISCOVERED THAT THE 2ND DEVIL, "GUBE BI", WAS ONE OF THE MASKED THIRTEEN. DURING THE LAST DECISIVE BATTLE, GUBE WAS FORCED OFF THE CLIFF TO HIS DEATH.
WHAT ARE THE WHERE-ABOUTS OF THE 12 REMAINING MASKED MEN?
WHEN YOU DISCOVERED THAT GUBE BI WAS ONE OF THE MASKED MEN, I WAS SHOCKED. WITH HIS PROWESS AND RENOWN IN THE MARTIAL ARTS WORLD, WHY WOULD HE ACT THE PART OF A ANONYMOUS MASKED MURDERER. THIS ONLY SHOWS THAT THE OTHER 12 MEN MUST BE OF EQUAL OR PERHAPS GREATER STATURE.
I HAVE GIVEN THIS MUCH THOUGHT, YET THE CAUSE STILL MYSTIFIES ME. WHAT IS THE LINK THAT LED THE MASKED MEN TO MURDER YOUR FAMILY? AND WHO IS THE MASTERMIND BEHIND THEM? WHO ARE THE OTHER 12 REMAINING MEMBERS?

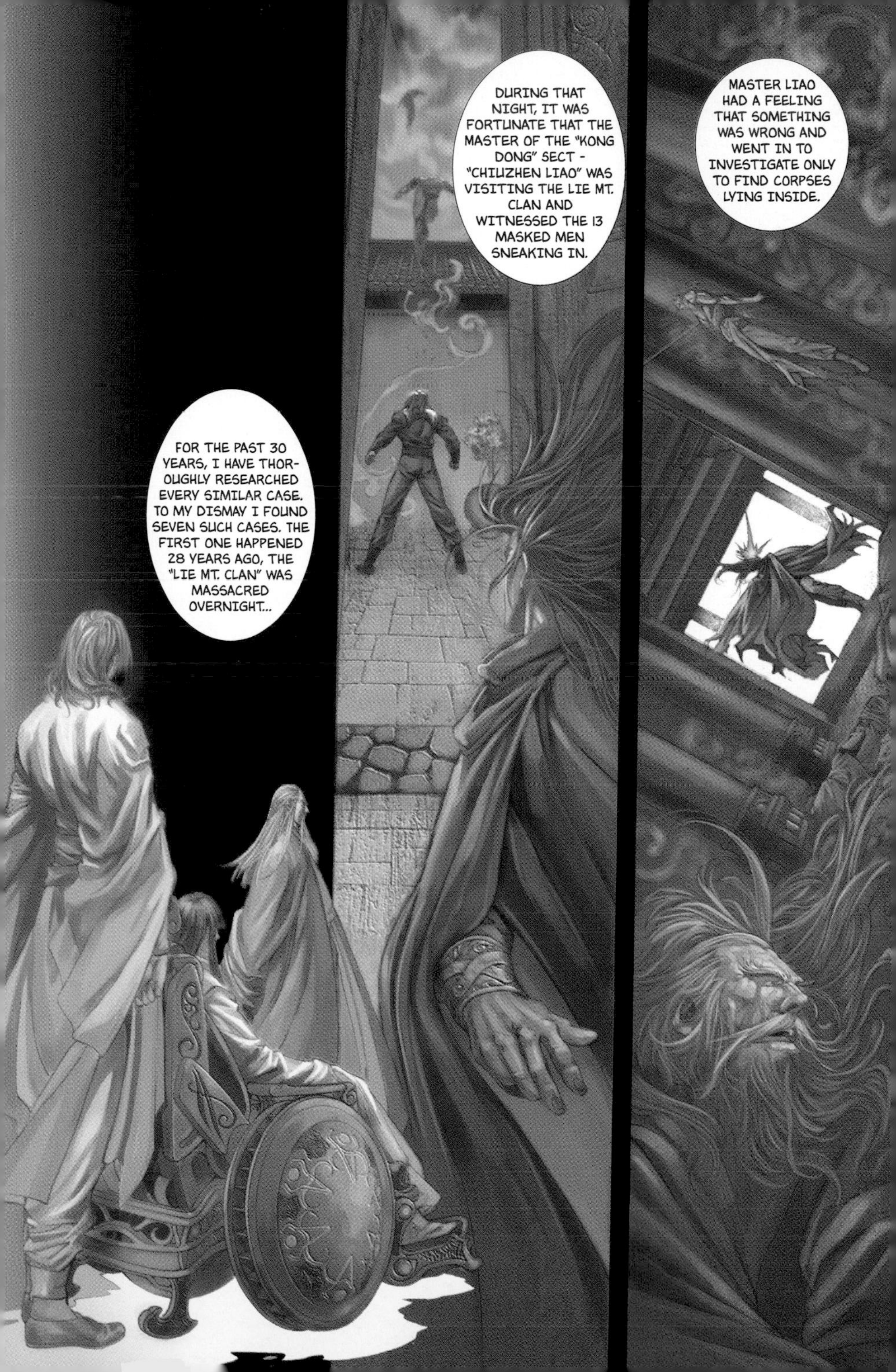
FOR THE PAST 30 YEARS, I HAVE THOROUGHLY RESEARCHED EVERY SIMILAR CASE. TO MY DISMAY I FOUND SEVEN SUCH CASES. THE FIRST ONE HAPPENED 28 YEARS AGO, THE "LIE MT. CLAN" WAS MASSACRED OVERNIGHT...
DURING THAT NIGHT, IT WAS FORTUNATE THAT THE MASTER OF THE "KONG DONG" SECT - "CHIUZHEN LIAO" WAS VISITING THE LIE MT. CLAN AND WITNESSED THE 13 MASKED MEN SNEAKING IN.
MASTER LIAO HAD A FEELING THAT SOMETHING WAS WRONG AND WENT IN TO INVESTIGATE ONLY TO FIND CORPSES LYING INSIDE.

ANOTHER CASE THAT OCCURRED 20 YEARS AGO INVOLVED "THE NINE PUZZLE MT.'S MA HOUSEHOLD." HIS ENTIRE FAMILY OF 24 WAS KILLED IN THE SAME IDENTICAL FASHION AS THE PREVIOUS CASES. THESE THREE CASES AND THE FOUR THAT FOLLOW ALL HAVE ONE SIMILARITY, THOUGH THE VICTIMS DIED FROM DIFFERENT WEAPONS...

NEXT CAME THE CASE OF THE "WU WEI" SECT 24 YEARS AGO. ALL 79 MEMBERS WERE RUTHLESSLY MURDERED IN THEIR TEMPLE. LUCKILY, A FARMER SAW THE MASKED MEN RUNNING UP TOWARD THE TEMPLE PRIOR TO THE INCIDENT.

THERE WAS ONE SPECIAL TYPE OF WOUND DISCOVERED; IT SEEMS TO BE CAUSED BY THE SPECIALTY WEAPON - "THE IRON LOTUS." THIS IS A RARELY SEEN WEAPON AND NOT FAVORED BY ANY KNOWN MASTERS. OR PERHAPS IT IS A SECRET TECHNIQUE NOT USED NORMALLY. NO ONE KNOWS FOR CERTAIN.

THE NEXT CASE SHOCKED THE MARTIAL ARTS WORLD. IT WAS THE DEATH OF THE KONG DONG CLAN MEMBERS 20 YEARS AGO. ACCORDING TO DISCIPLES OF THE KONG DONG CLAN, MASTER LIAO WAS SEEN SPEAKING TO ONE OF THE MASKED MEN. IT SEEMS THAT HE WAS AWARE OF THE MAN'S IDENTITY YET COULD NOT BELIEVE HIM CAPABLE OF SUCH A DEED...

MASTER LIAO PLANNED TO TALK THIS THROUGH FIRST, BUT BEFORE HE HAD A CHANCE, THEY STRUCK FIRST AND MURDERED HIM.

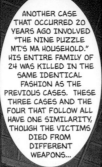

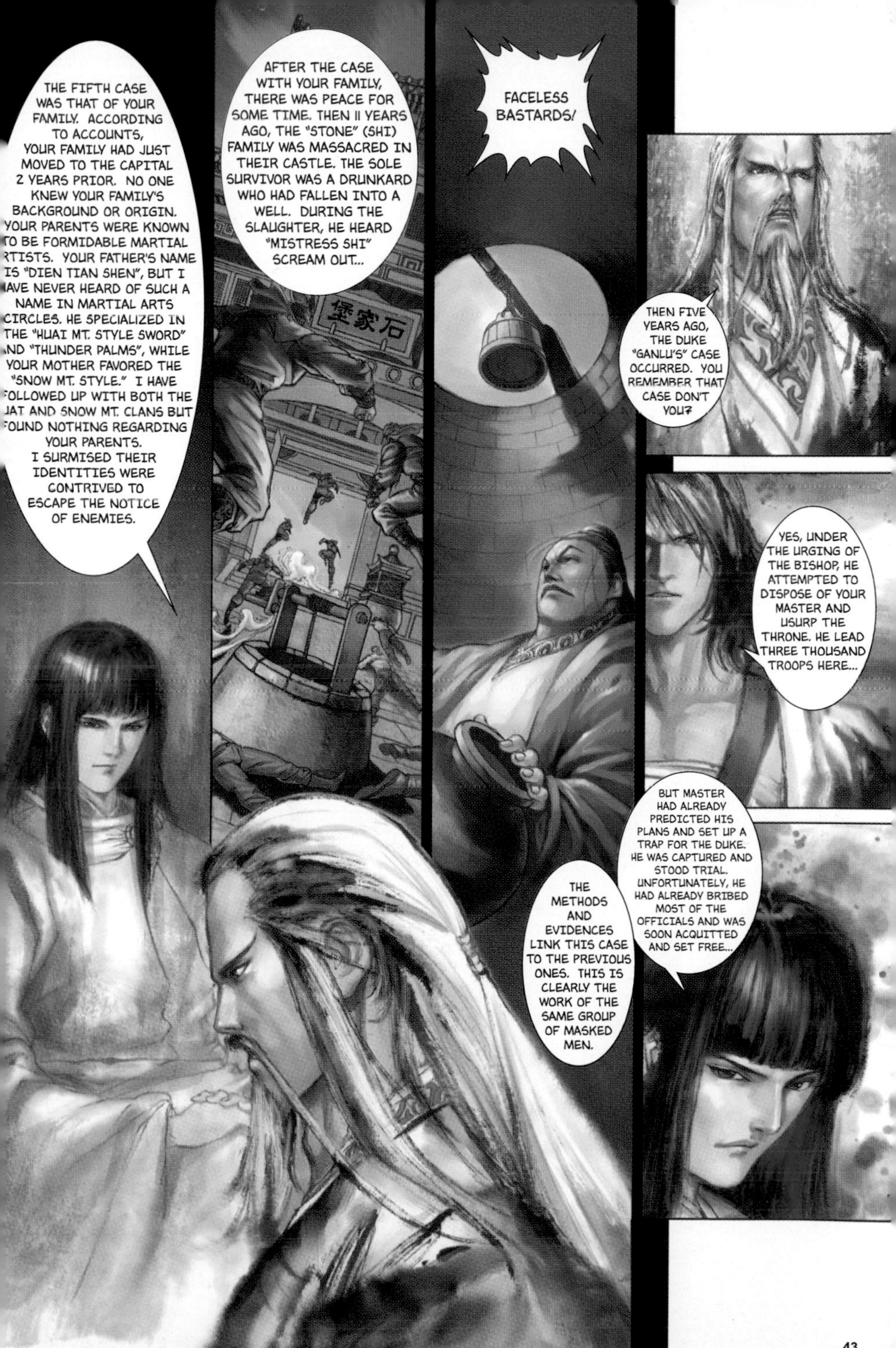

THE FIFTH CASE WAS THAT OF YOUR FAMILY. ACCORDING TO ACCOUNTS, YOUR FAMILY HAD JUST MOVED TO THE CAPITAL 2 YEARS PRIOR. NO ONE KNEW YOUR FAMILY'S BACKGROUND OR ORIGIN. YOUR PARENTS WERE KNOWN TO BE FORMIDABLE MARTIAL RTISTS. YOUR FATHER'S NAME IS "DIEN TIAN SHEN", BUT I AVE NEVER HEARD OF SUCH A NAME IN MARTIAL ARTS CIRCLES. HE SPECIALIZED IN THE "HUAI MT. STYLE SWORD" ND "THUNDER PALMS", WHILE YOUR MOTHER FAVORED THE "SNOW MT. STYLE." I HAVE OLLOWED UP WITH BOTH THE UAI AND SNOW MT. CLANS BUT OUND NOTHING REGARDING YOUR PARENTS. I SURMISED THEIR IDENTITIES WERE CONTRIVED TO ESCAPE THE NOTICE OF ENEMIES.
AFTER THE CASE WITH YOUR FAMILY, THERE WAS PEACE FOR SOME TIME. THEN 11 YEARS AGO, THE "STONE" (SHI) FAMILY WAS MASSACRED IN THEIR CASTLE. THE SOLE SURVIVOR WAS A DRUNKARD WHO HAD FALLEN INTO A WELL. DURING THE SLAUGHTER, HE HEARD "MISTRESS SHI" SCREAM OUT...
堡家石
FACELESS BASTARDS!
THEN FIVE YEARS AGO, THE DUKE "GANLU'S" CASE OCCURRED. YOU REMEMBER THAT CASE DON'T YOU?
YES, UNDER THE URGING OF THE BISHOP, HE ATTEMPTED TO DISPOSE OF YOUR MASTER AND USURP THE THRONE. HE LEAD THREE THOUSAND TROOPS HERE...
BUT MASTER HAD ALREADY PREDICTED HIS PLANS AND SET UP A TRAP FOR THE DUKE. HE WAS CAPTURED AND STOOD TRIAL. UNFORTUNATELY, HE HAD ALREADY BRIBED MOST OF THE OFFICIALS AND WAS SOON ACQUITTED AND SET FREE...
THE METHODS AND EVIDENCES LINK THIS CASE TO THE PREVIOUS ONES. THIS IS CLEARLY THE WORK OF THE SAME GROUP OF MASKED MEN.

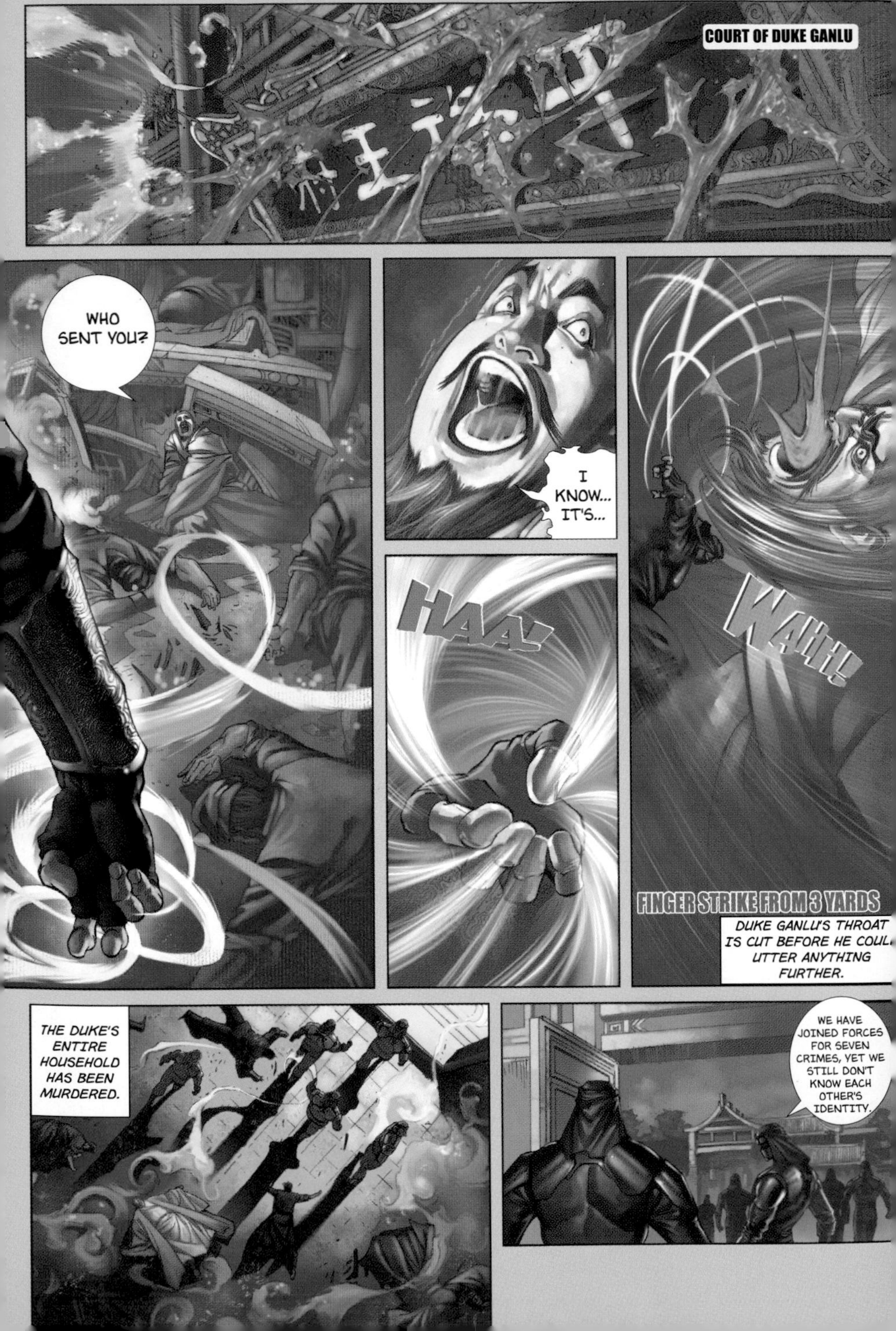
COURT OF DUKE GANLU
WHO SENT YOU?
I KNOW... IT'S...
HAAA!
WAHH!
FINGER STRIKE FROM 3 YARDS
DUKE GANLU'S THROAT IS CUT BEFORE HE COUL UTTER ANYTHING FURTHER.
THE DUKE'S ENTIRE HOUSEHOLD HAS BEEN MURDERED.
WE HAVE JOINED FORCES FOR SEVEN CRIMES, YET WE STILL DON'T KNOW EACH OTHER'S IDENTITY.

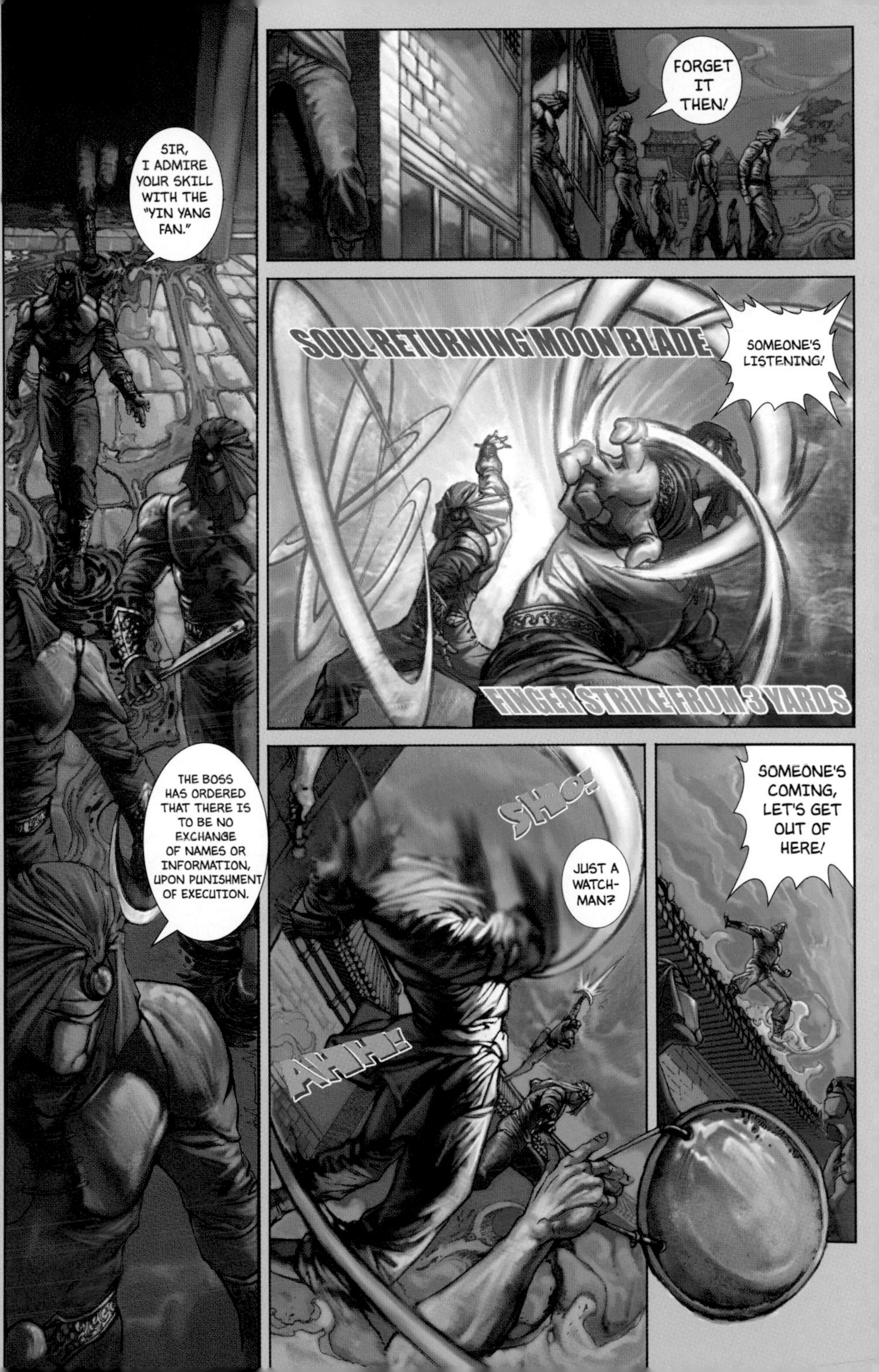
SIR, I ADMIRE YOUR SKILL WITH THE "YIN YANG FAN."
THE BOSS HAS ORDERED THAT THERE IS TO BE NO EXCHANGE OF NAMES OR INFORMATION, UPON PUNISHMENT OF EXECUTION.
FORGET IT THEN!
SOUL RETURNING MOON BLADE
SOMEONE'S LISTENING!
FINGER STRIKE FROM 3 YARDS
SHO!
JUST A WATCH-MAN?
AHH!
SOMEONE'S COMING, LET'S GET OUT OF HERE!

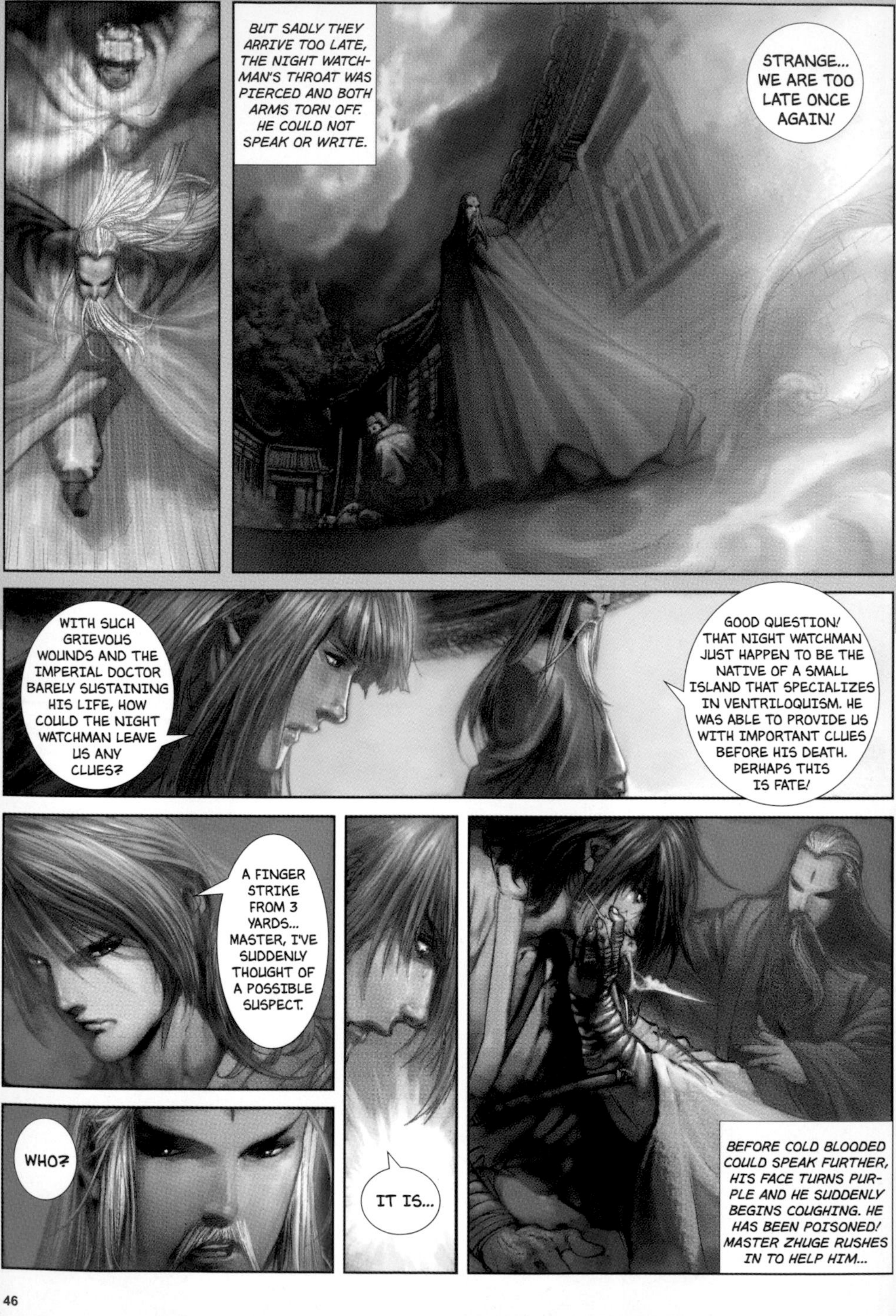
BUT SADLY THEY ARRIVE TOO LATE, THE NIGHT WATCH-MAN'S THROAT WAS PIERCED AND BOTH ARMS TORN OFF. HE COULD NOT SPEAK OR WRITE.
STRANGE... WE ARE TOO LATE ONCE AGAIN!
WITH SUCH GRIEVOUS WOUNDS AND THE IMPERIAL DOCTOR BARELY SUSTAINING HIS LIFE, HOW COULD THE NIGHT WATCHMAN LEAVE US ANY CLUES?
GOOD QUESTION! THAT NIGHT WATCHMAN JUST HAPPEN TO BE THE NATIVE OF A SMALL ISLAND THAT SPECIALIZES IN VENTRILOQUISM. HE WAS ABLE TO PROVIDE US WITH IMPORTANT CLUES BEFORE HIS DEATH. PERHAPS THIS IS FATE!
A FINGER STRIKE FROM 3 YARDS... MASTER, I'VE SUDDENLY THOUGHT OF A POSSIBLE SUSPECT.
WHO?
IT IS...
BEFORE COLD BLOODED COULD SPEAK FURTHER, HIS FACE TURNS PUR-PLE AND HE SUDDENLY BEGINS COUGHING. HE HAS BEEN POISONED! MASTER ZHUGE RUSHES IN TO HELP HIM...

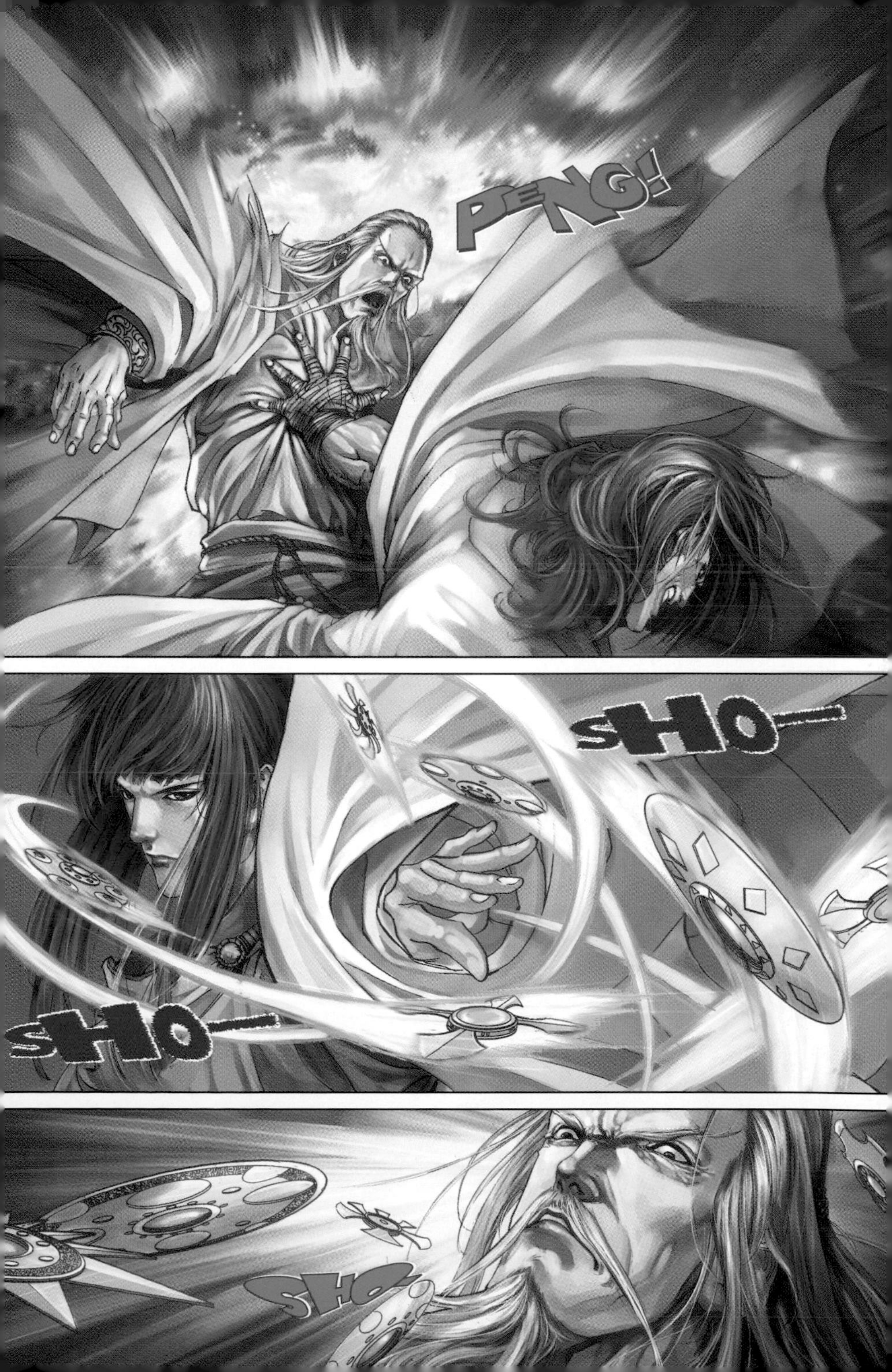
PENG!
SHO—
SHO—
SHO

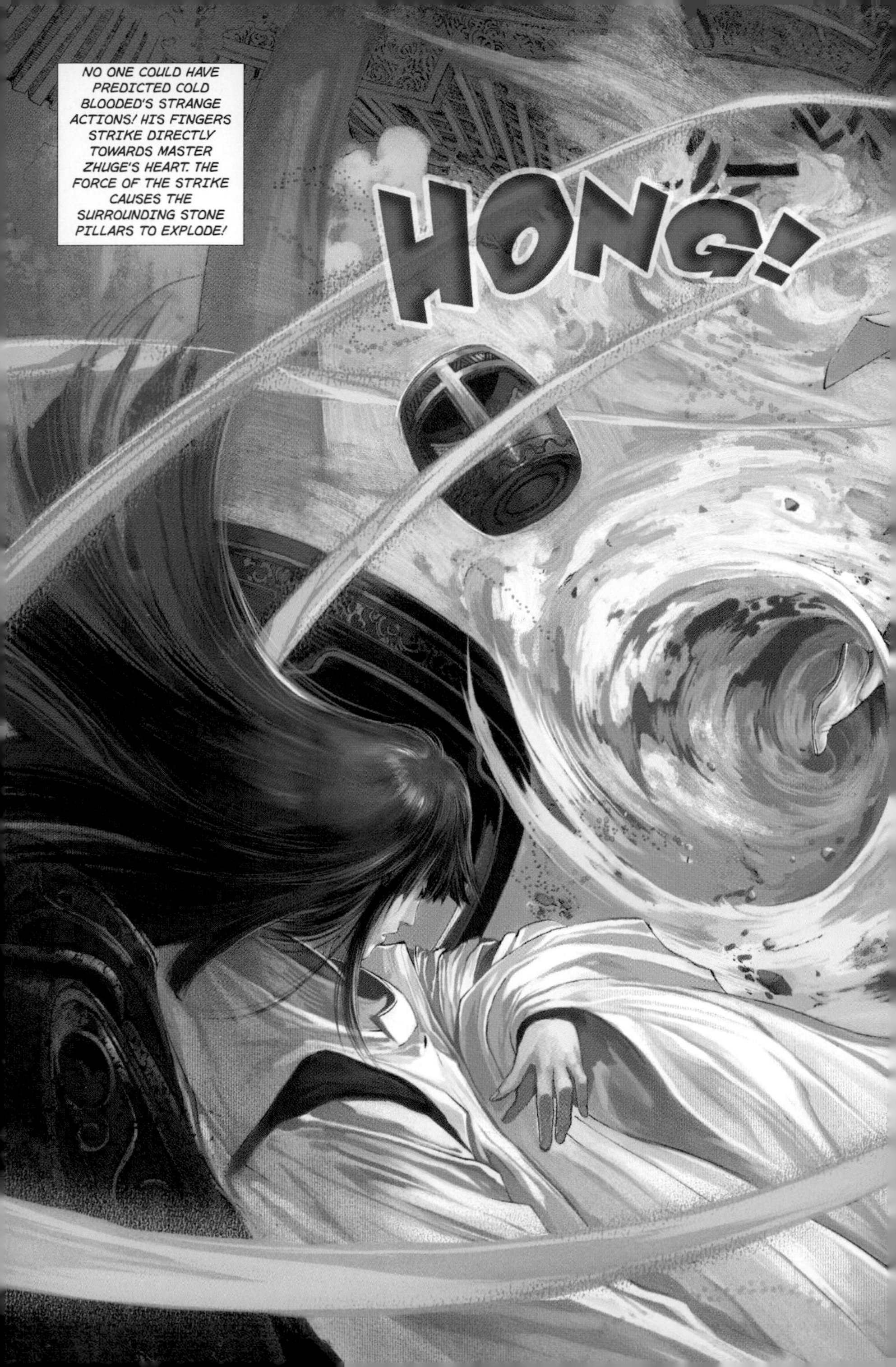
NO ONE COULD HAVE PREDICTED COLD BLOODED'S STRANGE ACTIONS! HIS FINGERS STRIKE DIRECTLY TOWARDS MASTER ZHUGE'S HEART. THE FORCE OF THE STRIKE CAUSES THE SURROUNDING STONE PILLARS TO EXPLODE!
HONG!

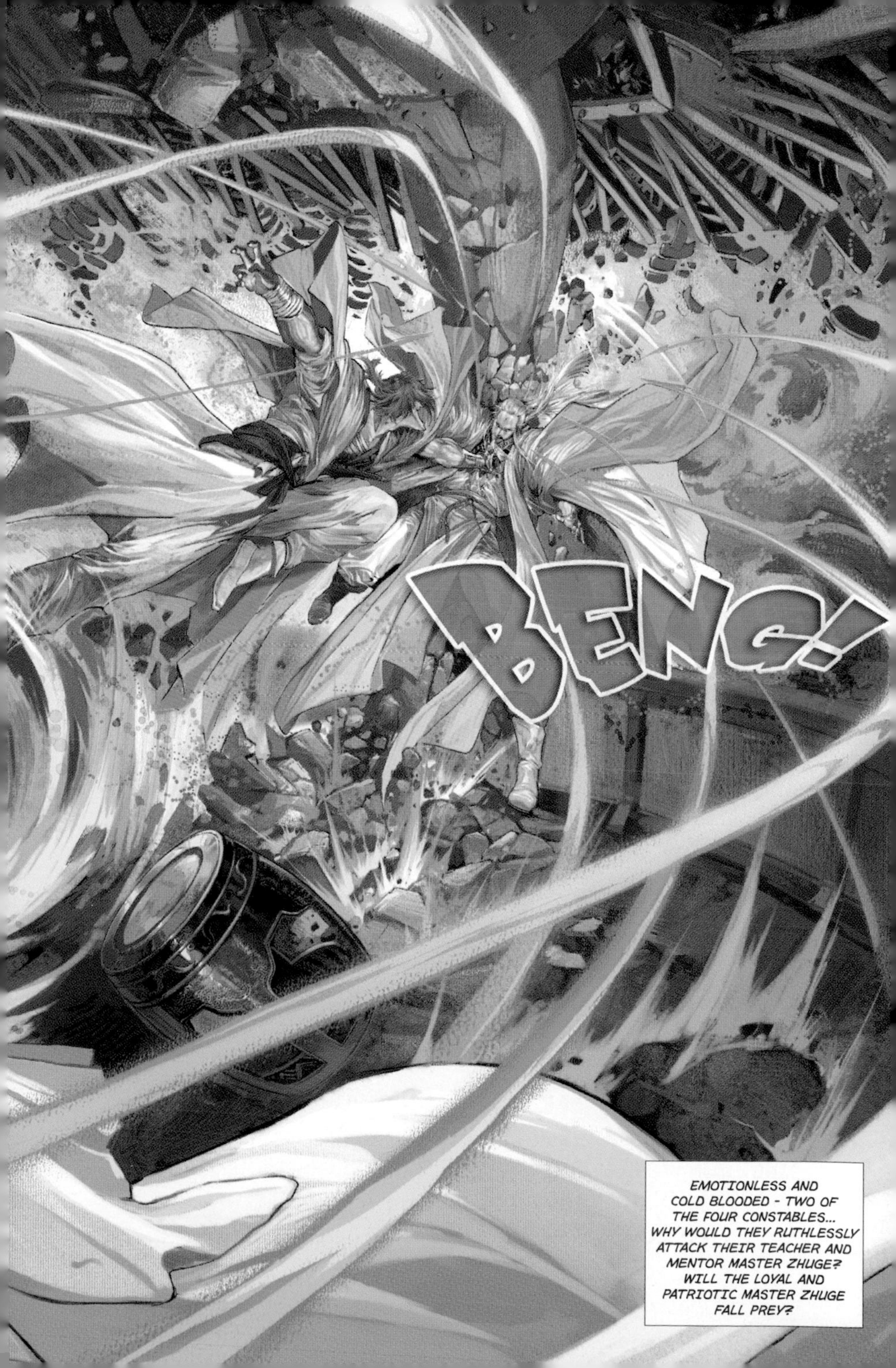
BENG!
EMOTIONLESS AND COLD BLOODED - TWO OF THE FOUR CONSTABLES... WHY WOULD THEY RUTHLESSLY ATTACK THEIR TEACHER AND MENTOR MASTER ZHUGE? WILL THE LOYAL AND PATRIOTIC MASTER ZHUGE FALL PREY?

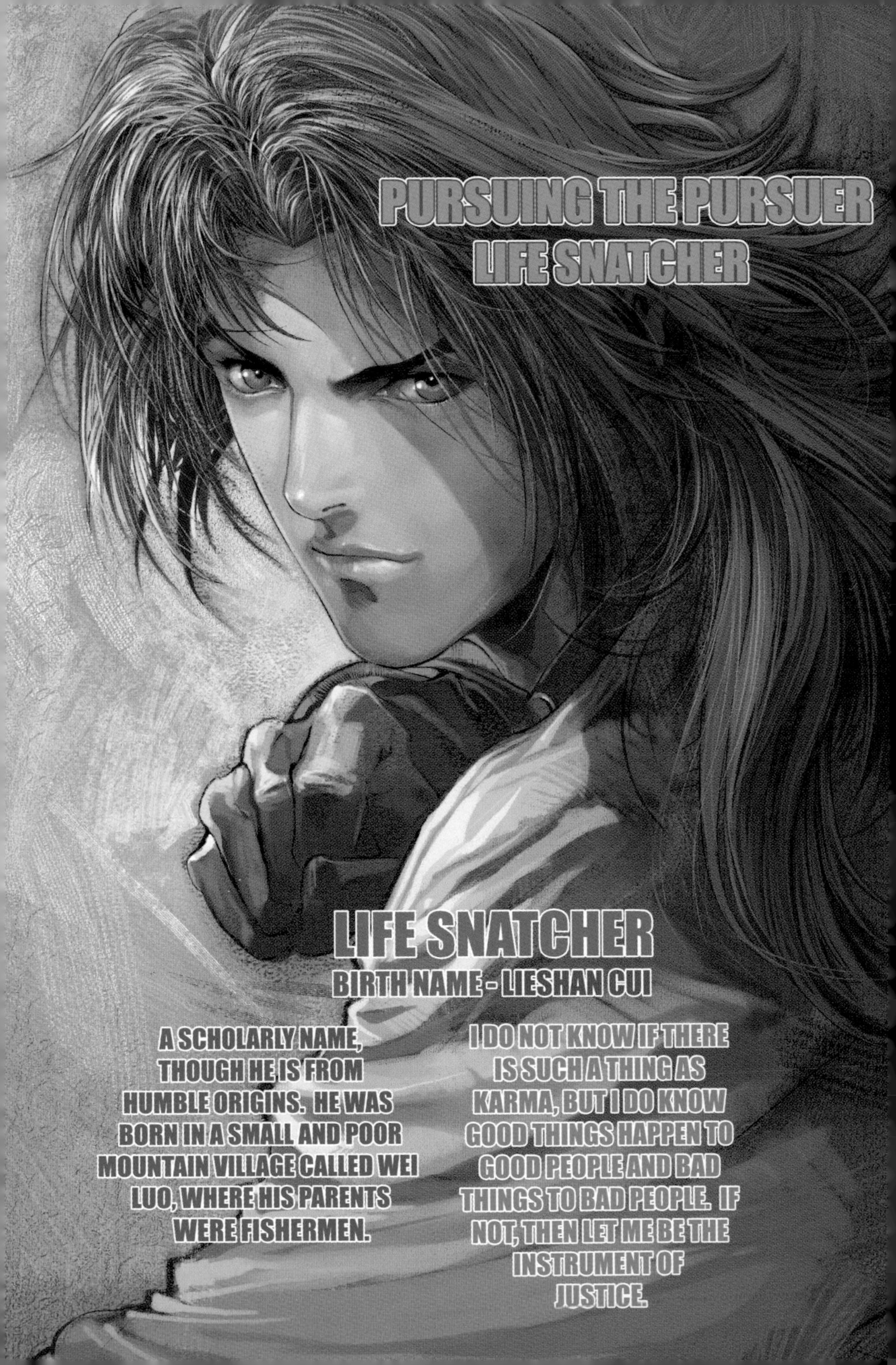
PURSUING THE PURSUER
LIFE SNATCHER
LIFE SNATCHER
BIRTH NAME - LIESHAN CUI
A SCHOLARLY NAME, THOUGH HE IS FROM HUMBLE ORIGINS. HE WAS BORN IN A SMALL AND POOR MOUNTAIN VILLAGE CALLED WEI LUO, WHERE HIS PARENTS WERE FISHERMEN.
I DO NOT KNOW IF THERE IS SUCH A THING AS KARMA, BUT I DO KNOW GOOD THINGS HAPPEN TO GOOD PEOPLE AND BAD THINGS TO BAD PEOPLE. IF NOT, THEN LET ME BE THE INSTRUMENT OF JUSTICE.

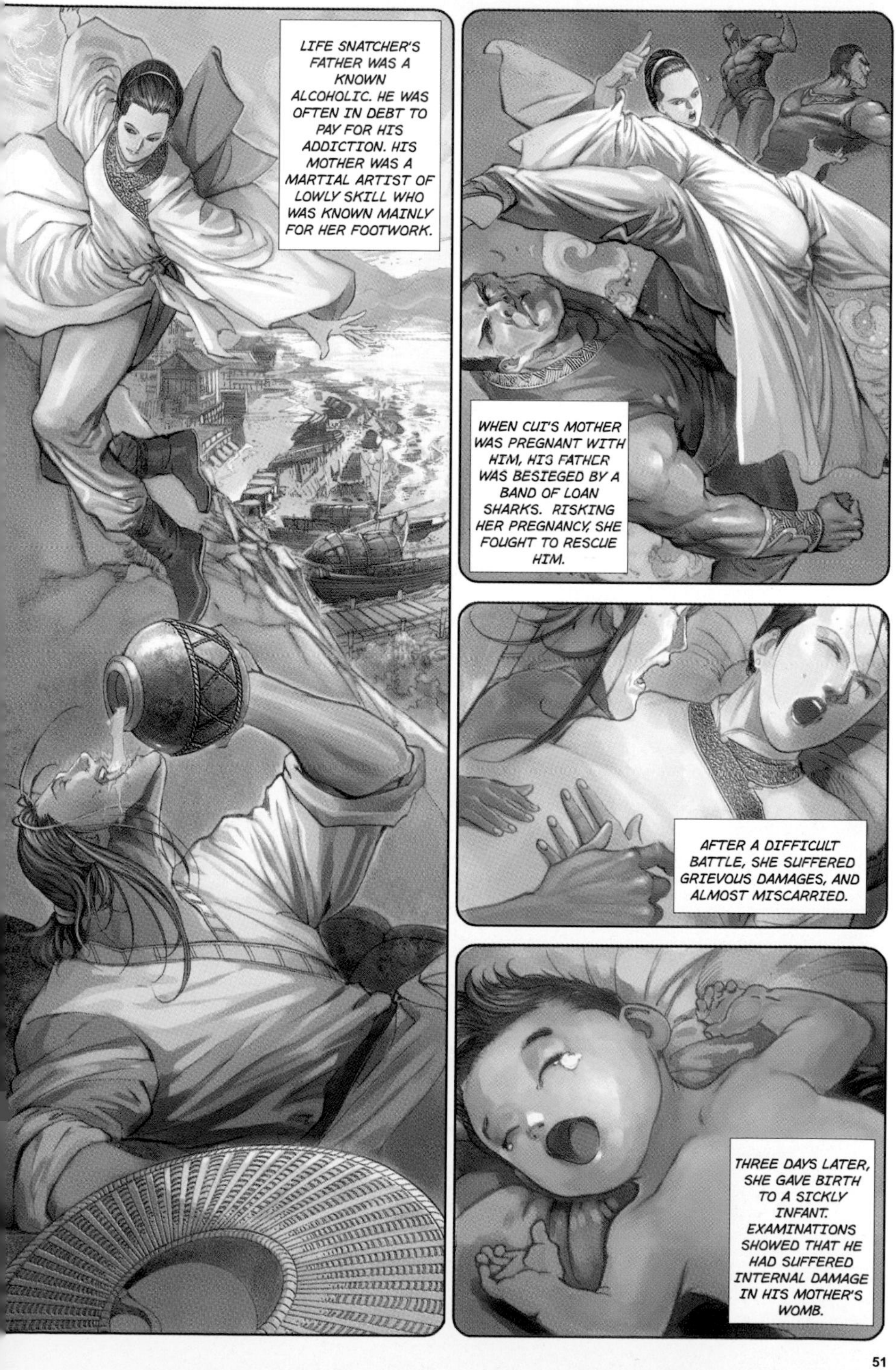
LIFE SNATCHER'S FATHER WAS A KNOWN ALCOHOLIC. HE WAS OFTEN IN DEBT TO PAY FOR HIS ADDICTION. HIS MOTHER WAS A MARTIAL ARTIST OF LOWLY SKILL WHO WAS KNOWN MAINLY FOR HER FOOTWORK.
WHEN CUI'S MOTHER WAS PREGNANT WITH HIM, HIS FATHER WAS BESIEGED BY A BAND OF LOAN SHARKS. RISKING HER PREGNANCY, SHE FOUGHT TO RESCUE HIM.
AFTER A DIFFICULT BATTLE, SHE SUFFERED GRIEVOUS DAMAGES, AND ALMOST MISCARRIED.
THREE DAYS LATER, SHE GAVE BIRTH TO A SICKLY INFANT. EXAMINATIONS SHOWED THAT HE HAD SUFFERED INTERNAL DAMAGE IN HIS MOTHER'S WOMB.

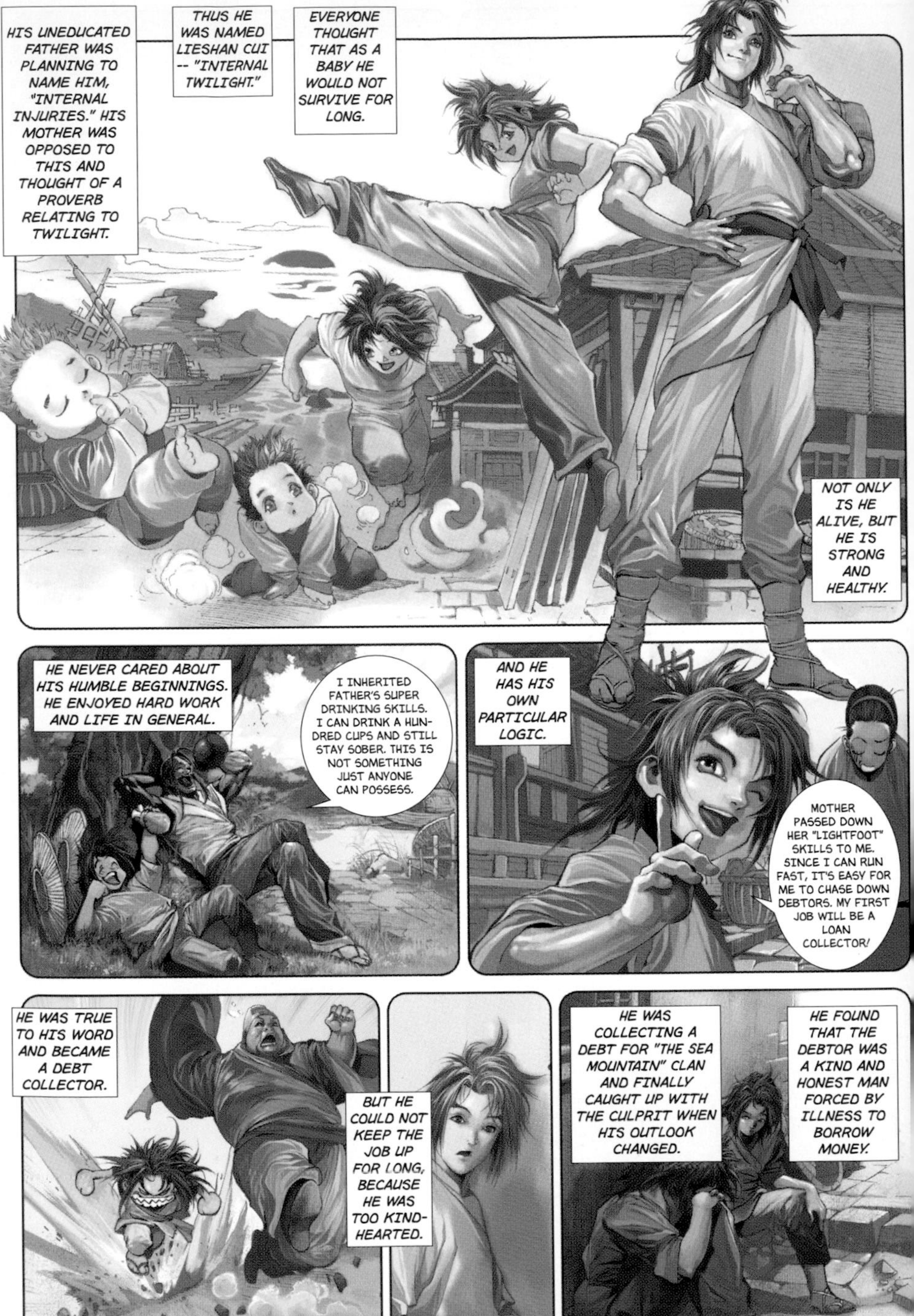
HIS UNEDUCATED FATHER WAS PLANNING TO NAME HIM, "INTERNAL INJURIES." HIS MOTHER WAS OPPOSED TO THIS AND THOUGHT OF A PROVERB RELATING TO TWILIGHT.
THUS HE WAS NAMED LIESHAN CUI -- "INTERNAL TWILIGHT."
EVERYONE THOUGHT THAT AS A BABY HE WOULD NOT SURVIVE FOR LONG.
NOT ONLY IS HE ALIVE, BUT HE IS STRONG AND HEALTHY.
HE NEVER CARED ABOUT HIS HUMBLE BEGINNINGS. HE ENJOYED HARD WORK AND LIFE IN GENERAL.
I INHERITED FATHER'S SUPER DRINKING SKILLS. I CAN DRINK A HUNDRED CUPS AND STILL STAY SOBER. THIS IS NOT SOMETHING JUST ANYONE CAN POSSESS.
AND HE HAS HIS OWN PARTICULAR LOGIC.
MOTHER PASSED DOWN HER "LIGHTFOOT" SKILLS TO ME. SINCE I CAN RUN FAST, IT'S EASY FOR ME TO CHASE DOWN DEBTORS. MY FIRST JOB WILL BE A LOAN COLLECTOR!
HE WAS TRUE TO HIS WORD AND BECAME A DEBT COLLECTOR.
BUT HE COULD NOT KEEP THE JOB UP FOR LONG, BECAUSE HE WAS TOO KIND-HEARTED.
HE WAS COLLECTING A DEBT FOR "THE SEA MOUNTAIN" CLAN AND FINALLY CAUGHT UP WITH THE CULPRIT WHEN HIS OUTLOOK CHANGED.
HE FOUND THAT THE DEBTOR WAS A KIND AND HONEST MAN FORCED BY ILLNESS TO BORROW MONEY.

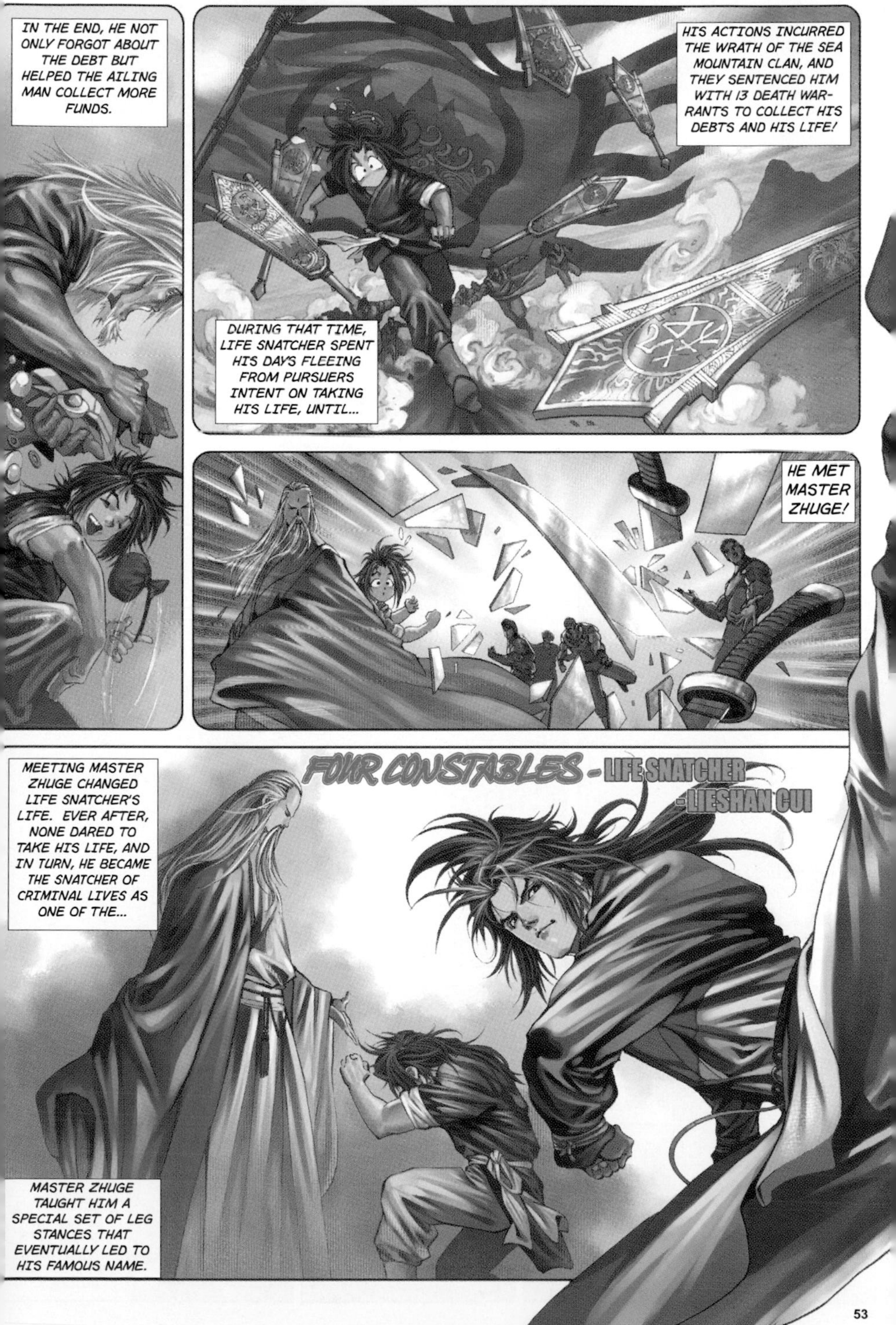
IN THE END, HE NOT ONLY FORGOT ABOUT THE DEBT BUT HELPED THE AILING MAN COLLECT MORE FUNDS.
HIS ACTIONS INCURRED THE WRATH OF THE SEA MOUNTAIN CLAN, AND THEY SENTENCED HIM WITH 13 DEATH WARRANTS TO COLLECT HIS DEBTS AND HIS LIFE!
DURING THAT TIME, LIFE SNATCHER SPENT HIS DAY'S FLEEING FROM PURSUERS INTENT ON TAKING HIS LIFE, UNTIL...
HE MET MASTER ZHUGE!
MEETING MASTER ZHUGE CHANGED LIFE SNATCHER'S LIFE. EVER AFTER, NONE DARED TO TAKE HIS LIFE, AND IN TURN, HE BECAME THE SNATCHER OF CRIMINAL LIVES AS ONE OF THE...
FOUR CONSTABLES - LIFE SNATCHER
- LIESHAN CUI
MASTER ZHUGE TAUGHT HIM A SPECIAL SET OF LEG STANCES THAT EVENTUALLY LED TO HIS FAMOUS NAME.

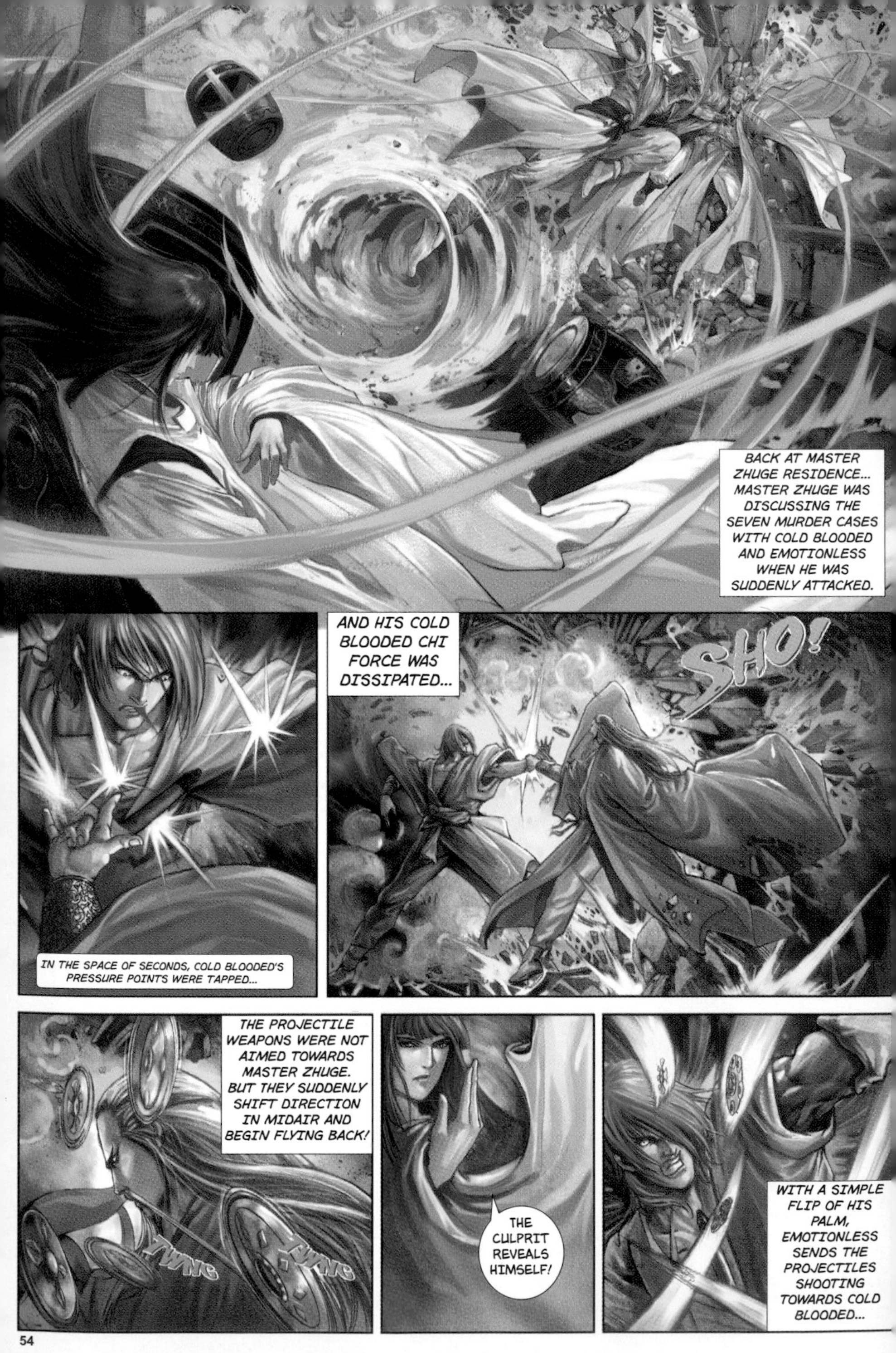
BACK AT MASTER ZHUGE RESIDENCE... MASTER ZHUGE WAS DISCUSSING THE SEVEN MURDER CASES WITH COLD BLOODED AND EMOTIONLESS WHEN HE WAS SUDDENLY ATTACKED.
IN THE SPACE OF SECONDS, COLD BLOODED'S PRESSURE POINTS WERE TAPPED...
AND HIS COLD BLOODED CHI FORCE WAS DISSIPATED...
SHO!
THE PROJECTILE WEAPONS WERE NOT AIMED TOWARDS MASTER ZHUGE. BUT THEY SUDDENLY SHIFT DIRECTION IN MIDAIR AND BEGIN FLYING BACK!
TWANG
TWANG
THE CULPRIT REVEALS HIMSELF!
WITH A SIMPLE FLIP OF HIS PALM, EMOTIONLESS SENDS THE PROJECTILES SHOOTING TOWARDS COLD BLOODED...

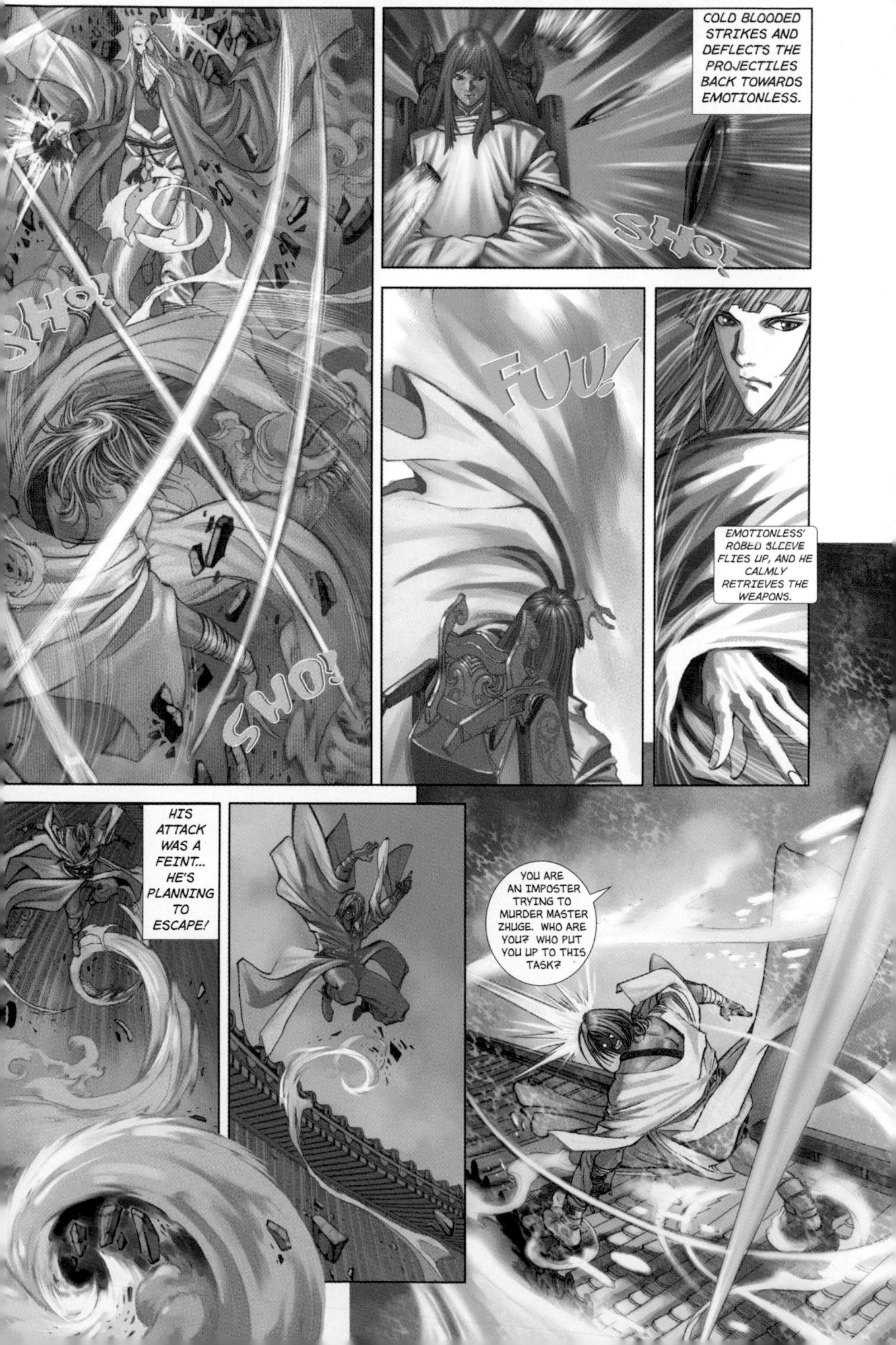
SHO!
SHO!
COLD BLOODED STRIKES AND DEFLECTS THE PROJECTILES BACK TOWARDS EMOTIONLESS.
SHO!
FUU!
EMOTIONLESS' ROBED SLEEVE FLIES UP, AND HE CALMLY RETRIEVES THE WEAPONS.
HIS ATTACK WAS A FEINT... HE'S PLANNING TO ESCAPE!
YOU ARE AN IMPOSTER TRYING TO MURDER MASTER ZHUGE. WHO ARE YOU? WHO PUT YOU UP TO THIS TASK?

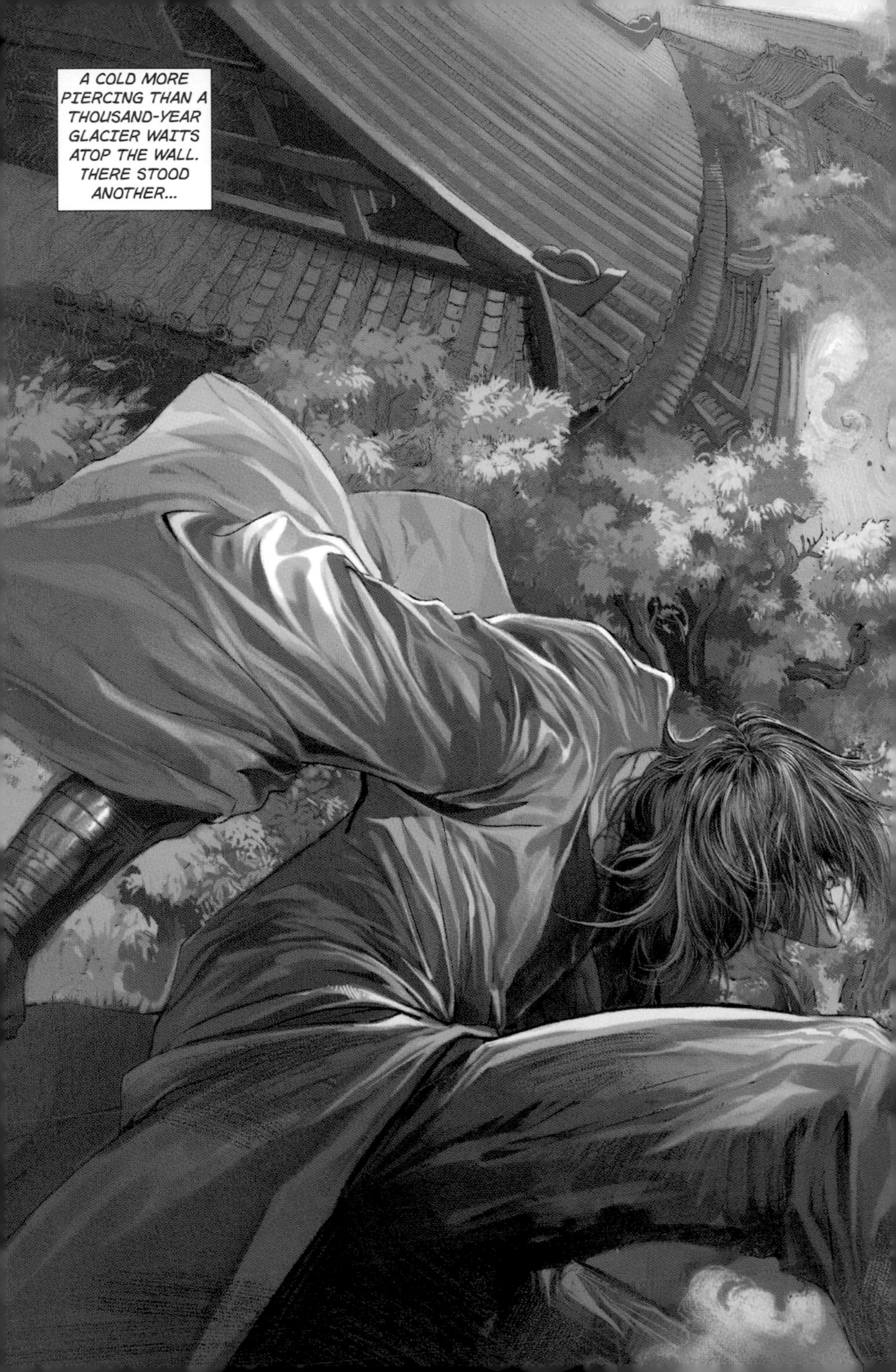
A COLD MORE PIERCING THAN A THOUSAND-YEAR GLACIER WAITS ATOP THE WALL. THERE STOOD ANOTHER...

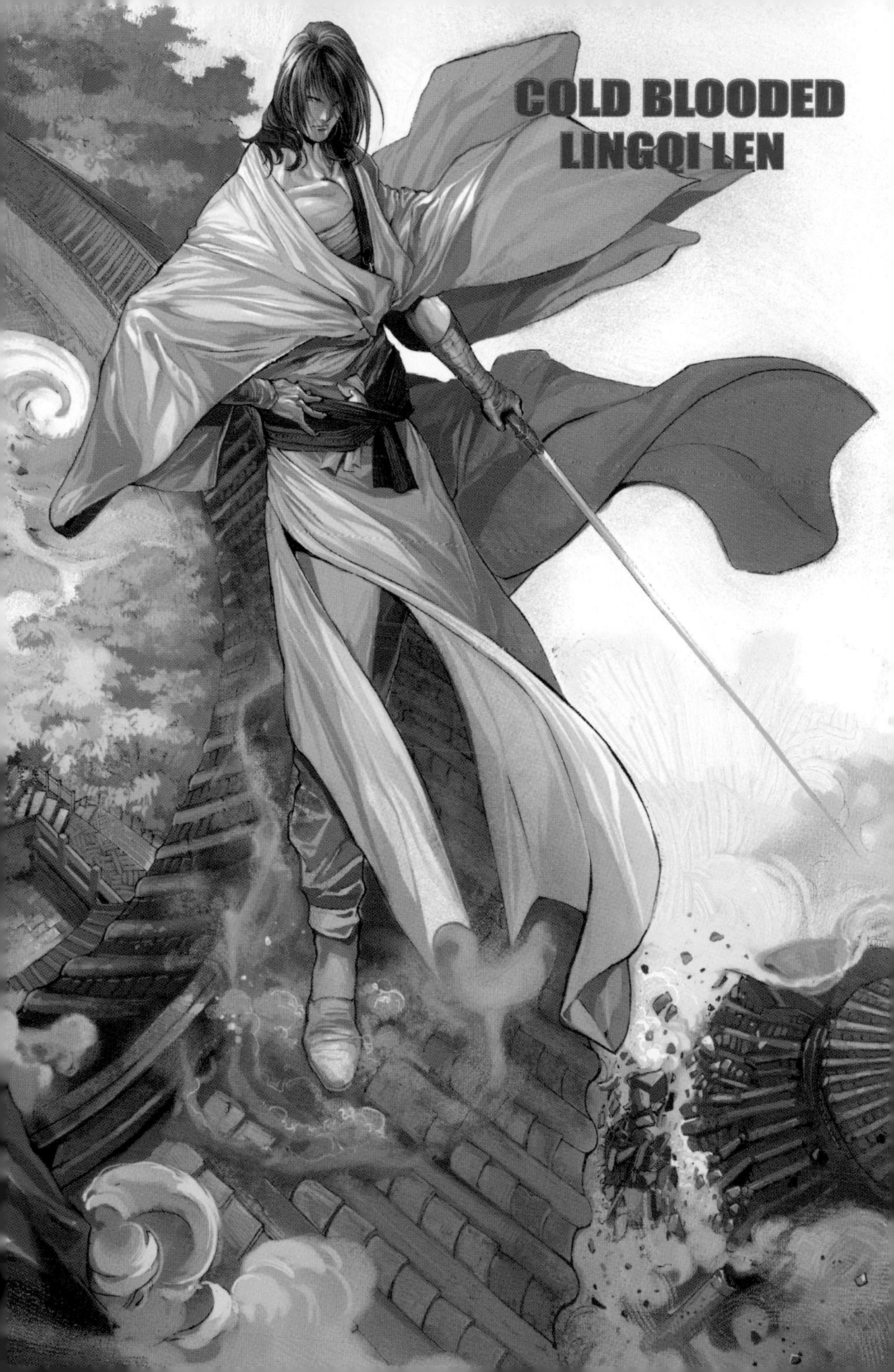
COLD BLOODED
LINGQI LEN

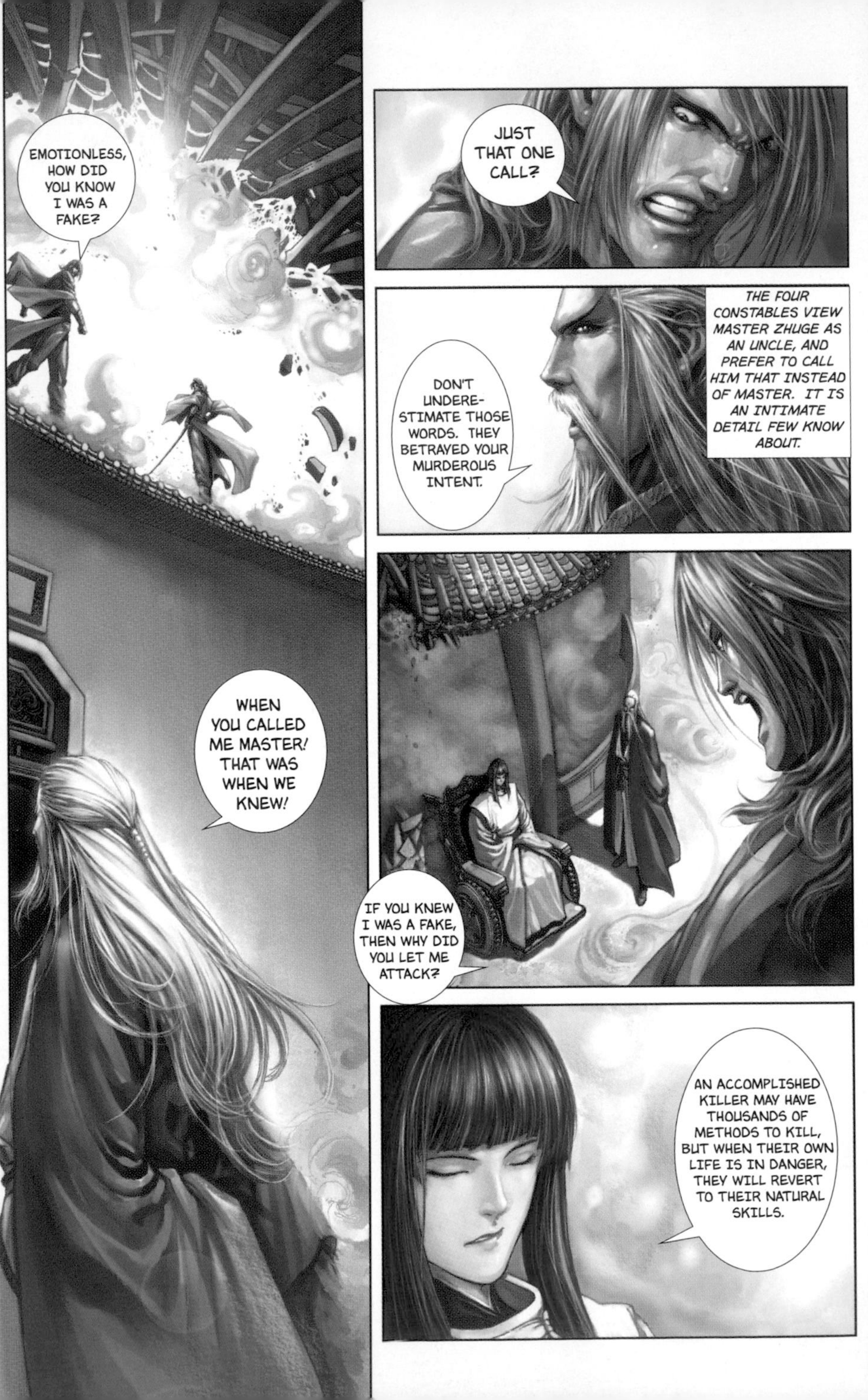
EMOTIONLESS, HOW DID YOU KNOW I WAS A FAKE?
WHEN YOU CALLED ME MASTER! THAT WAS WHEN WE KNEW!
JUST THAT ONE CALL?
THE FOUR CONSTABLES VIEW MASTER ZHUGE AS AN UNCLE, AND PREFER TO CALL HIM THAT INSTEAD OF MASTER. IT IS AN INTIMATE DETAIL FEW KNOW ABOUT.
DON'T UNDERE-STIMATE THOSE WORDS. THEY BETRAYED YOUR MURDEROUS INTENT.
IF YOU KNEW I WAS A FAKE, THEN WHY DID YOU LET ME ATTACK?
AN ACCOMPLISHED KILLER MAY HAVE THOUSANDS OF METHODS TO KILL, BUT WHEN THEIR OWN LIFE IS IN DANGER, THEY WILL REVERT TO THEIR NATURAL SKILLS.

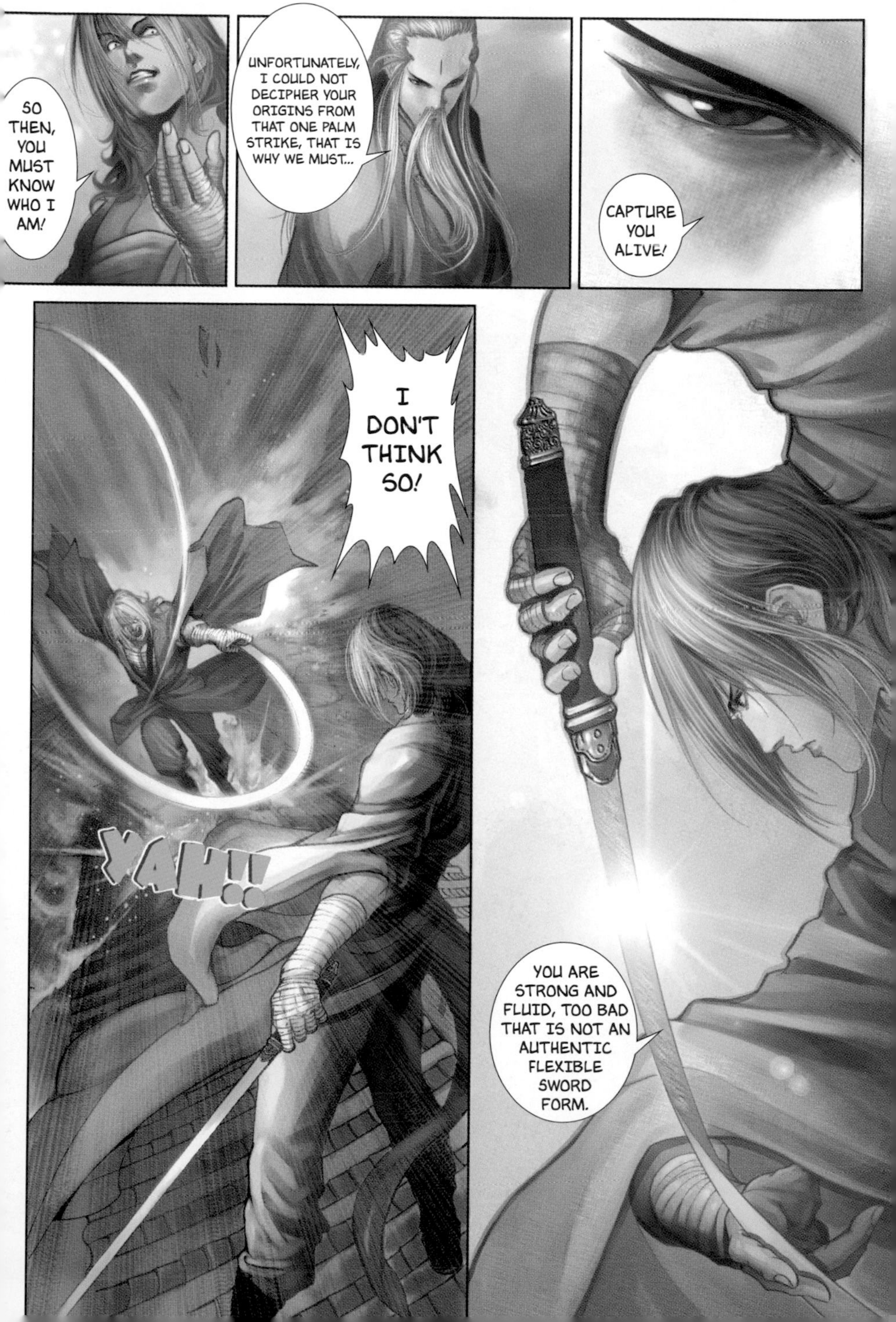
SO THEN, YOU MUST KNOW WHO I AM!
UNFORTUNATELY, I COULD NOT DECIPHER YOUR ORIGINS FROM THAT ONE PALM STRIKE, THAT IS WHY WE MUST...
CAPTURE YOU ALIVE!
I DON'T THINK SO!
YAH!!
YOU ARE STRONG AND FLUID, TOO BAD THAT IS NOT AN AUTHENTIC FLEXIBLE SWORD FORM.

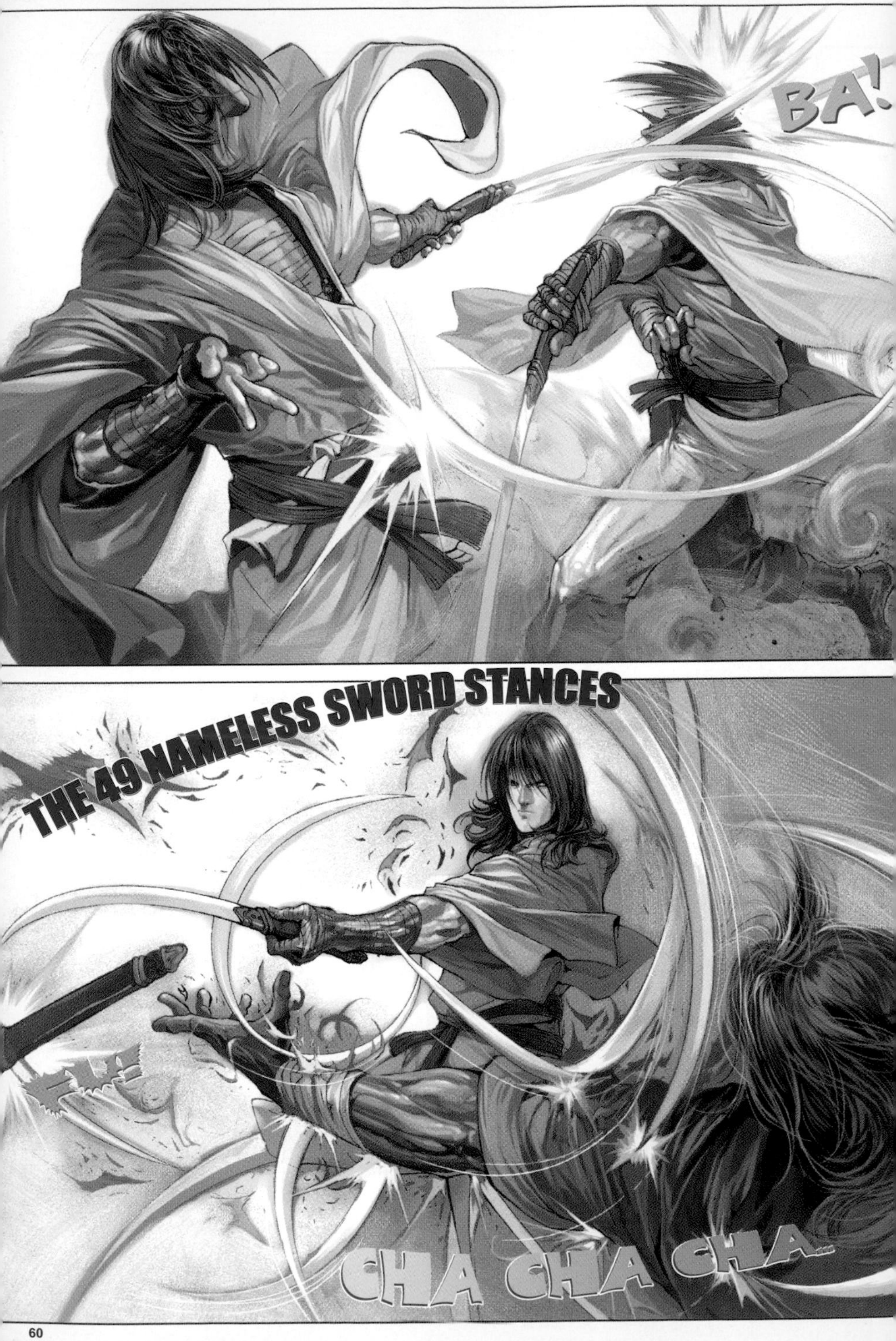
BA!
THE 49 NAMELESS SWORD STANCES
CHA CHA CHA...

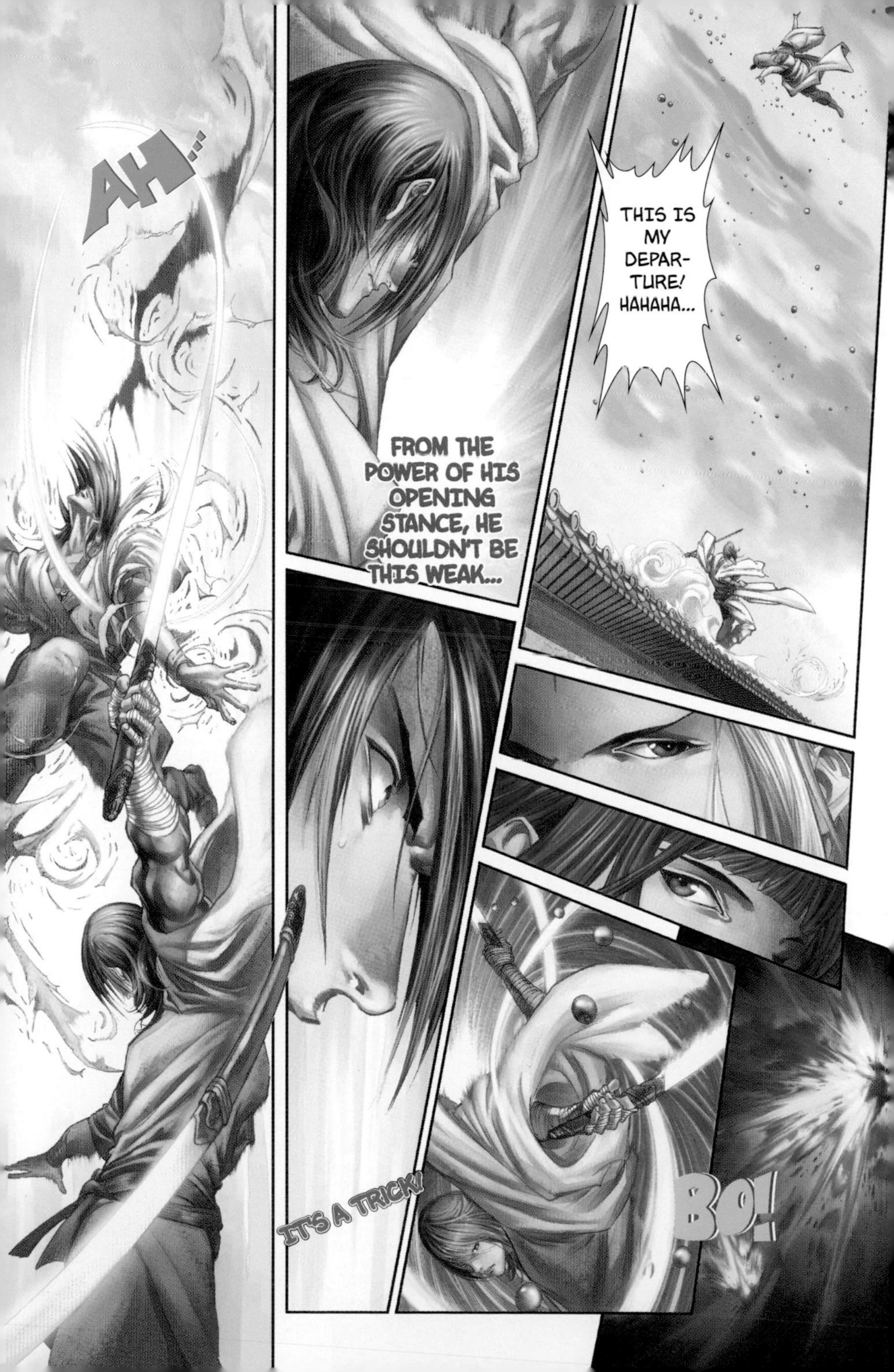
AH...
THIS IS MY DEPAR-TURE! HAHAHA...
FROM THE POWER OF HIS OPENING STANCE, HE SHOULDN'T BE THIS WEAK...
IT'S A TRICK!
BO!

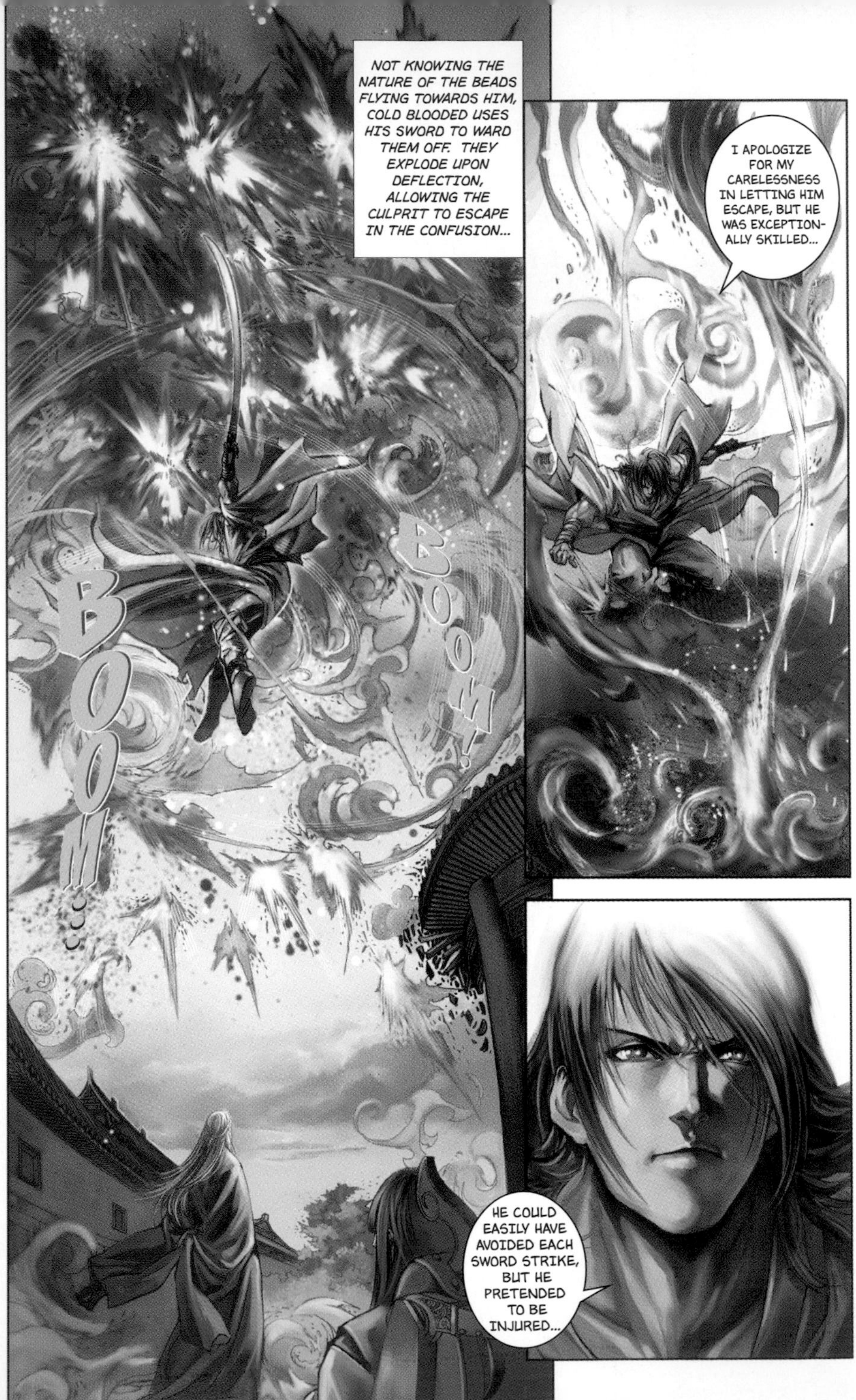
NOT KNOWING THE NATURE OF THE BEADS FLYING TOWARDS HIM, COLD BLOODED USES HIS SWORD TO WARD THEM OFF. THEY EXPLODE UPON DEFLECTION, ALLOWING THE CULPRIT TO ESCAPE IN THE CONFUSION...
BOOM!
BOOM!...
I APOLOGIZE FOR MY CARELESSNESS IN LETTING HIM ESCAPE, BUT HE WAS EXCEPTION-ALLY SKILLED...
HE COULD EASILY HAVE AVOIDED EACH SWORD STRIKE, BUT HE PRETENDED TO BE INJURED...

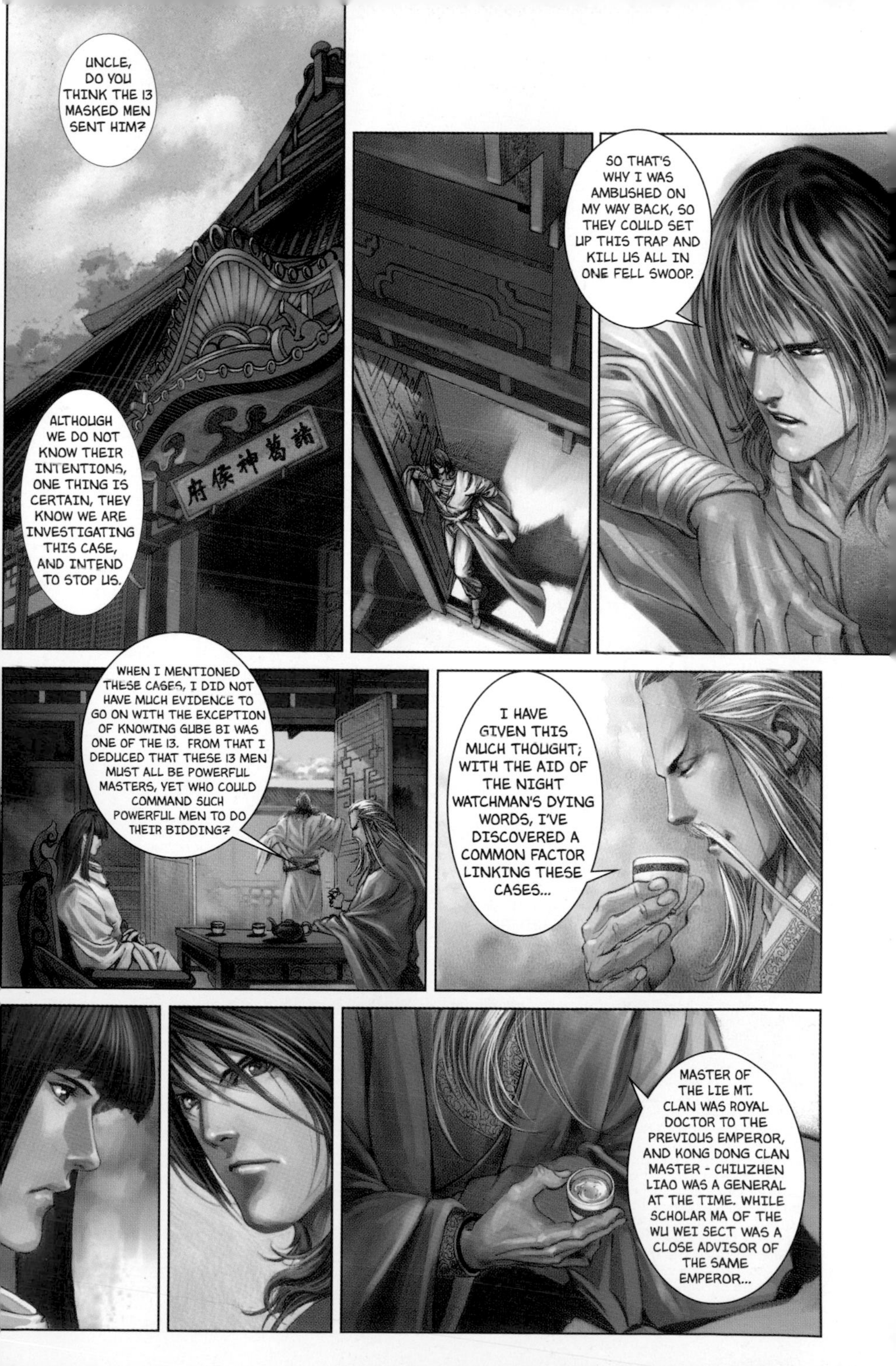
UNCLE, DO YOU THINK THE 13 MASKED MEN SENT HIM?
ALTHOUGH WE DO NOT KNOW THEIR INTENTIONS, ONE THING IS CERTAIN, THEY KNOW WE ARE INVESTIGATING THIS CASE, AND INTEND TO STOP US.
諸葛神侯府
SO THAT'S WHY I WAS AMBUSHED ON MY WAY BACK, SO THEY COULD SET UP THIS TRAP AND KILL US ALL IN ONE FELL SWOOP.
WHEN I MENTIONED THESE CASES, I DID NOT HAVE MUCH EVIDENCE TO GO ON WITH THE EXCEPTION OF KNOWING GUBE BI WAS ONE OF THE 13. FROM THAT I DEDUCED THAT THESE 13 MEN MUST ALL BE POWERFUL MASTERS, YET WHO COULD COMMAND SUCH POWERFUL MEN TO DO THEIR BIDDING?
I HAVE GIVEN THIS MUCH THOUGHT; WITH THE AID OF THE NIGHT WATCHMAN'S DYING WORDS, I'VE DISCOVERED A COMMON FACTOR LINKING THESE CASES...
MASTER OF THE LIE MT. CLAN WAS ROYAL DOCTOR TO THE PREVIOUS EMPEROR, AND KONG DONG CLAN MASTER - CHIUZHEN LIAO WAS A GENERAL AT THE TIME. WHILE SCHOLAR MA OF THE WU WEI SECT WAS A CLOSE ADVISOR OF THE SAME EMPEROR...

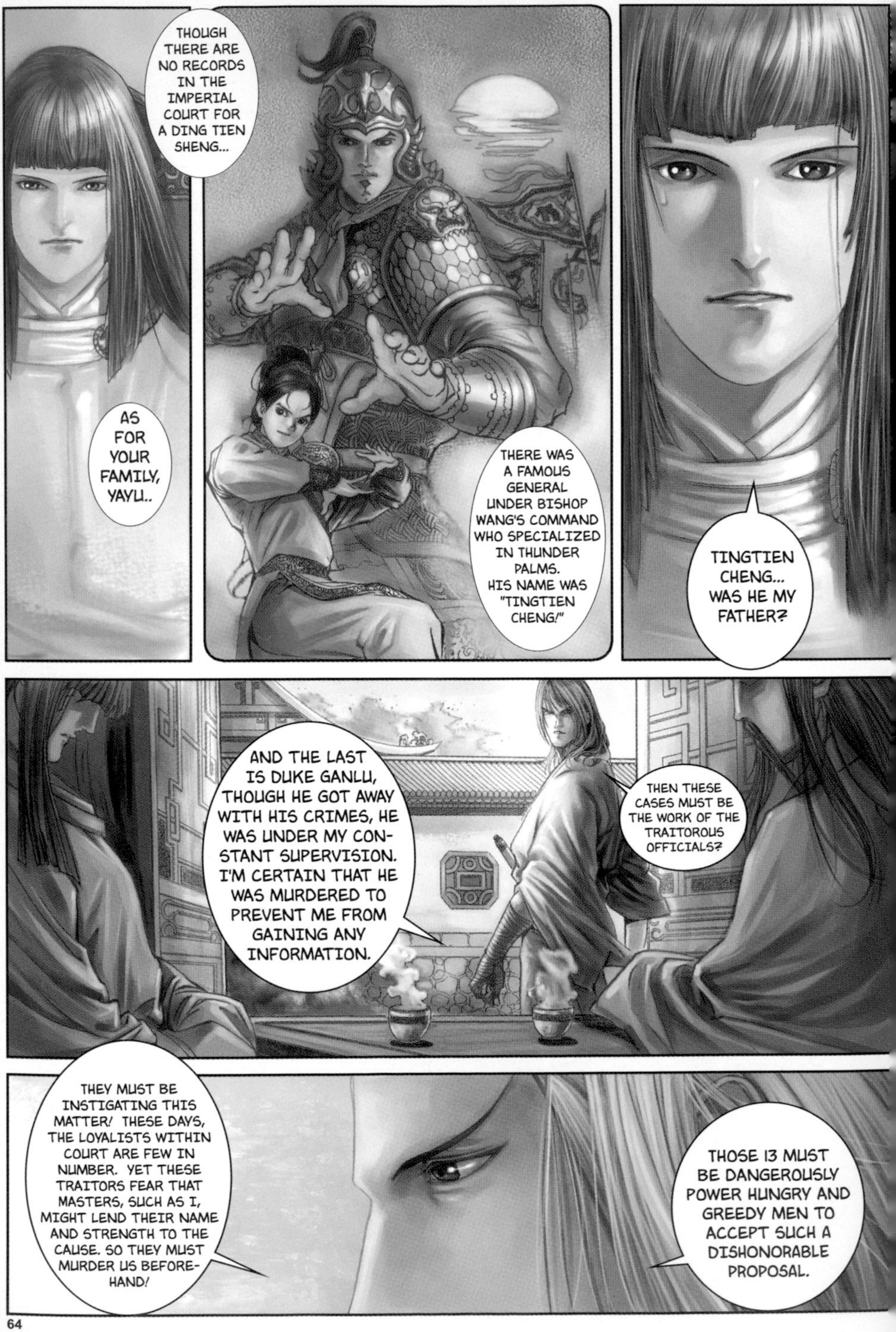
THOUGH THERE ARE NO RECORDS IN THE IMPERIAL COURT FOR A DING TIEN SHENG...
AS FOR YOUR FAMILY, YAYU..
THERE WAS A FAMOUS GENERAL UNDER BISHOP WANG'S COMMAND WHO SPECIALIZED IN THUNDER PALMS. HIS NAME WAS "TINGTIEN CHENG!"
TINGTIEN CHENG... WAS HE MY FATHER?
AND THE LAST IS DUKE GANLU, THOUGH HE GOT AWAY WITH HIS CRIMES, HE WAS UNDER MY CONSTANT SUPERVISION. I'M CERTAIN THAT HE WAS MURDERED TO PREVENT ME FROM GAINING ANY INFORMATION.
THEN THESE CASES MUST BE THE WORK OF THE TRAITOROUS OFFICIALS?
THEY MUST BE INSTIGATING THIS MATTER! THESE DAYS, THE LOYALISTS WITHIN COURT ARE FEW IN NUMBER. YET THESE TRAITORS FEAR THAT MASTERS, SUCH AS I, MIGHT LEND THEIR NAME AND STRENGTH TO THE CAUSE. SO THEY MUST MURDER US BEFOREHAND!
THOSE 13 MUST BE DANGEROUSLY POWER HUNGRY AND GREEDY MEN TO ACCEPT SUCH A DISHONORABLE PROPOSAL.

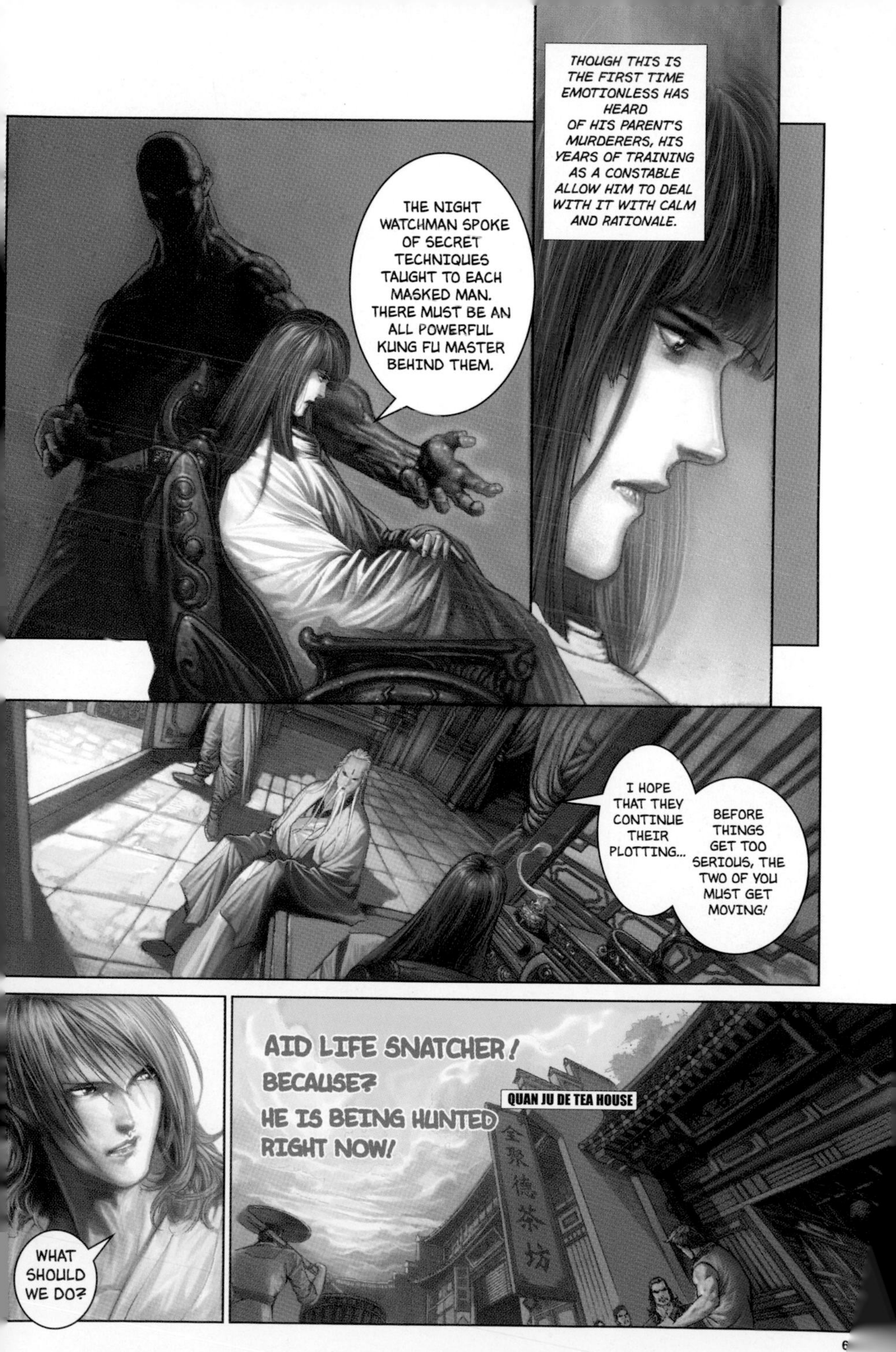
THOUGH THIS IS THE FIRST TIME EMOTIONLESS HAS HEARD OF HIS PARENT'S MURDERERS, HIS YEARS OF TRAINING AS A CONSTABLE ALLOW HIM TO DEAL WITH IT WITH CALM AND RATIONALE.
THE NIGHT WATCHMAN SPOKE OF SECRET TECHNIQUES TAUGHT TO EACH MASKED MAN. THERE MUST BE AN ALL POWERFUL KUNG FU MASTER BEHIND THEM.
I HOPE THAT THEY CONTINUE THEIR PLOTTING...
BEFORE THINGS GET TOO SERIOUS, THE TWO OF YOU MUST GET MOVING!
WHAT SHOULD WE DO?
AID LIFE SNATCHER!
BECAUSE?
HE IS BEING HUNTED RIGHT NOW!
QUAN JU DE TEA HOUSE
全聚德茶坊

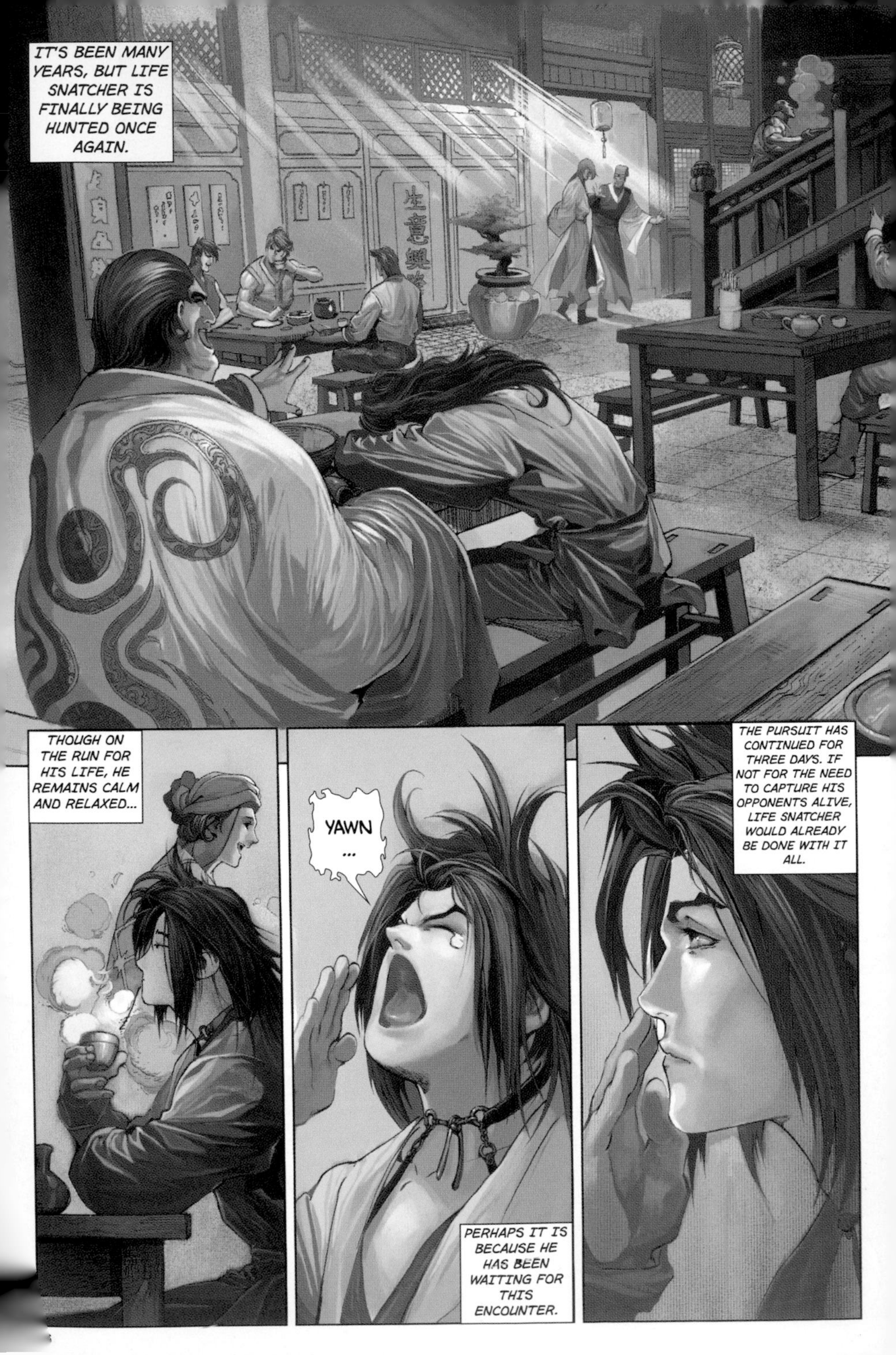
IT'S BEEN MANY YEARS, BUT LIFE SNATCHER IS FINALLY BEING HUNTED ONCE AGAIN.
THOUGH ON THE RUN FOR HIS LIFE, HE REMAINS CALM AND RELAXED...
YAWN ...
PERHAPS IT IS BECAUSE HE HAS BEEN WAITING FOR THIS ENCOUNTER.
THE PURSUIT HAS CONTINUED FOR THREE DAYS. IF NOT FOR THE NEED TO CAPTURE HIS OPPONENTS ALIVE, LIFE SNATCHER WOULD ALREADY BE DONE WITH IT ALL.

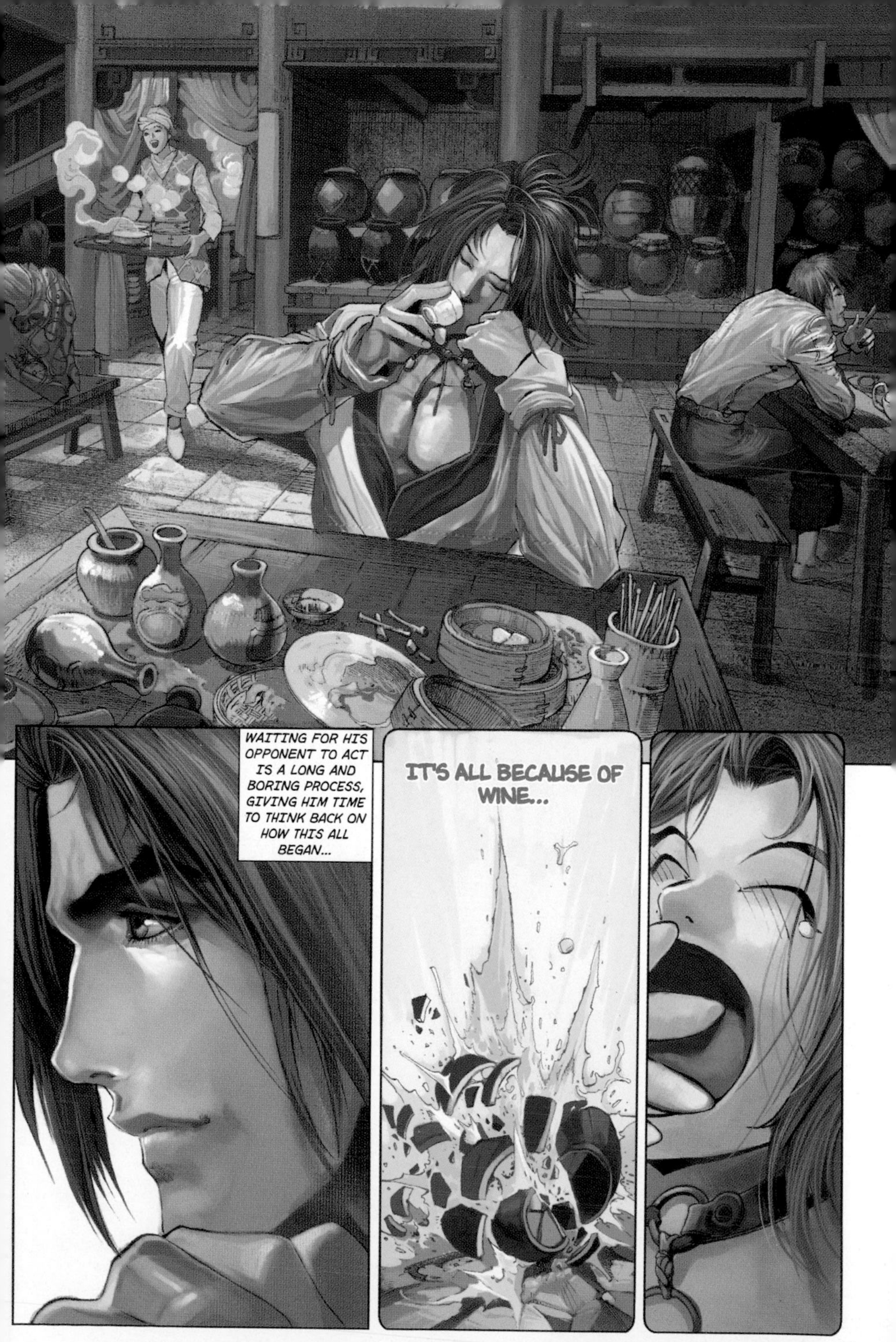
WAITING FOR HIS OPPONENT TO ACT IS A LONG AND BORING PROCESS, GIVING HIM TIME TO THINK BACK ON HOW THIS ALL BEGAN...
IT'S ALL BECAUSE OF WINE...

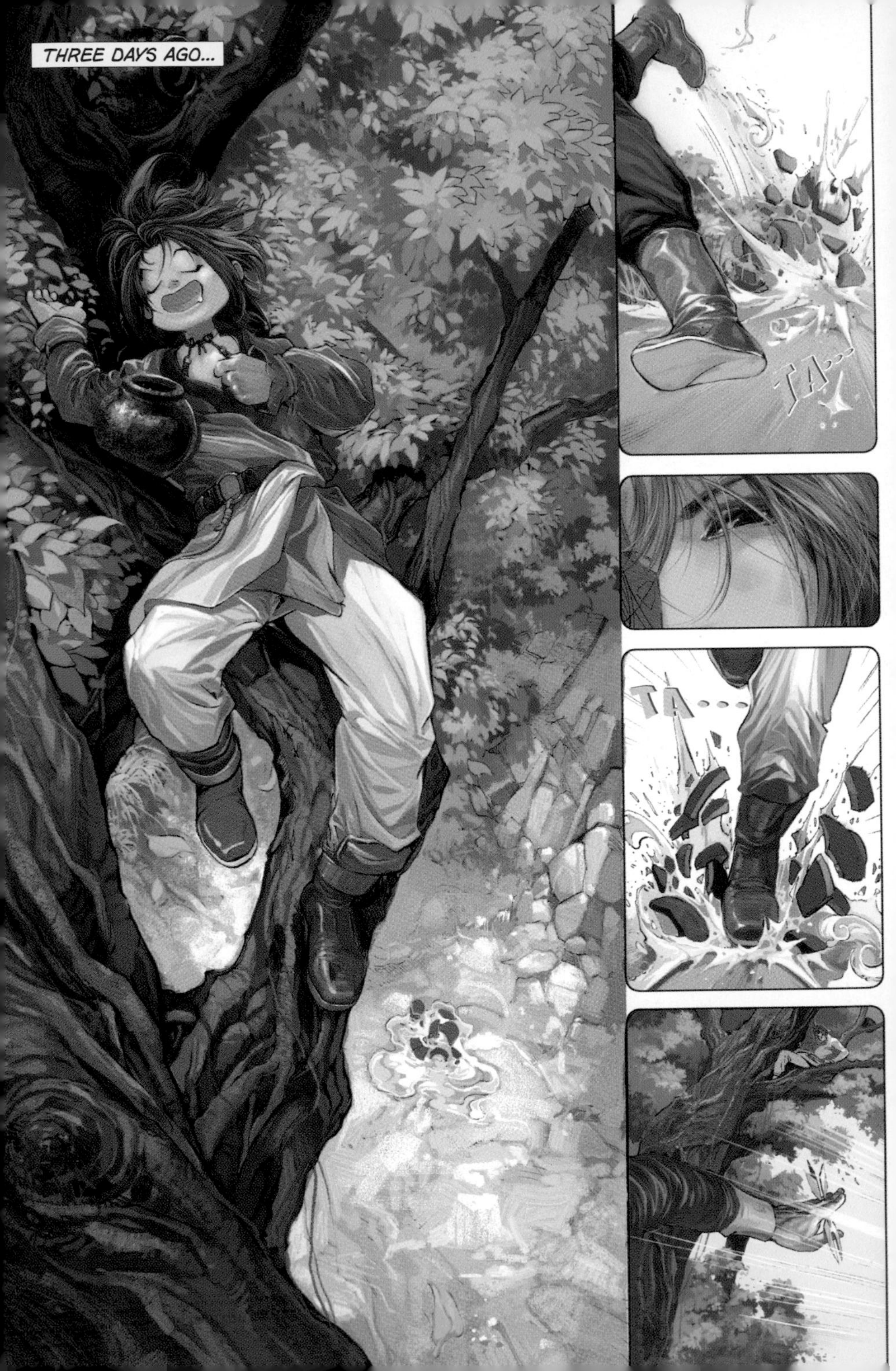
THREE DAYS AGO...
TA...
TA...

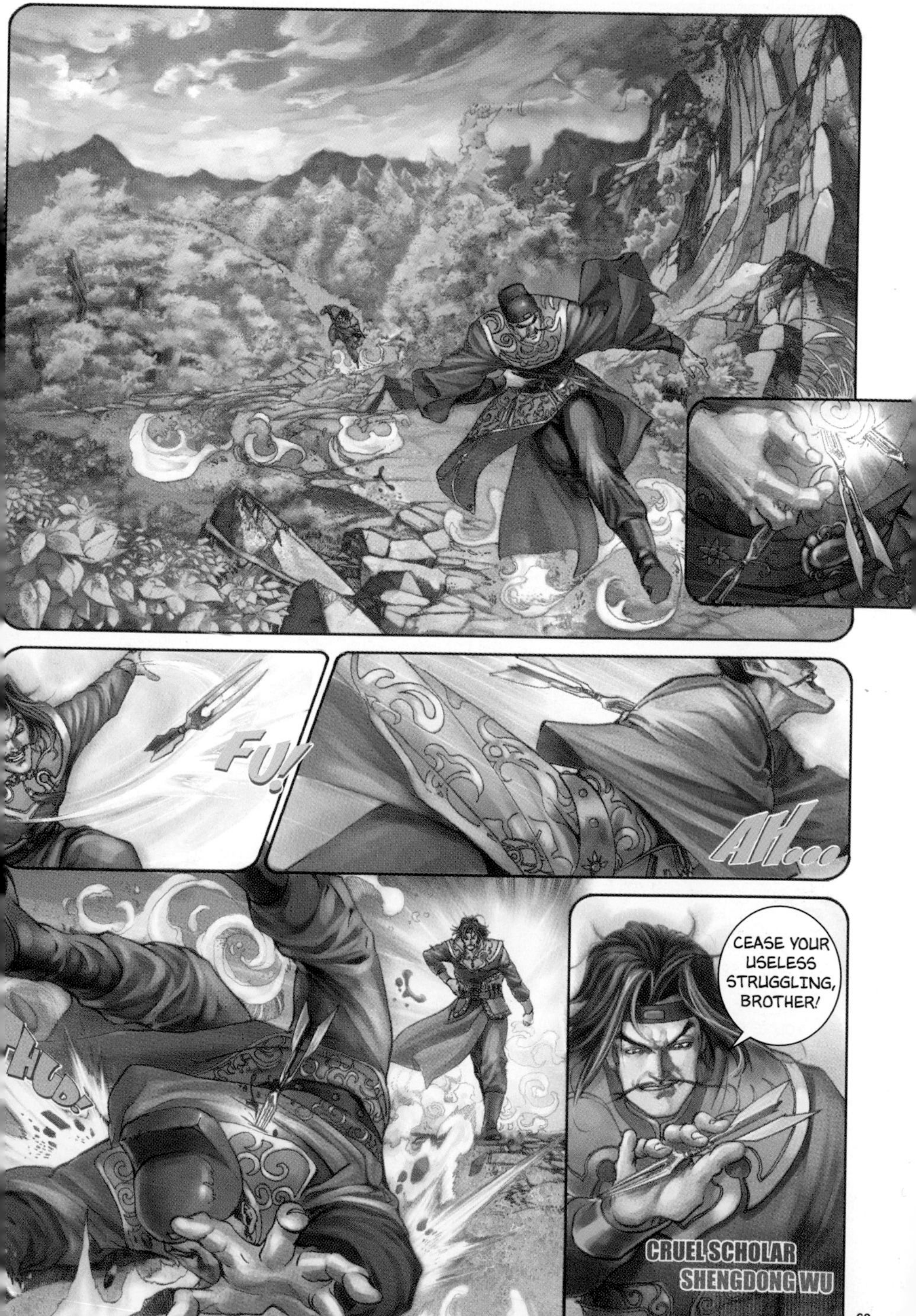
FU!
AH...
THUD!
CEASE YOUR USELESS STRUGGLING, BROTHER!
CRUEL SCHOLAR SHENGDONG WU

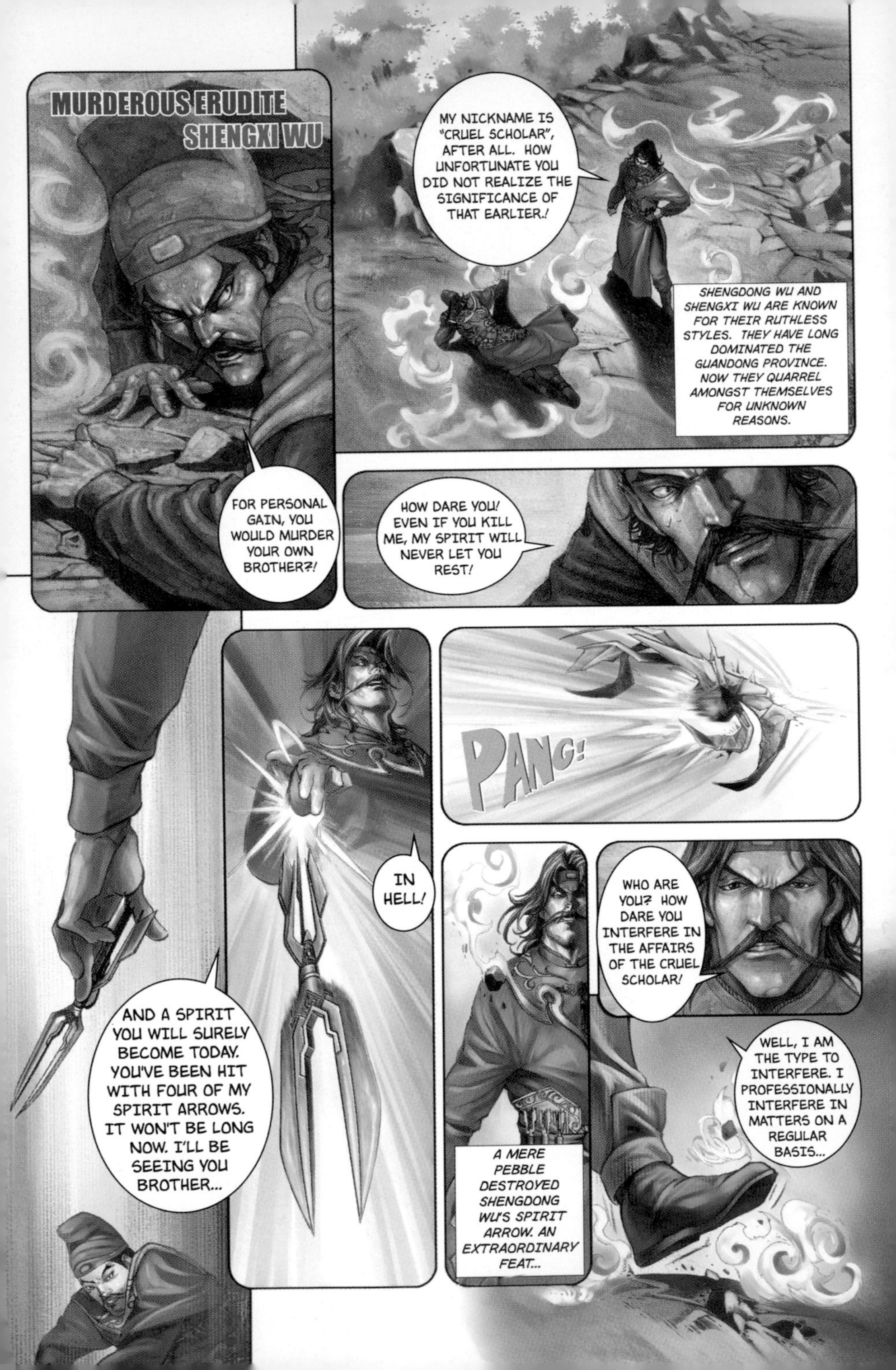
MURDEROUS ERUDITE
SHENGXI WU
MY NICKNAME IS "CRUEL SCHOLAR", AFTER ALL. HOW UNFORTUNATE YOU DID NOT REALIZE THE SIGNIFICANCE OF THAT EARLIER.!
SHENGDONG WU AND SHENGXI WU ARE KNOWN FOR THEIR RUTHLESS STYLES. THEY HAVE LONG DOMINATED THE GUANDONG PROVINCE. NOW THEY QUARREL AMONGST THEMSELVES FOR UNKNOWN REASONS.
FOR PERSONAL GAIN, YOU WOULD MURDER YOUR OWN BROTHER?!
HOW DARE YOU! EVEN IF YOU KILL ME, MY SPIRIT WILL NEVER LET YOU REST!
AND A SPIRIT YOU WILL SURELY BECOME TODAY. YOU'VE BEEN HIT WITH FOUR OF MY SPIRIT ARROWS. IT WON'T BE LONG NOW. I'LL BE SEEING YOU BROTHER...
IN HELL!
PANG!
WHO ARE YOU? HOW DARE YOU INTERFERE IN THE AFFAIRS OF THE CRUEL SCHOLAR!
A MERE PEBBLE DESTROYED SHENGDONG WU'S SPIRIT ARROW. AN EXTRAORDINARY FEAT...
WELL, I AM THE TYPE TO INTERFERE. I PROFESSIONALLY INTERFERE IN MATTERS ON A REGULAR BASIS...

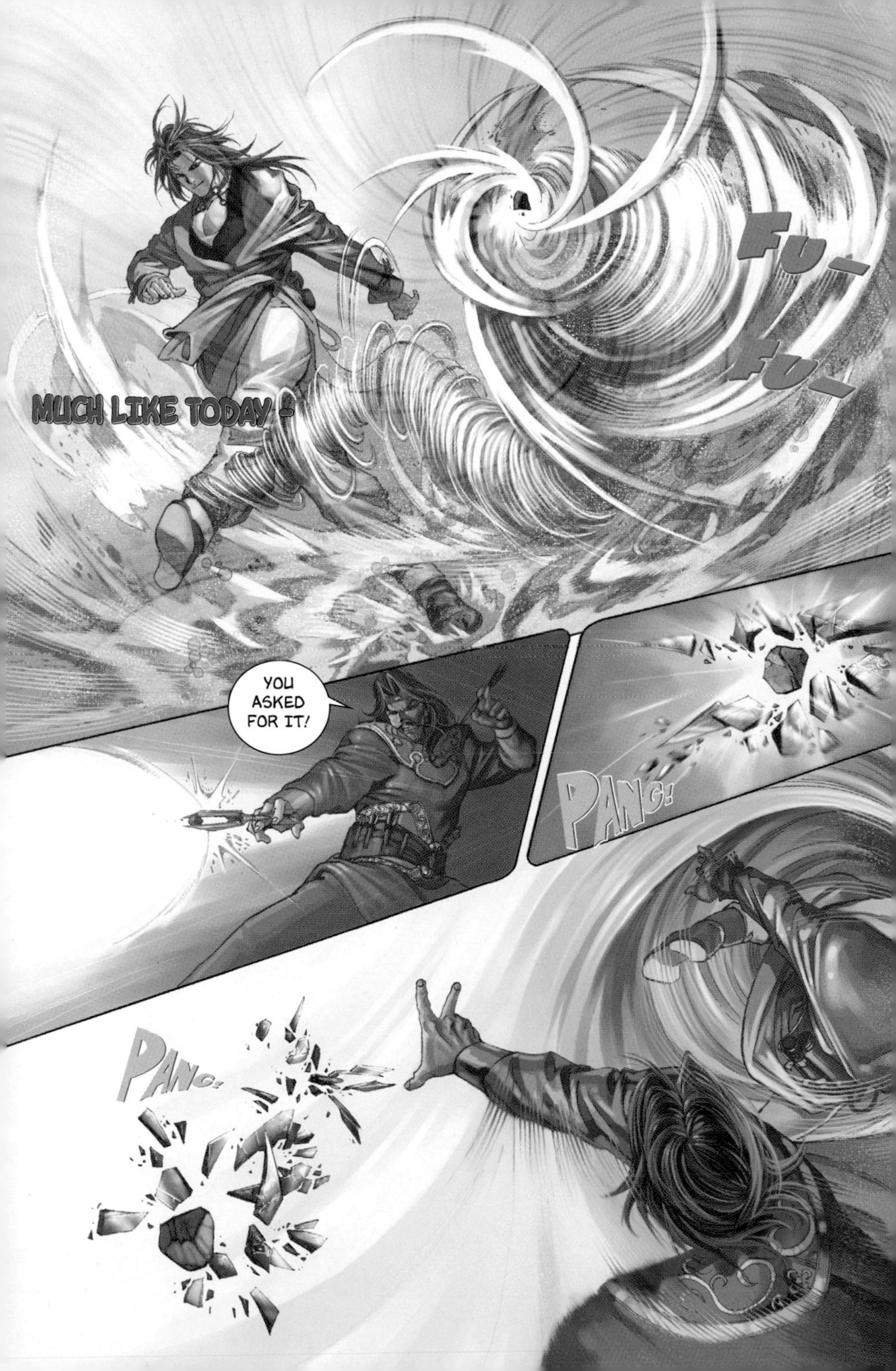
FU-
FU-
MUCH LIKE TODAY -
YOU ASKED FOR IT!
PANG!
PANG!

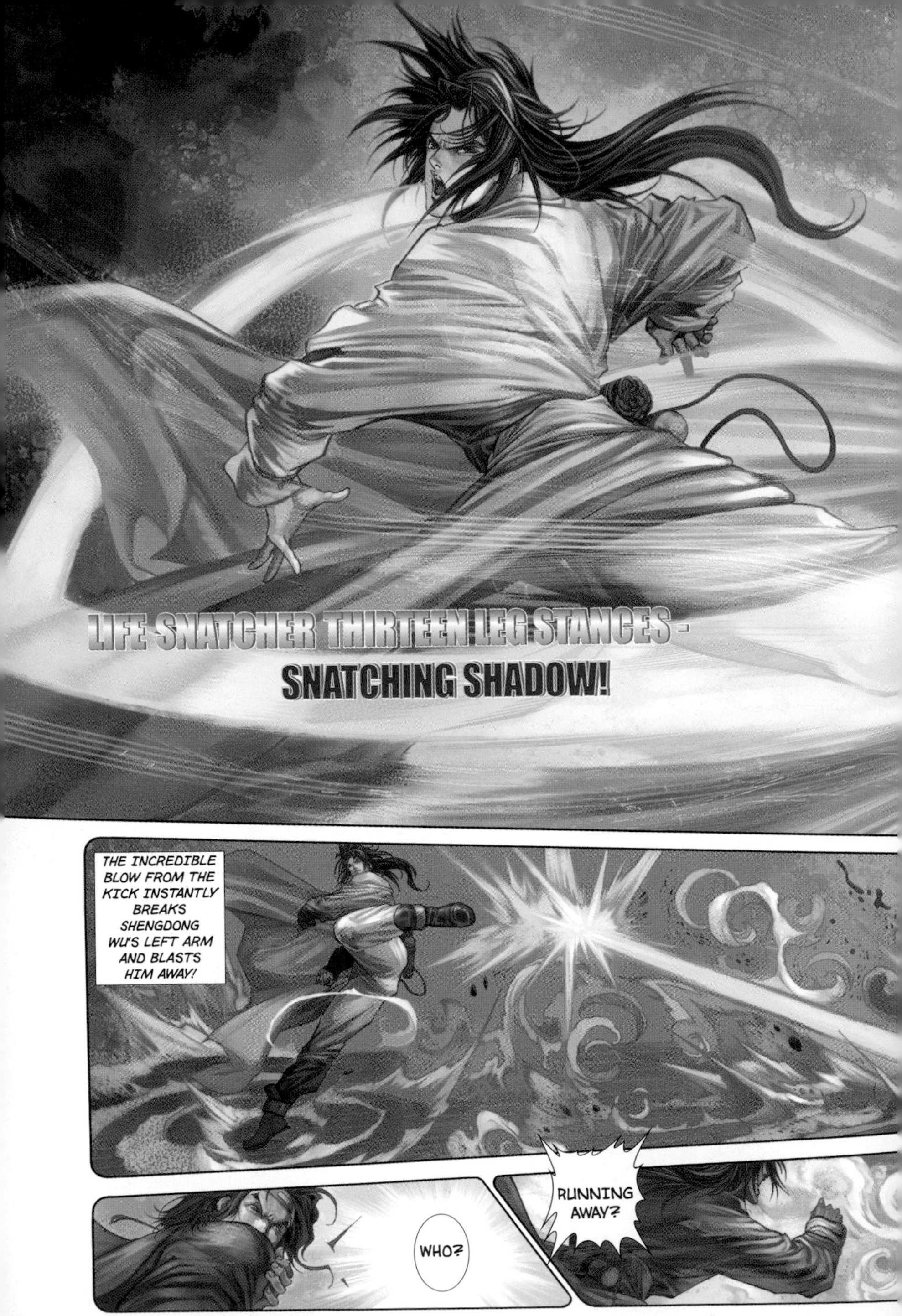
LIFE SNATCHER THIRTEEN LEG STANCES -
SNATCHING SHADOW!
THE INCREDIBLE BLOW FROM THE KICK INSTANTLY BREAKS SHENGDONG WU'S LEFT ARM AND BLASTS HIM AWAY!
RUNNING AWAY?
WHO?

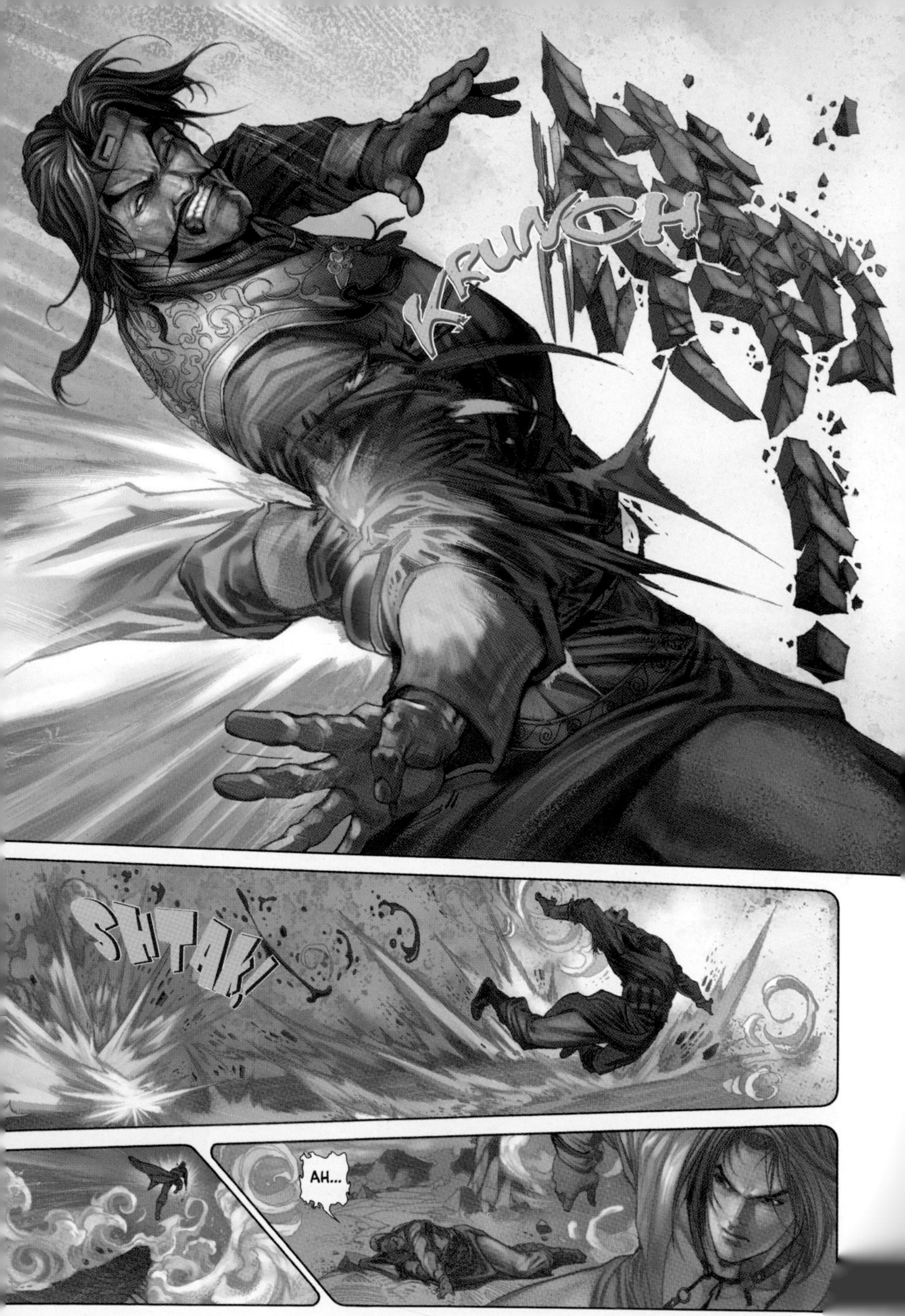
KRUNCH
SHTAK!
AH...

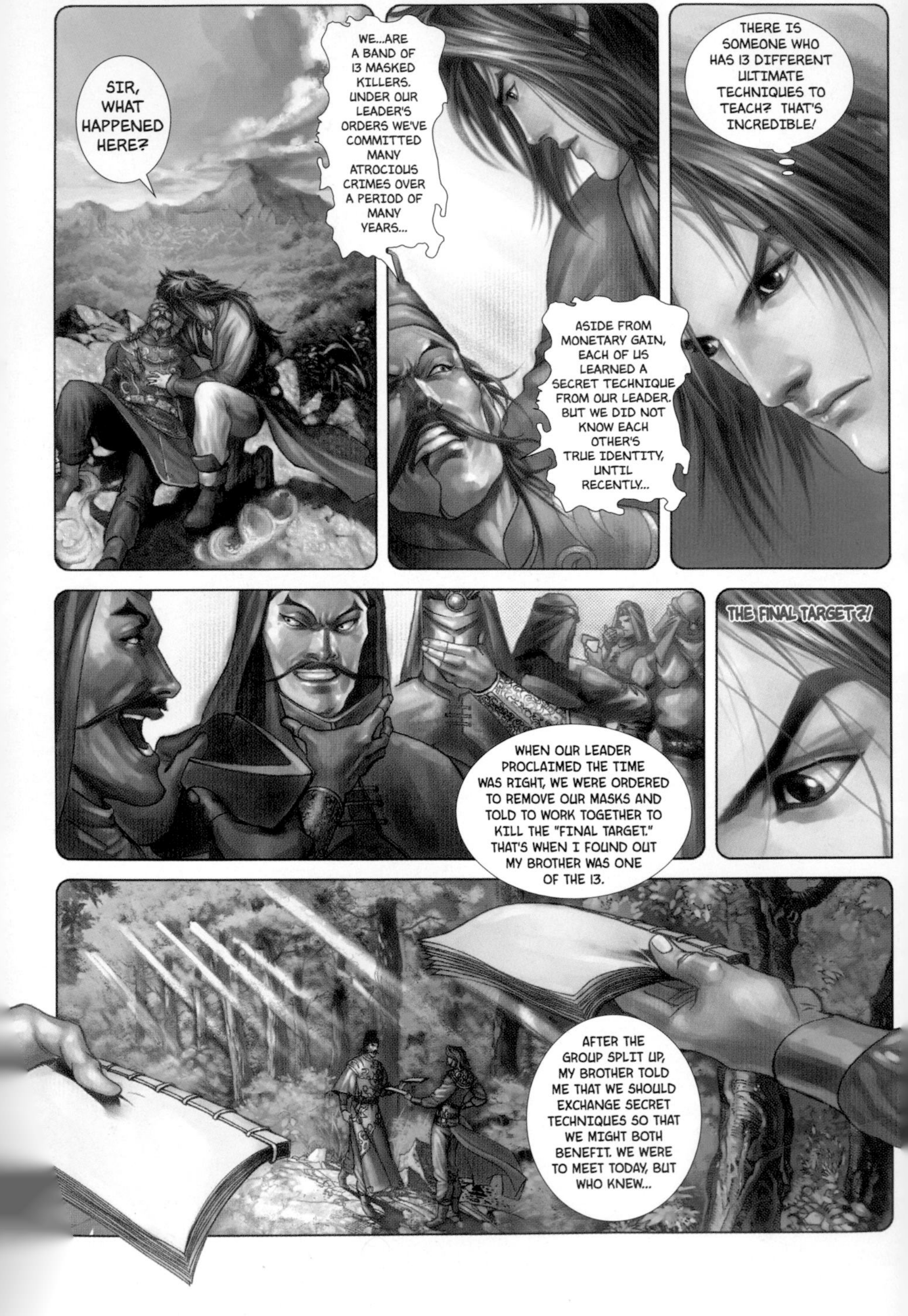
SIR, WHAT HAPPENED HERE?
WE...ARE A BAND OF 13 MASKED KILLERS. UNDER OUR LEADER'S ORDERS WE'VE COMMITTED MANY ATROCIOUS CRIMES OVER A PERIOD OF MANY YEARS...
ASIDE FROM MONETARY GAIN, EACH OF US LEARNED A SECRET TECHNIQUE FROM OUR LEADER. BUT WE DID NOT KNOW EACH OTHER'S TRUE IDENTITY, UNTIL RECENTLY...
THERE IS SOMEONE WHO HAS 13 DIFFERENT ULTIMATE TECHNIQUES TO TEACH? THAT'S INCREDIBLE!
WHEN OUR LEADER PROCLAIMED THE TIME WAS RIGHT, WE WERE ORDERED TO REMOVE OUR MASKS AND TOLD TO WORK TOGETHER TO KILL THE "FINAL TARGET." THAT'S WHEN I FOUND OUT MY BROTHER WAS ONE OF THE 13.
THE FINAL TARGET?!
AFTER THE GROUP SPLIT UP, MY BROTHER TOLD ME THAT WE SHOULD EXCHANGE SECRET TECHNIQUES SO THAT WE MIGHT BOTH BENEFIT. WE WERE TO MEET TODAY, BUT WHO KNEW...

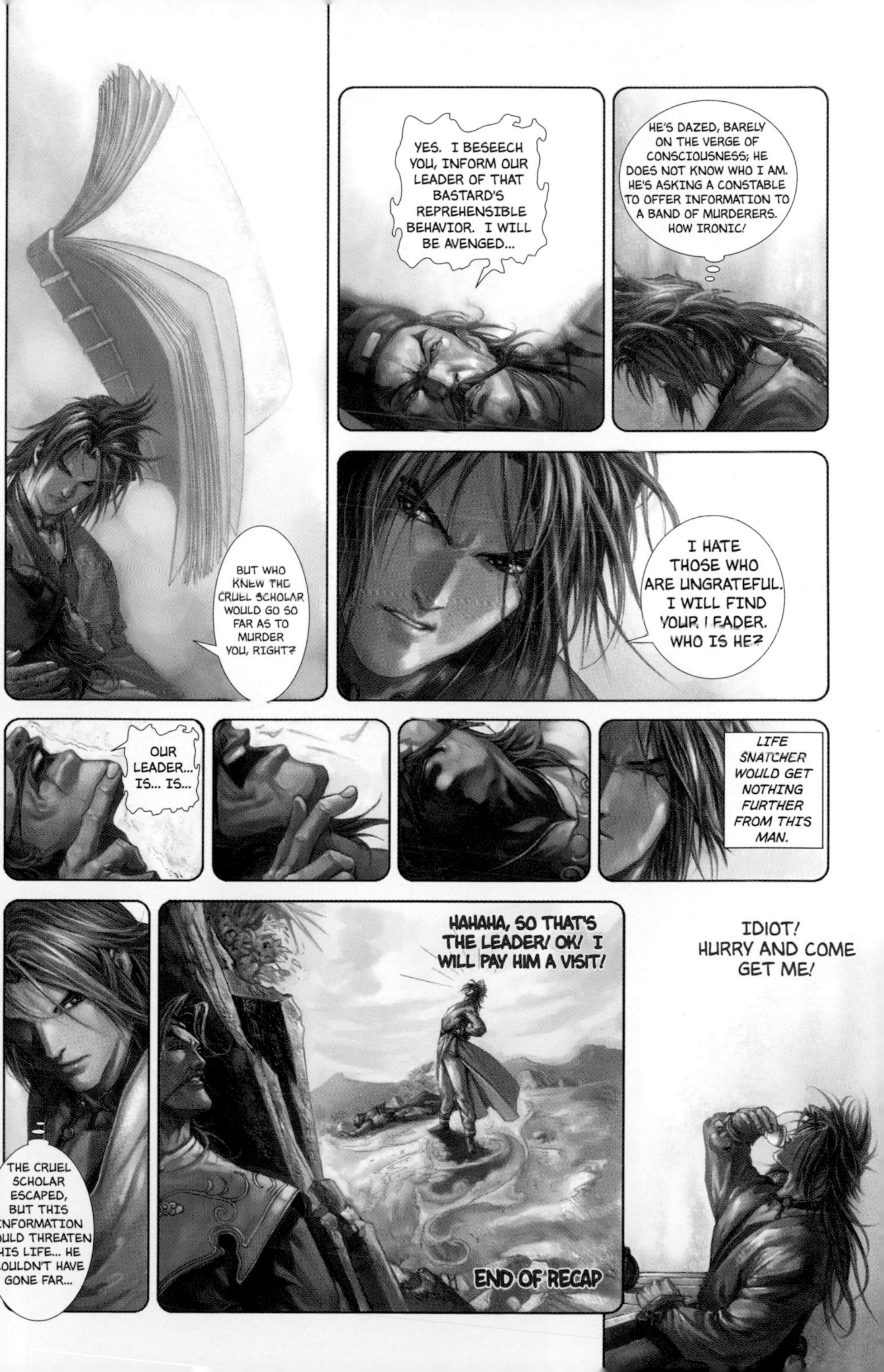
BUT WHO KNEW THE CRUEL SCHOLAR WOULD GO SO FAR AS TO MURDER YOU, RIGHT?
YES. I BESEECH YOU, INFORM OUR LEADER OF THAT BASTARD'S REPREHENSIBLE BEHAVIOR. I WILL BE AVENGED...
HE'S DAZED, BARELY ON THE VERGE OF CONSCIOUSNESS; HE DOES NOT KNOW WHO I AM. HE'S ASKING A CONSTABLE TO OFFER INFORMATION TO A BAND OF MURDERERS. HOW IRONIC!
I HATE THOSE WHO ARE UNGRATEFUL. I WILL FIND YOUR LEADER. WHO IS HE?
OUR LEADER... IS... IS...
LIFE SNATCHER WOULD GET NOTHING FURTHER FROM THIS MAN.
THE CRUEL SCHOLAR ESCAPED, BUT THIS INFORMATION OULD THREATEN HIS LIFE... HE COULDN'T HAVE GONE FAR...
HAHAHA, SO THAT'S THE LEADER! OK! I WILL PAY HIM A VISIT!
END OF RECAP
IDIOT! HURRY AND COME GET ME!

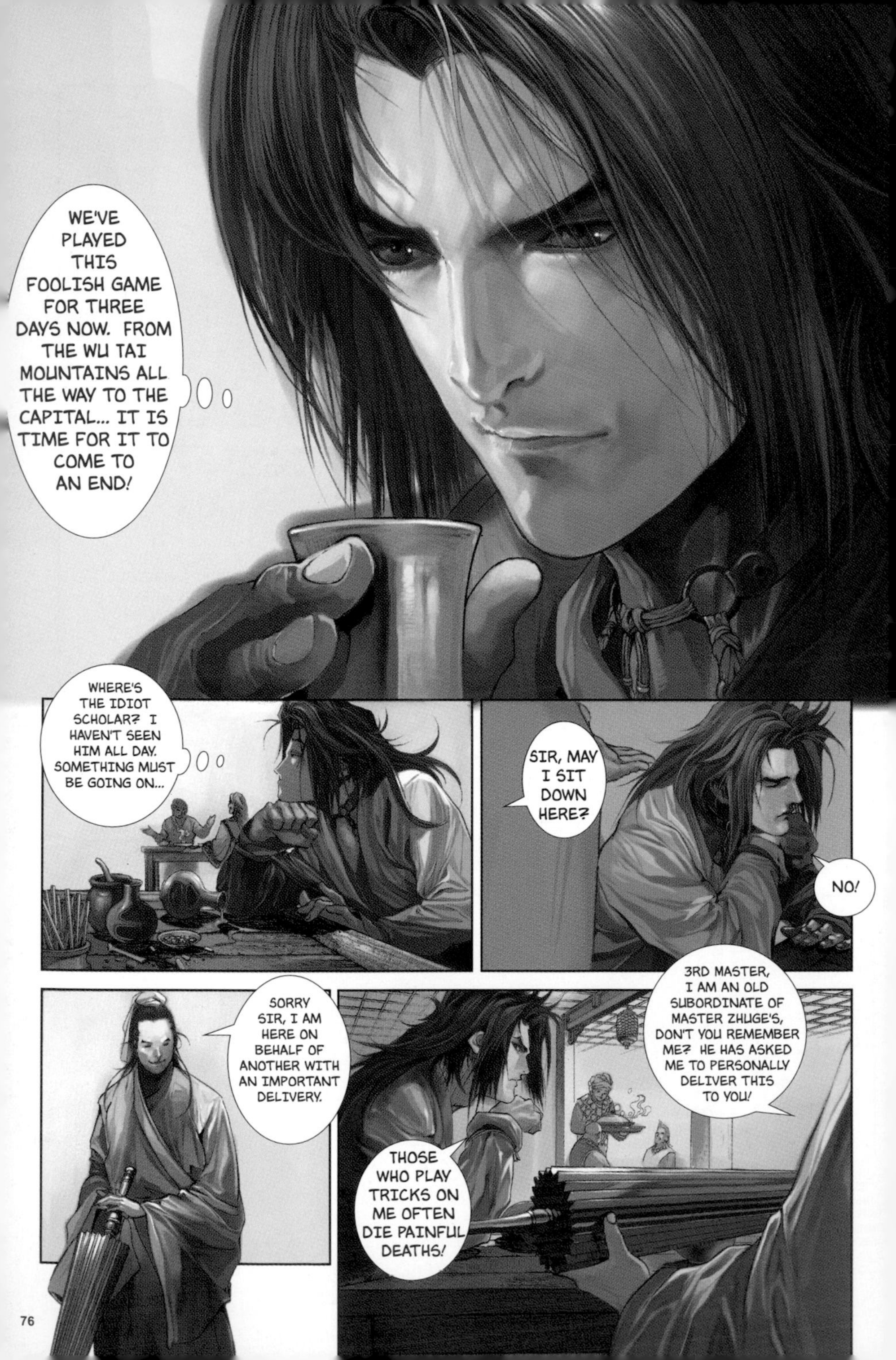
WE'VE PLAYED THIS FOOLISH GAME FOR THREE DAYS NOW. FROM THE WU TAI MOUNTAINS ALL THE WAY TO THE CAPITAL... IT IS TIME FOR IT TO COME TO AN END!
WHERE'S THE IDIOT SCHOLAR? I HAVEN'T SEEN HIM ALL DAY. SOMETHING MUST BE GOING ON...
SIR, MAY I SIT DOWN HERE?
NO!
SORRY SIR, I AM HERE ON BEHALF OF ANOTHER WITH AN IMPORTANT DELIVERY.
3RD MASTER, I AM AN OLD SUBORDINATE OF MASTER ZHUGE'S, DON'T YOU REMEMBER ME? HE HAS ASKED ME TO PERSONALLY DELIVER THIS TO YOU!
THOSE WHO PLAY TRICKS ON ME OFTEN DIE PAINFUL DEATHS!

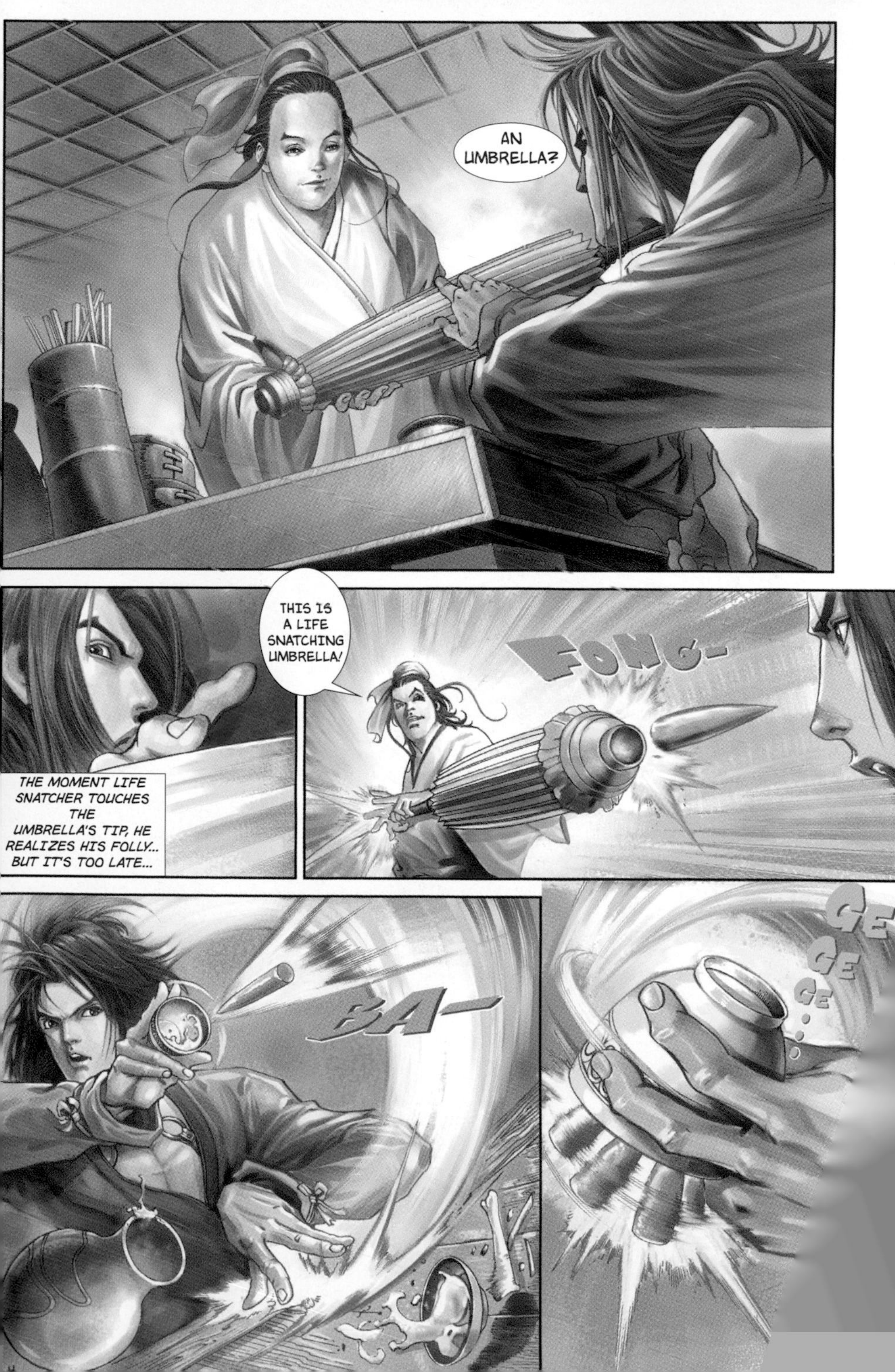
AN UMBRELLA?
THIS IS A LIFE SNATCHING UMBRELLA!
THE MOMENT LIFE SNATCHER TOUCHES THE UMBRELLA'S TIP, HE REALIZES HIS FOLLY... BUT IT'S TOO LATE...
FONG-
BA-
GE GE GE

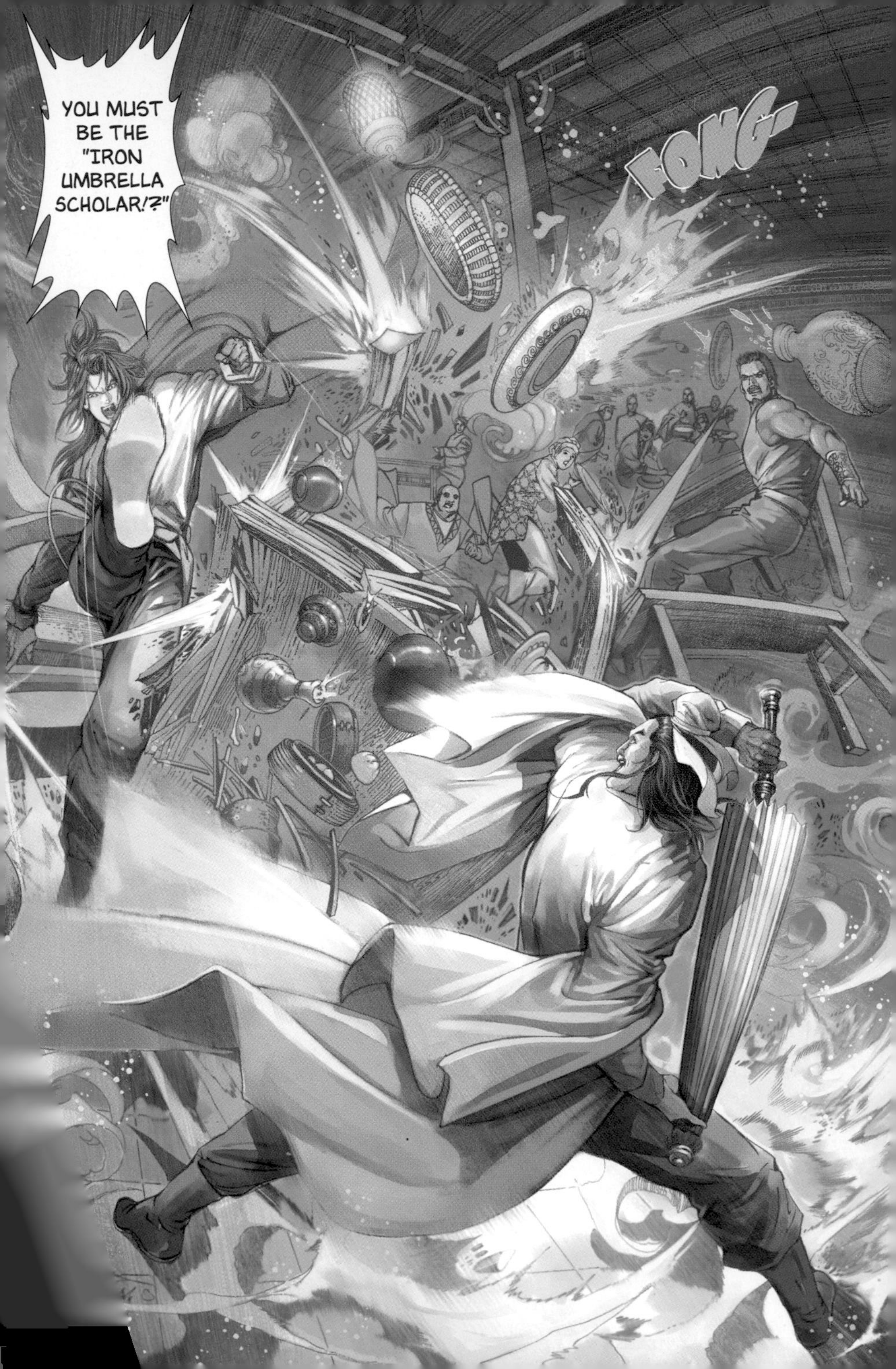
YOU MUST BE THE "IRON UMBRELLA SCHOLAR!?"
FOMG-

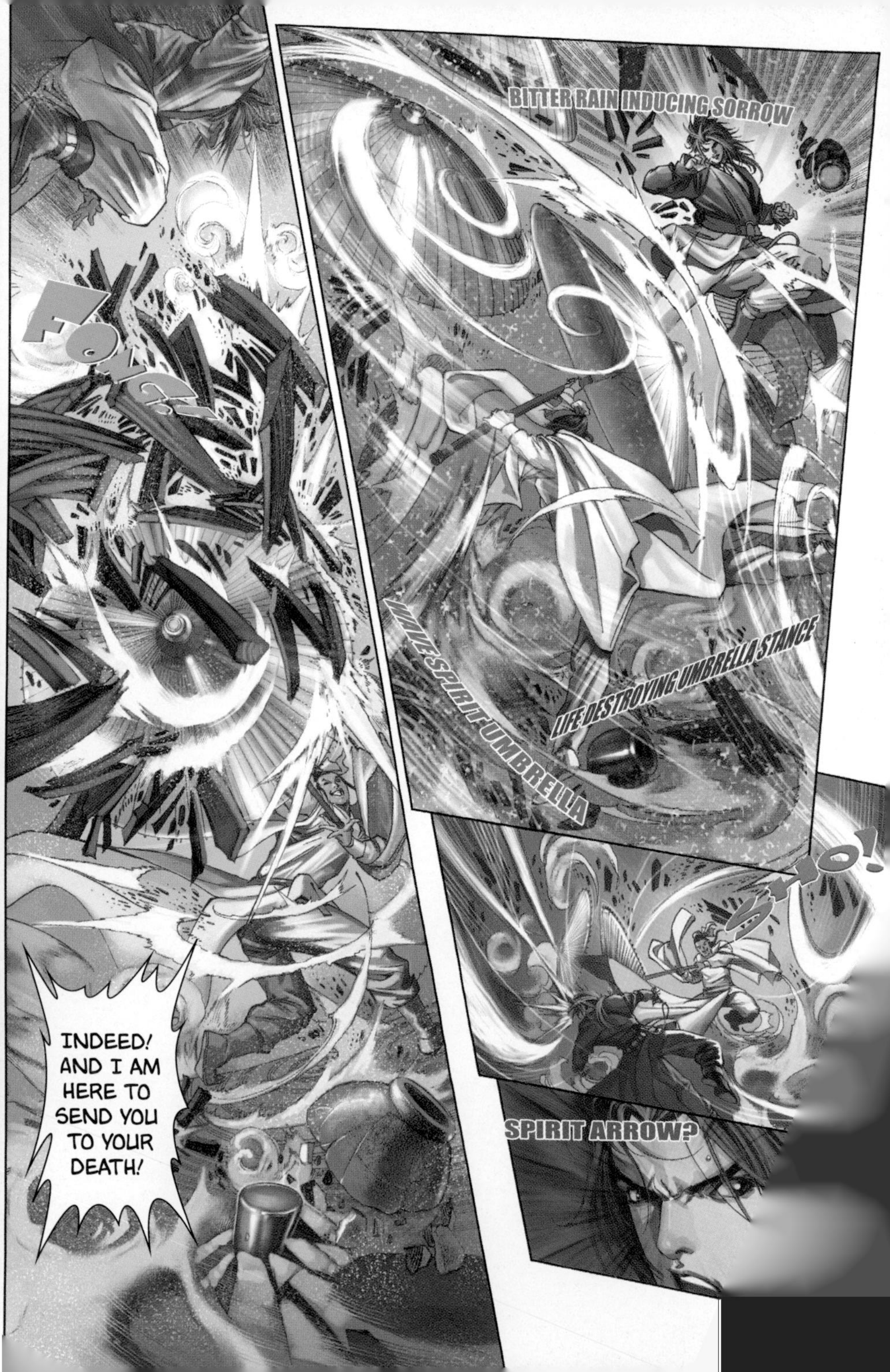
FONG!!
BITTER RAIN INDUCING SORROW
WHITE SPIRIT UMBRELLA
LIFE DESTROYING UMBRELLA STANCE
SHO!
INDEED! AND I AM HERE TO SEND YOU TO YOUR DEATH!
SPIRIT ARROW?

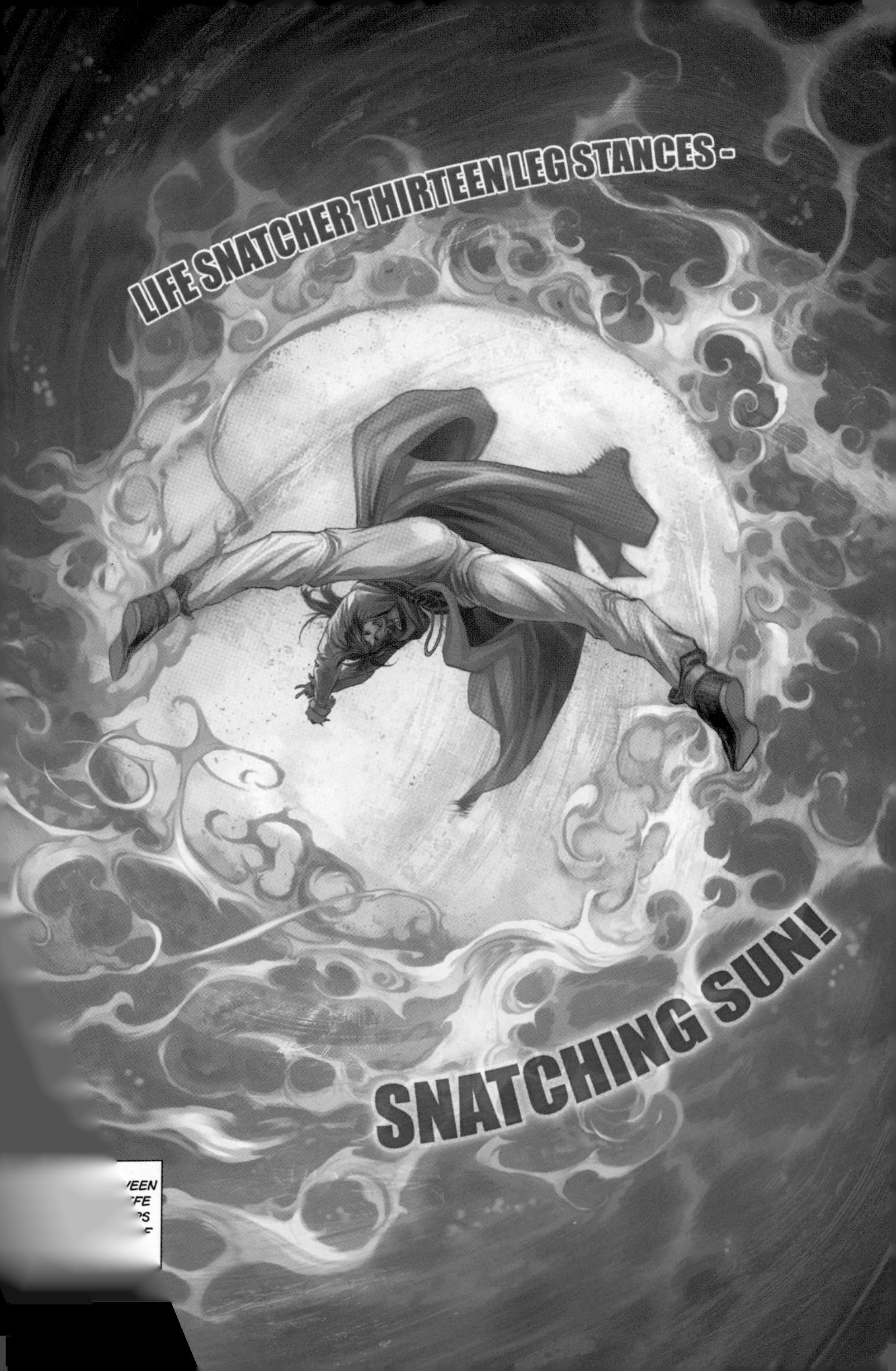
LIFE SNATCHER THIRTEEN LEG STANCES -
SNATCHING SUN!

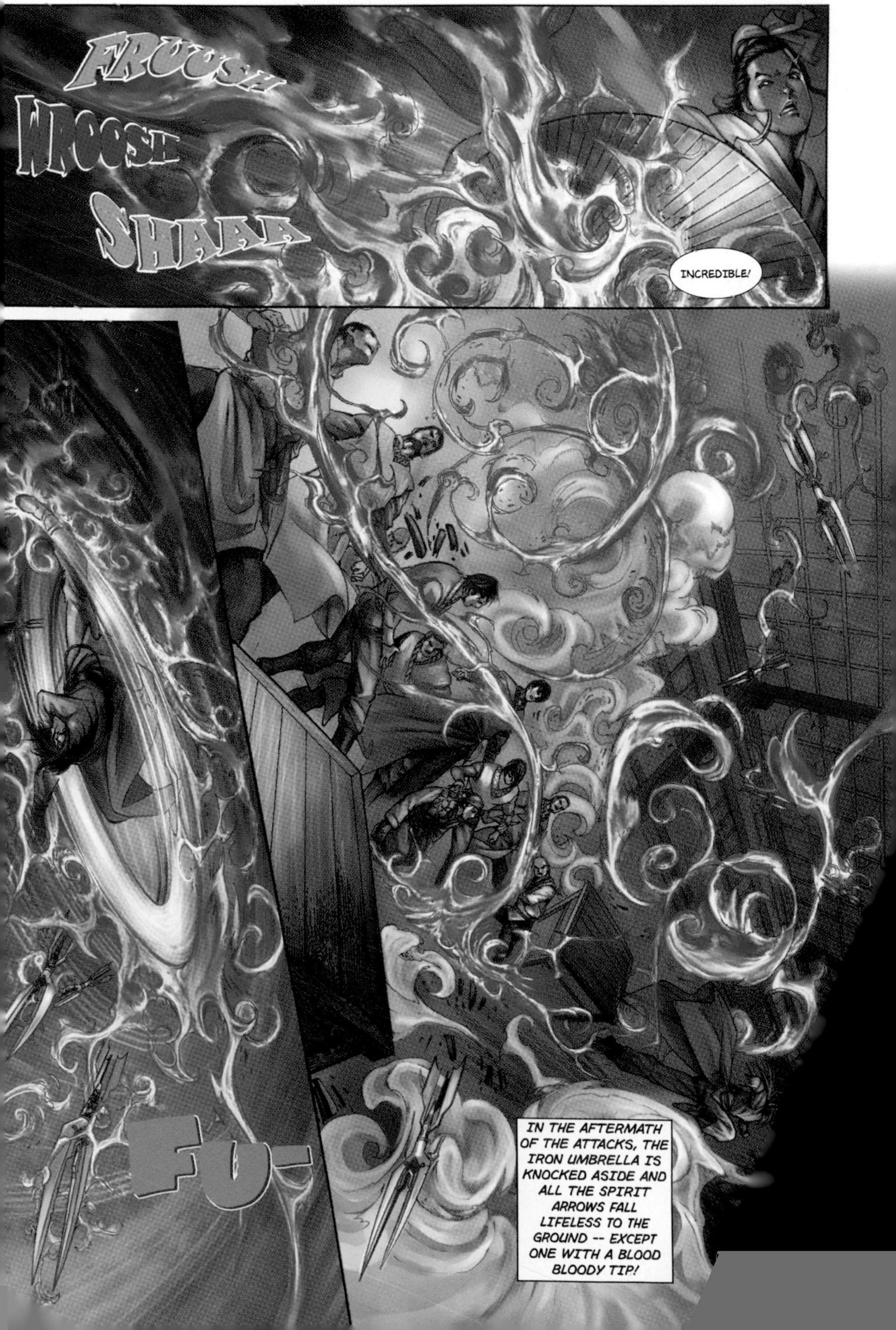
FROOSH
WROOSH
SHAAA
INCREDIBLE!
FU-
IN THE AFTERMATH OF THE ATTACKS, THE IRON UMBRELLA IS KNOCKED ASIDE AND ALL THE SPIRIT ARROWS FALL LIFELESS TO THE GROUND -- EXCEPT ONE WITH A BLOOD BLOODY TIP!

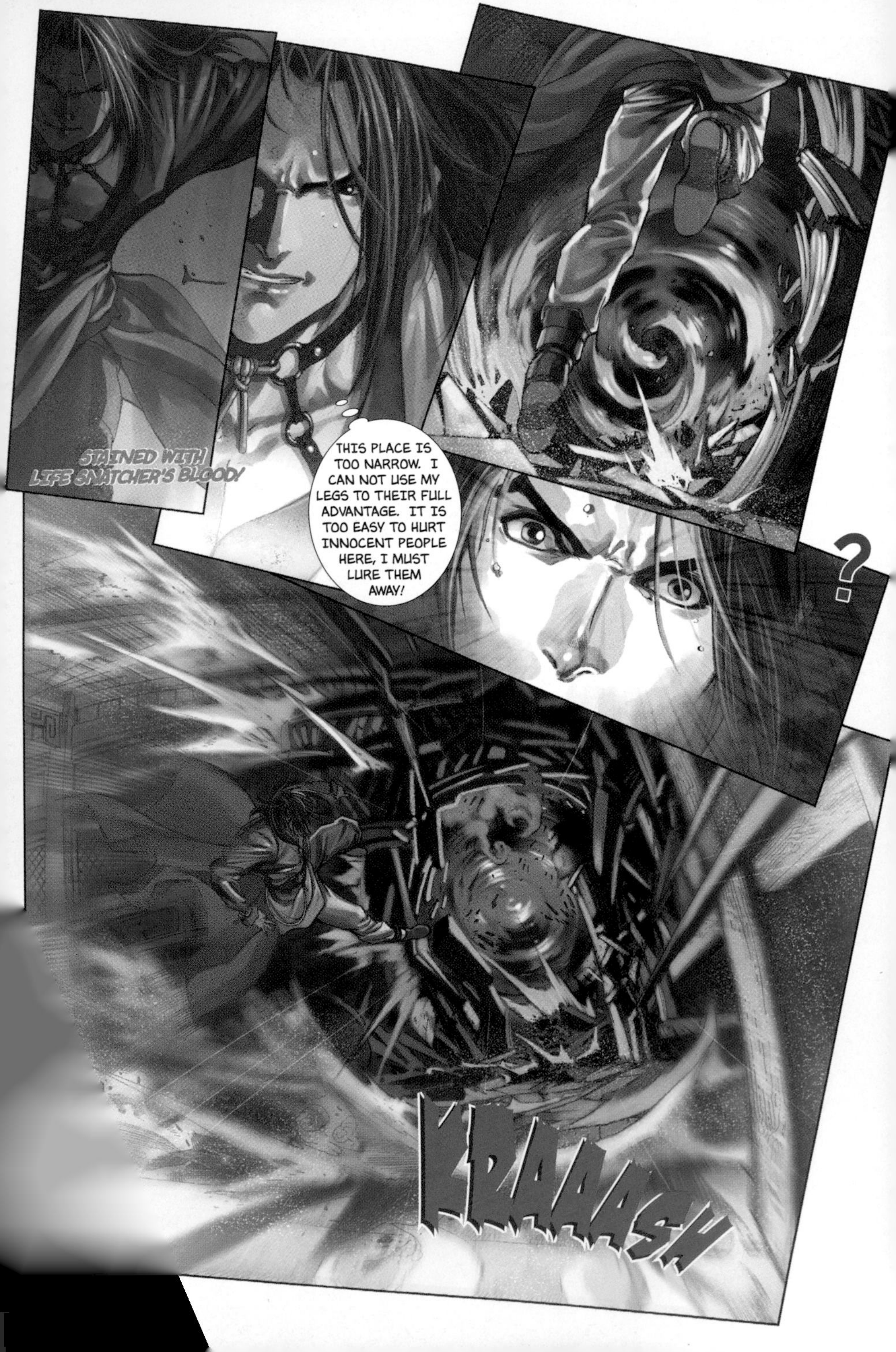
STAINED WITH LIFE SNATCHER'S BLOOD!
THIS PLACE IS TOO NARROW. I CAN NOT USE MY LEGS TO THEIR FULL ADVANTAGE. IT IS TOO EASY TO HURT INNOCENT PEOPLE HERE, I MUST LURE THEM AWAY!
?
KRAAASH

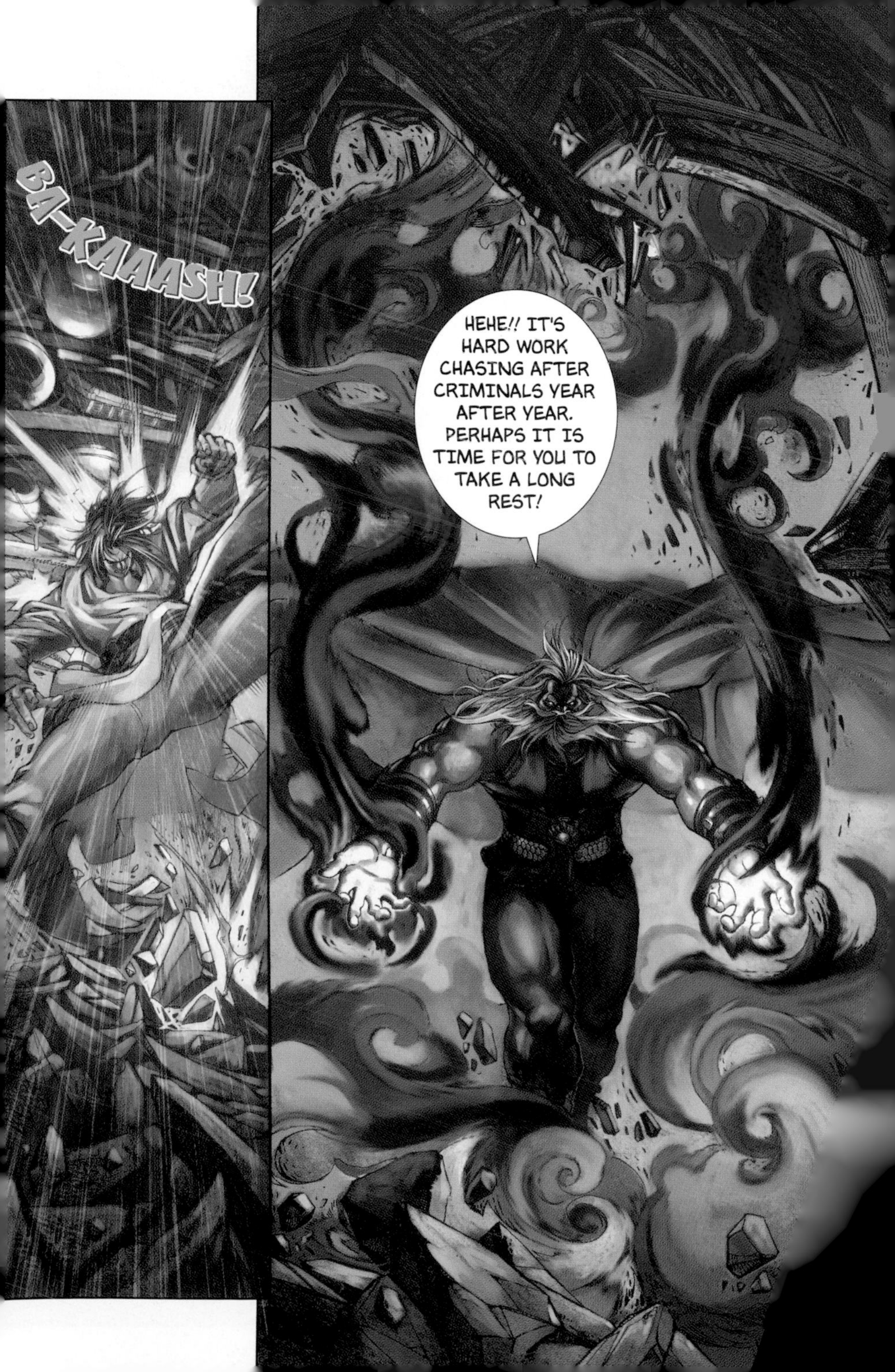
BA-KAAASH!
HEHE!! IT'S HARD WORK CHASING AFTER CRIMINALS YEAR AFTER YEAR. PERHAPS IT IS TIME FOR YOU TO TAKE A LONG REST!

BLACK DEATH PALMS
ELDER GUAN

W ASIDE FROM THE
UMBRELLA SCHOLAR
HE CRUEL SCHOLAR,
R HAS JOINED THE
ROM THE BLACK
ETING FROM HIS
E LOOKS TO BE
ER TOUGH
R. NOW IT IS
THREE FOR
ER. DANGER
MS!

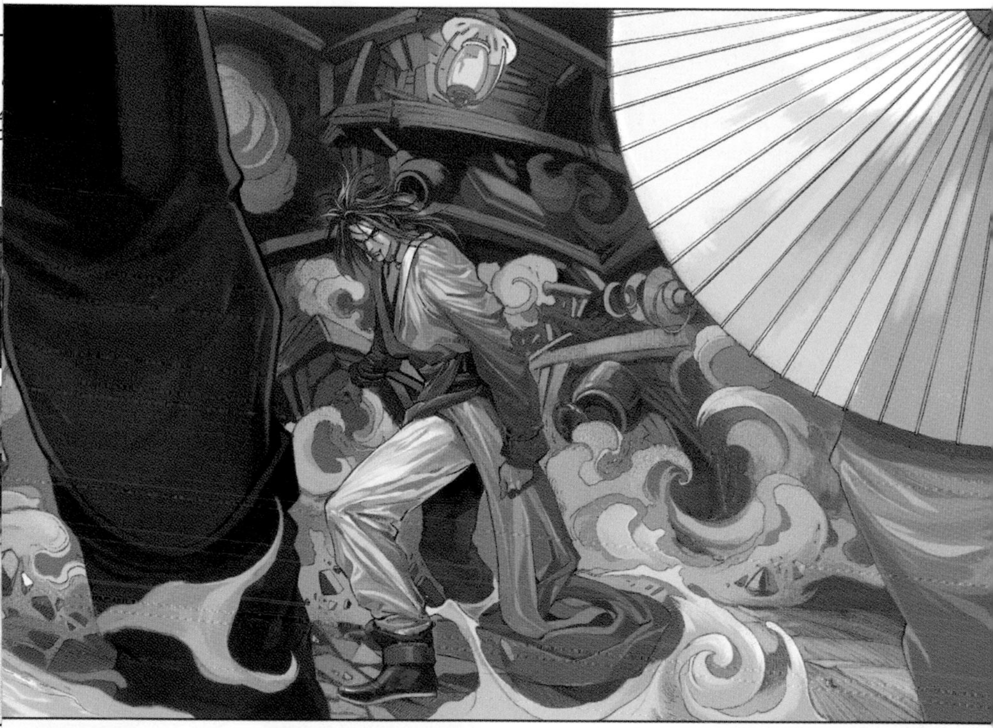

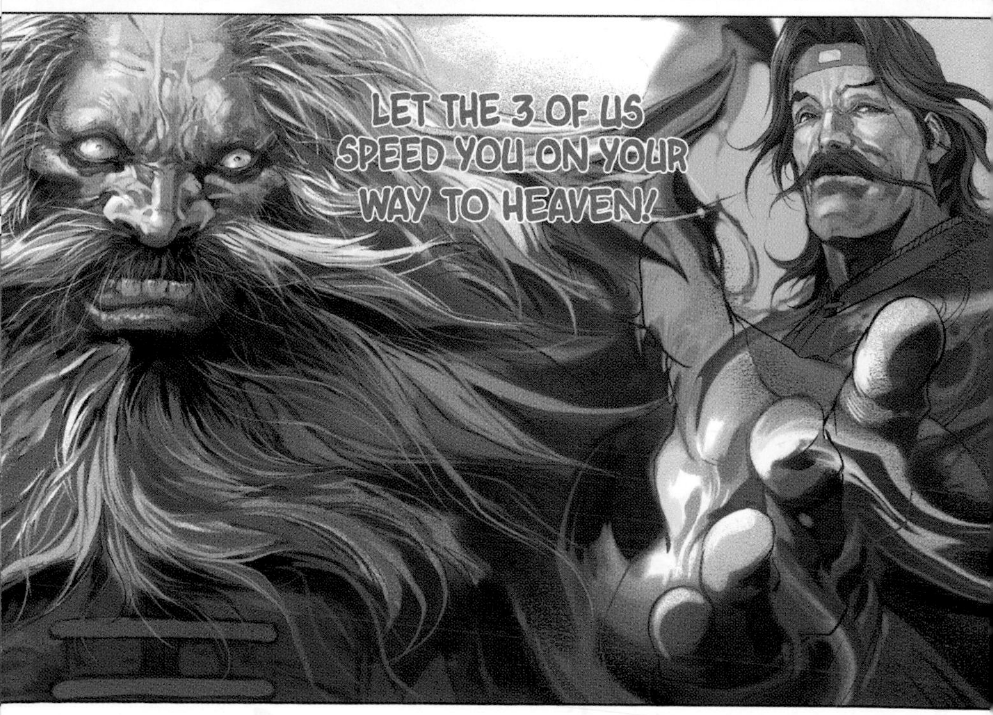
LET THE 3 OF US SPEED YOU ON YOUR WAY TO HEAVEN!

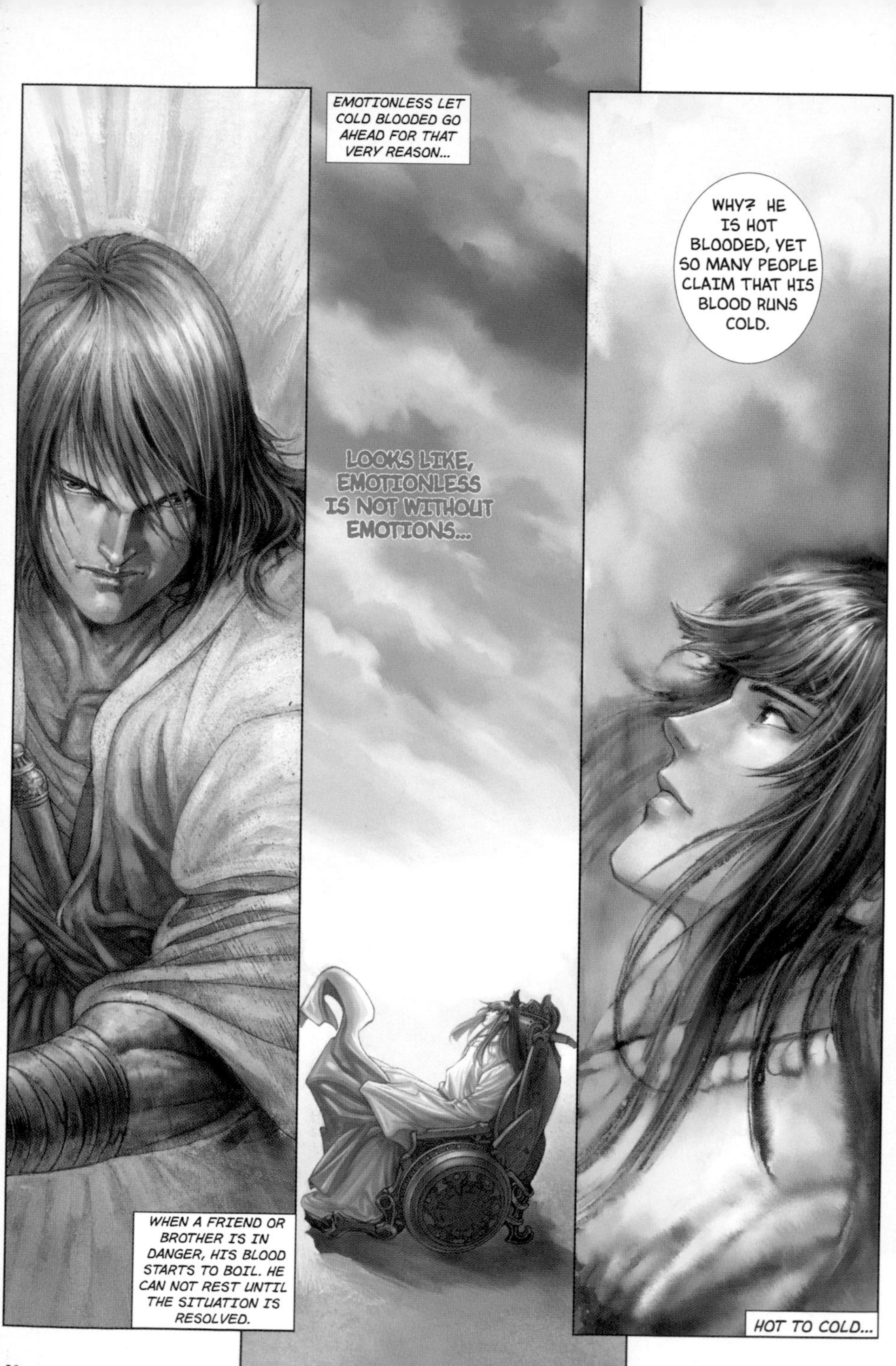
EMOTIONLESS LET COLD BLOODED GO AHEAD FOR THAT VERY REASON...
WHY? HE IS HOT BLOODED, YET SO MANY PEOPLE CLAIM THAT HIS BLOOD RUNS COLD.
LOOKS LIKE, EMOTIONLESS IS NOT WITHOUT EMOTIONS...
WHEN A FRIEND OR BROTHER IS IN DANGER, HIS BLOOD STARTS TO BOIL. HE CAN NOT REST UNTIL THE SITUATION IS RESOLVED.
HOT TO COLD...

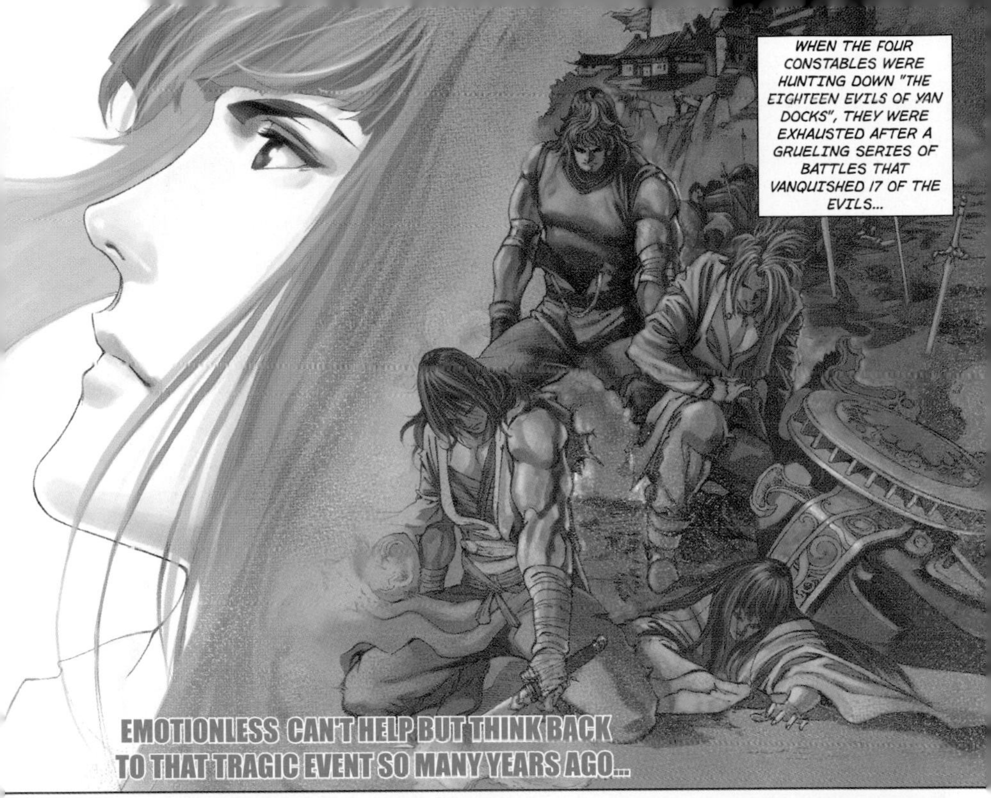
WHEN THE FOUR CONSTABLES WERE HUNTING DOWN "THE EIGHTEEN EVILS OF YAN DOCKS", THEY WERE EXHAUSTED AFTER A GRUELING SERIES OF BATTLES THAT VANQUISHED 17 OF THE EVILS...
EMOTIONLESS CAN'T HELP BUT THINK BACK TO THAT TRAGIC EVENT SO MANY YEARS AGO...

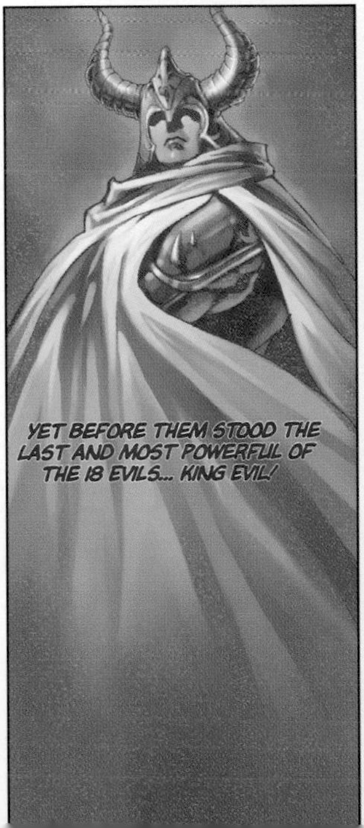
YET BEFORE THEM STOOD THE LAST AND MOST POWERFUL OF THE 18 EVILS... KING EVIL!

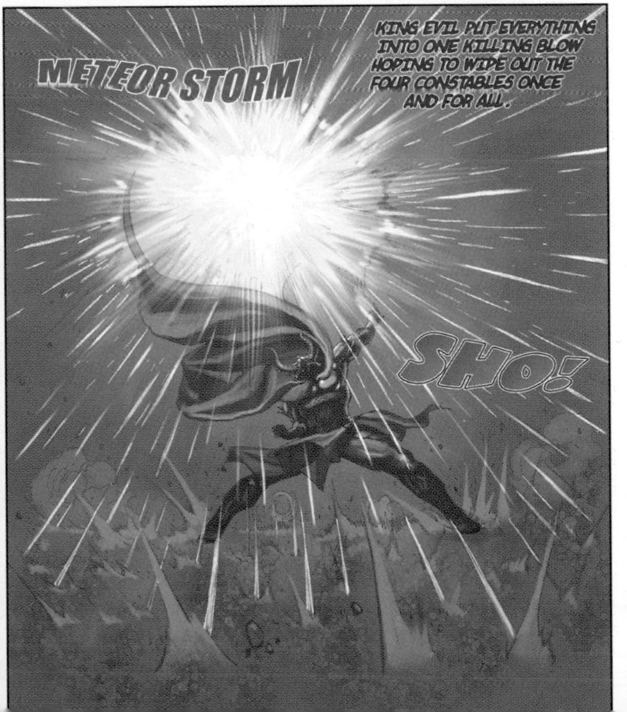
KING EVIL PUT EVERYTHING INTO ONE KILLING BLOW HOPING TO WIPE OUT THE FOUR CONSTABLES ONCE AND FOR ALL.
METEOR STORM
SHO!

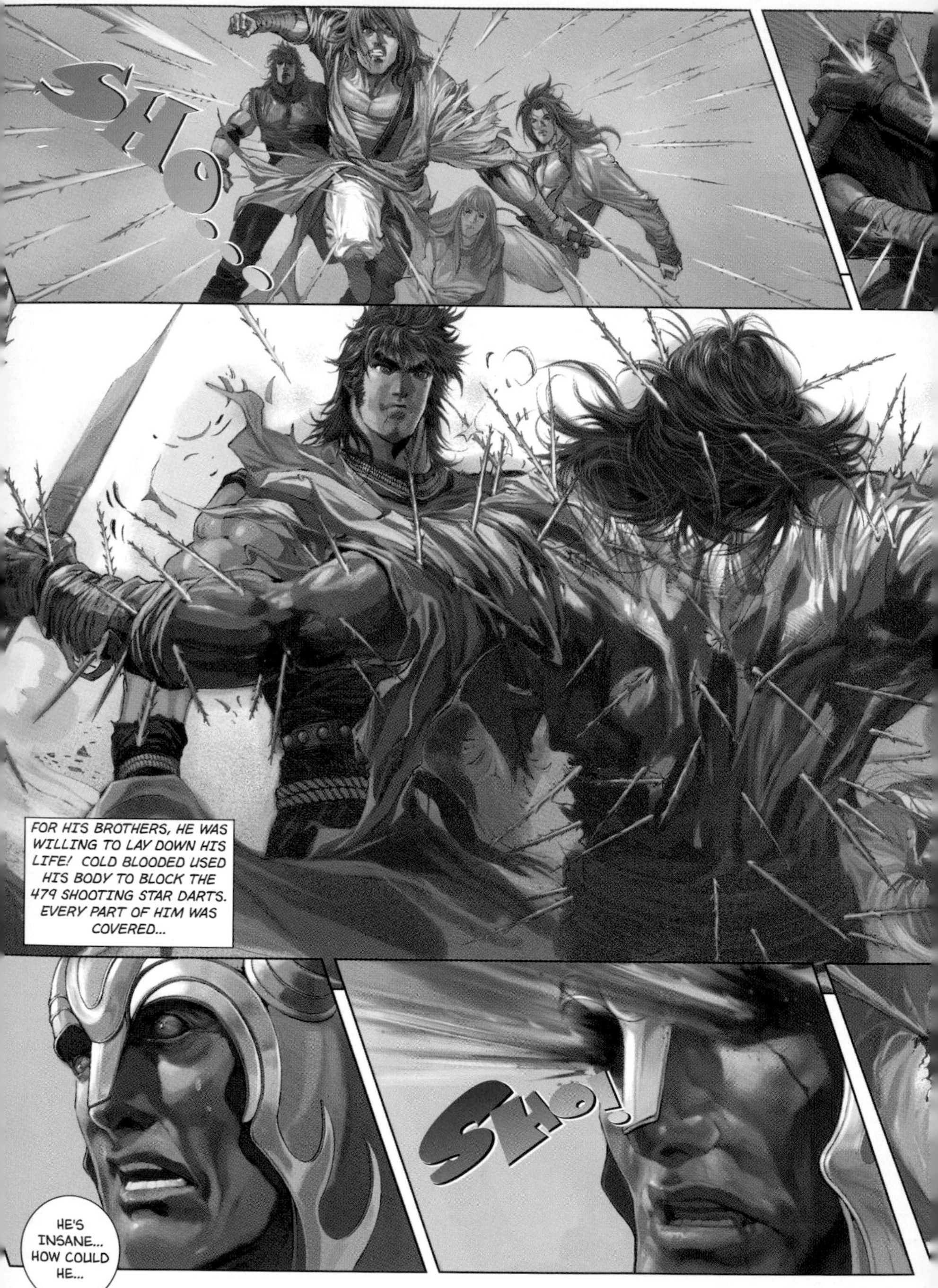
SHO...
FOR HIS BROTHERS, HE WAS WILLING TO LAY DOWN HIS LIFE! COLD BLOODED USED HIS BODY TO BLOCK THE 479 SHOOTING STAR DARTS. EVERY PART OF HIM WAS COVERED...
HE'S INSANE... HOW COULD HE...
SHO!

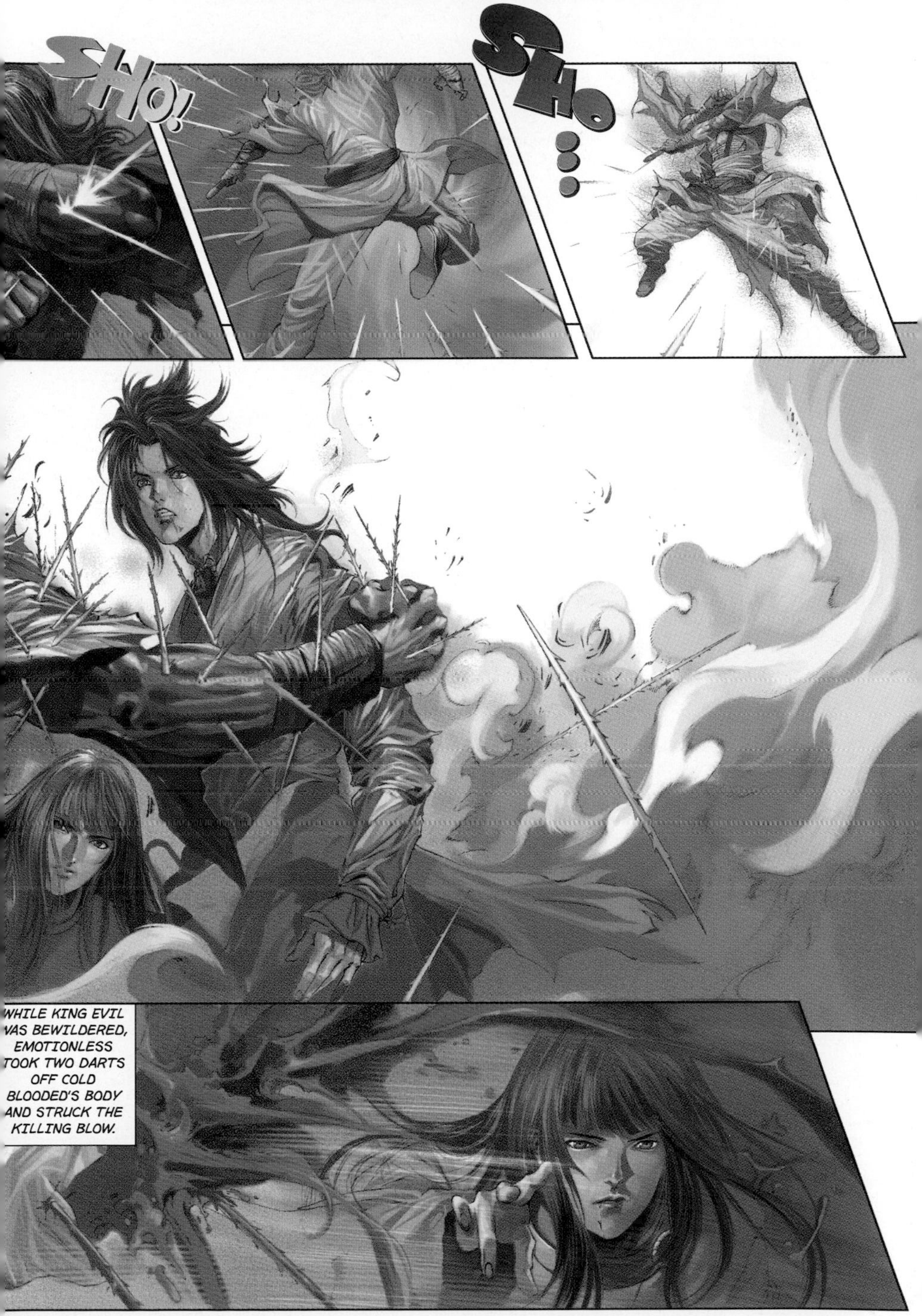
SHO!
SHO...
WHILE KING EVIL WAS BEWILDERED, EMOTIONLESS TOOK TWO DARTS OFF COLD BLOODED'S BODY AND STRUCK THE KILLING BLOW.

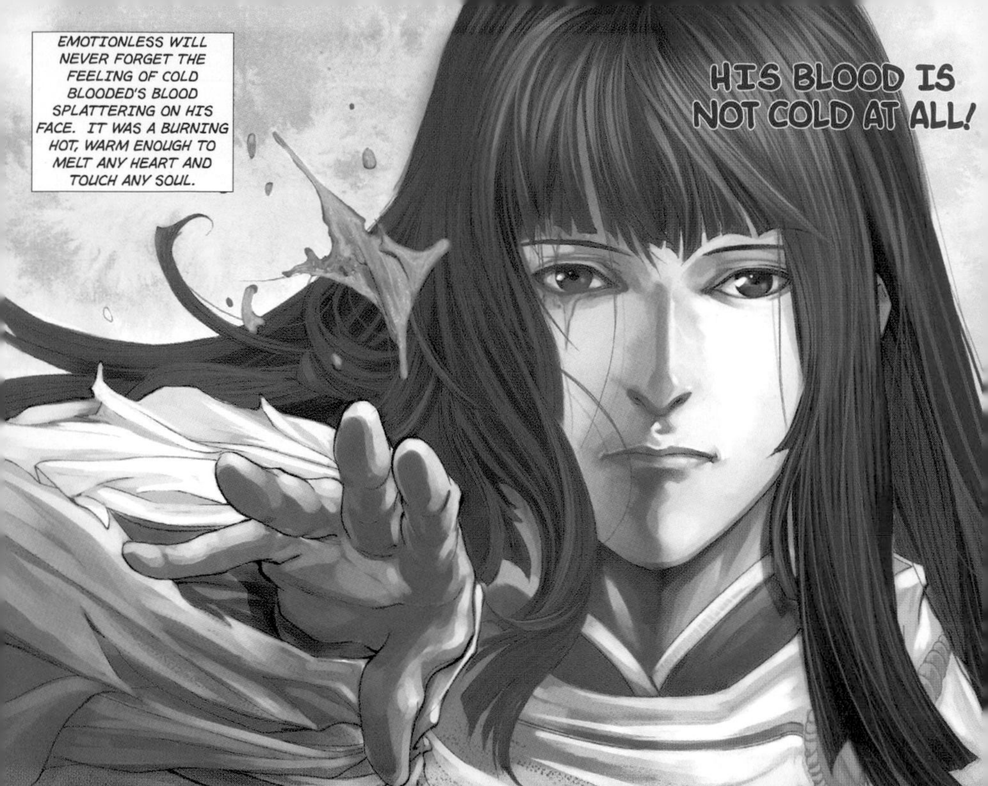
EMOTIONLESS WILL NEVER FORGET THE FEELING OF COLD BLOODED'S BLOOD SPLATTERING ON HIS FACE. IT WAS A BURNING HOT, WARM ENOUGH TO MELT ANY HEART AND TOUCH ANY SOUL.
HIS BLOOD IS NOT COLD AT ALL!

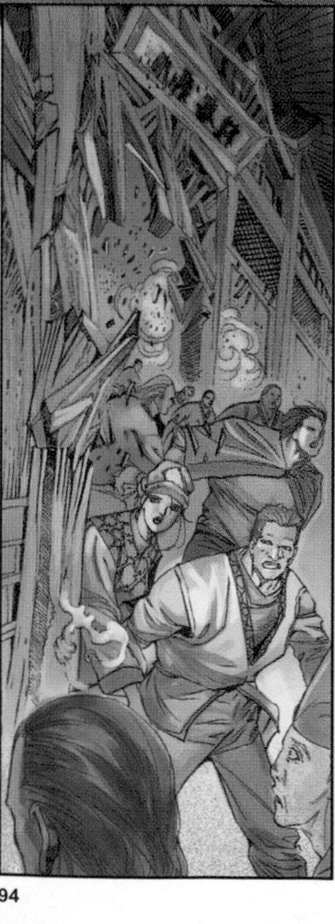

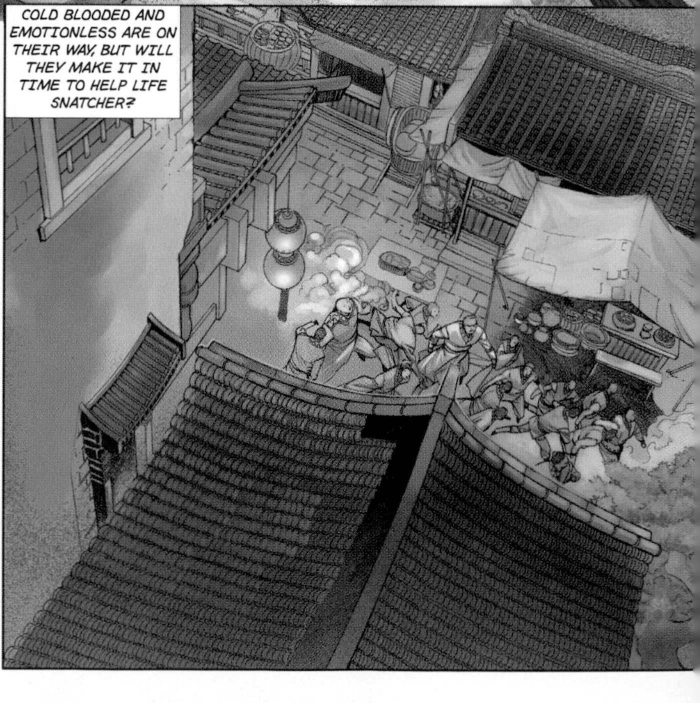
COLD BLOODED AND EMOTIONLESS ARE ON THEIR WAY, BUT WILL THEY MAKE IT IN TIME TO HELP LIFE SNATCHER?

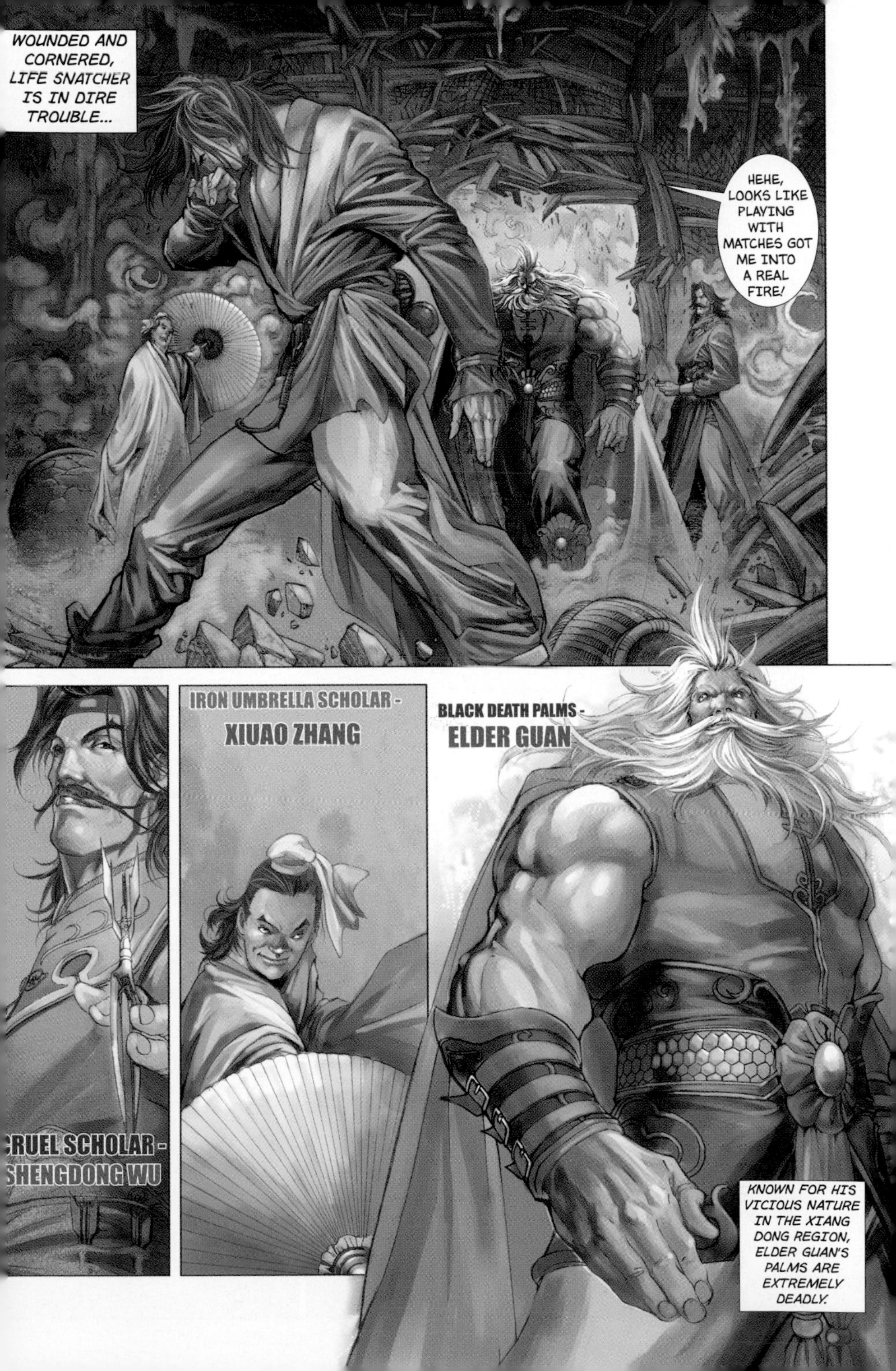
WOUNDED AND CORNERED, LIFE SNATCHER IS IN DIRE TROUBLE...
HEHE, LOOKS LIKE PLAYING WITH MATCHES GOT ME INTO A REAL FIRE!
IRON UMBRELLA SCHOLAR - XIUAO ZHANG
BLACK DEATH PALMS - ELDER GUAN
CRUEL SCHOLAR - SHENGDONG WU
KNOWN FOR HIS VICIOUS NATURE IN THE XIANG DONG REGION, ELDER GUAN'S PALMS ARE EXTREMELY DEADLY.

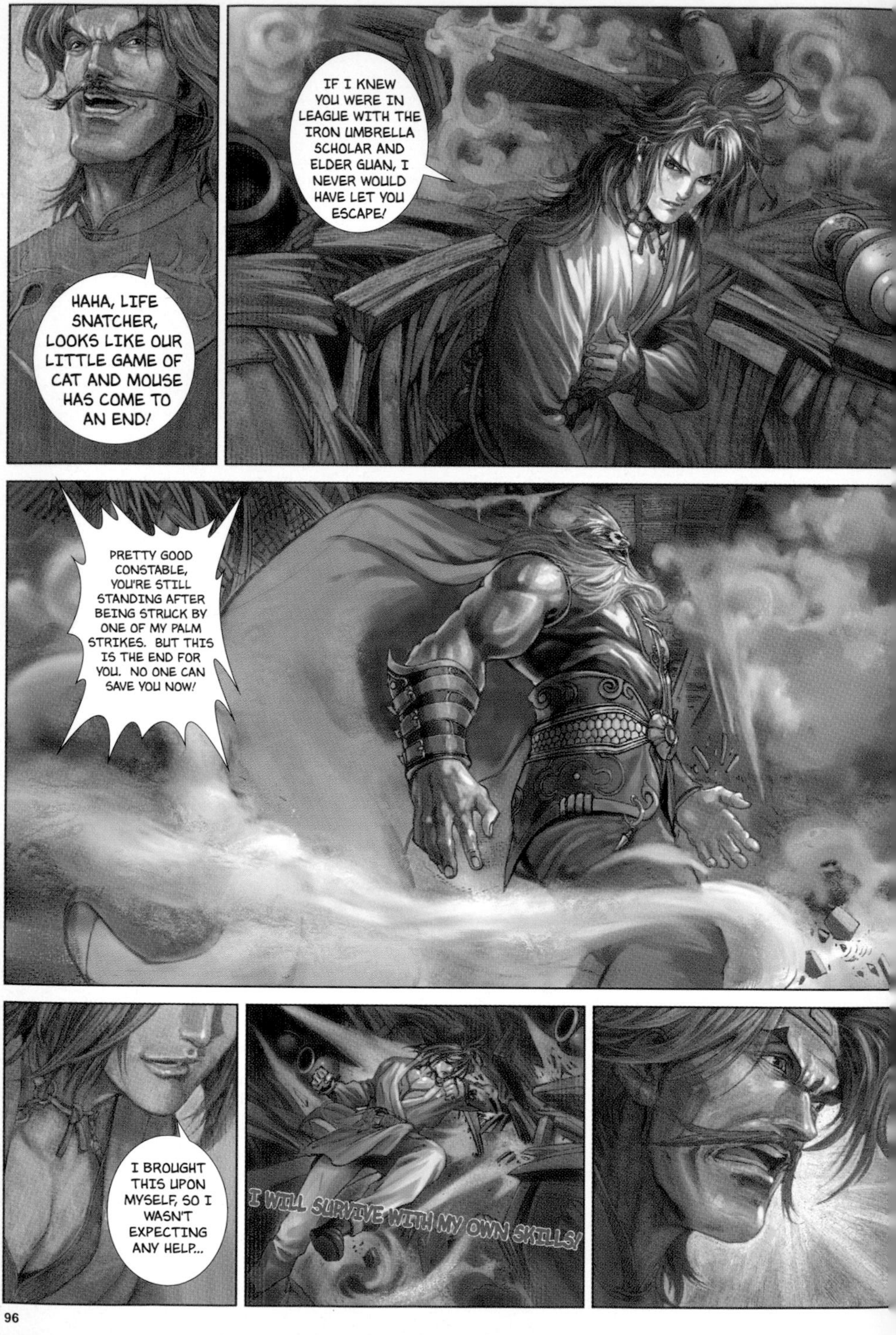
HAHA, LIFE SNATCHER, LOOKS LIKE OUR LITTLE GAME OF CAT AND MOUSE HAS COME TO AN END!
IF I KNEW YOU WERE IN LEAGUE WITH THE IRON UMBRELLA SCHOLAR AND ELDER GUAN, I NEVER WOULD HAVE LET YOU ESCAPE!
PRETTY GOOD CONSTABLE, YOU'RE STILL STANDING AFTER BEING STRUCK BY ONE OF MY PALM STRIKES. BUT THIS IS THE END FOR YOU. NO ONE CAN SAVE YOU NOW!
I BROUGHT THIS UPON MYSELF, SO I WASN'T EXPECTING ANY HELP...
I WILL SURVIVE WITH MY OWN SKILLS!

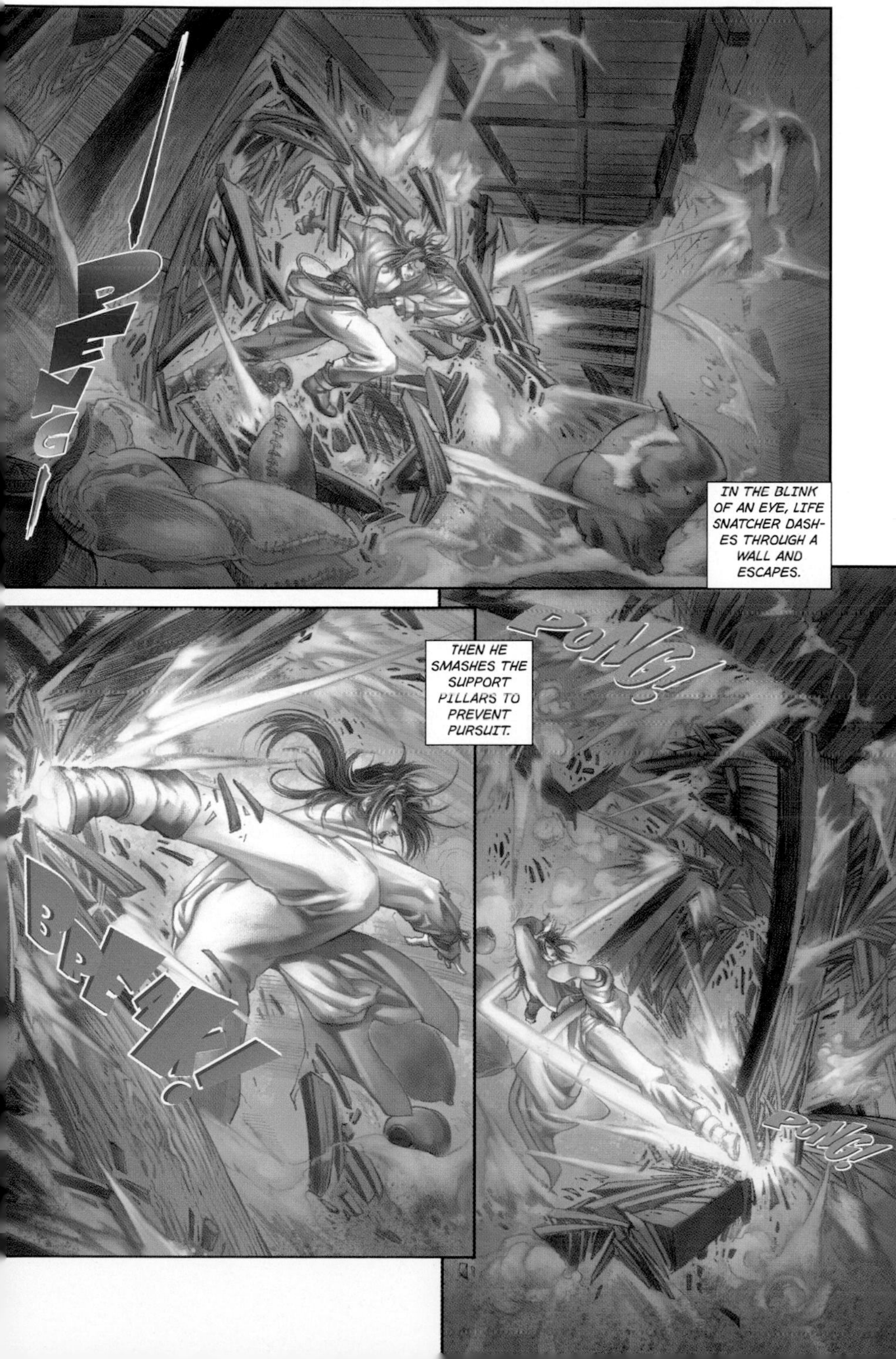
PENG!
IN THE BLINK OF AN EYE, LIFE SNATCHER DASH-ES THROUGH A WALL AND ESCAPES.
THEN HE SMASHES THE SUPPORT PILLARS TO PREVENT PURSUIT.
BREAK!
PONG!
PONG!

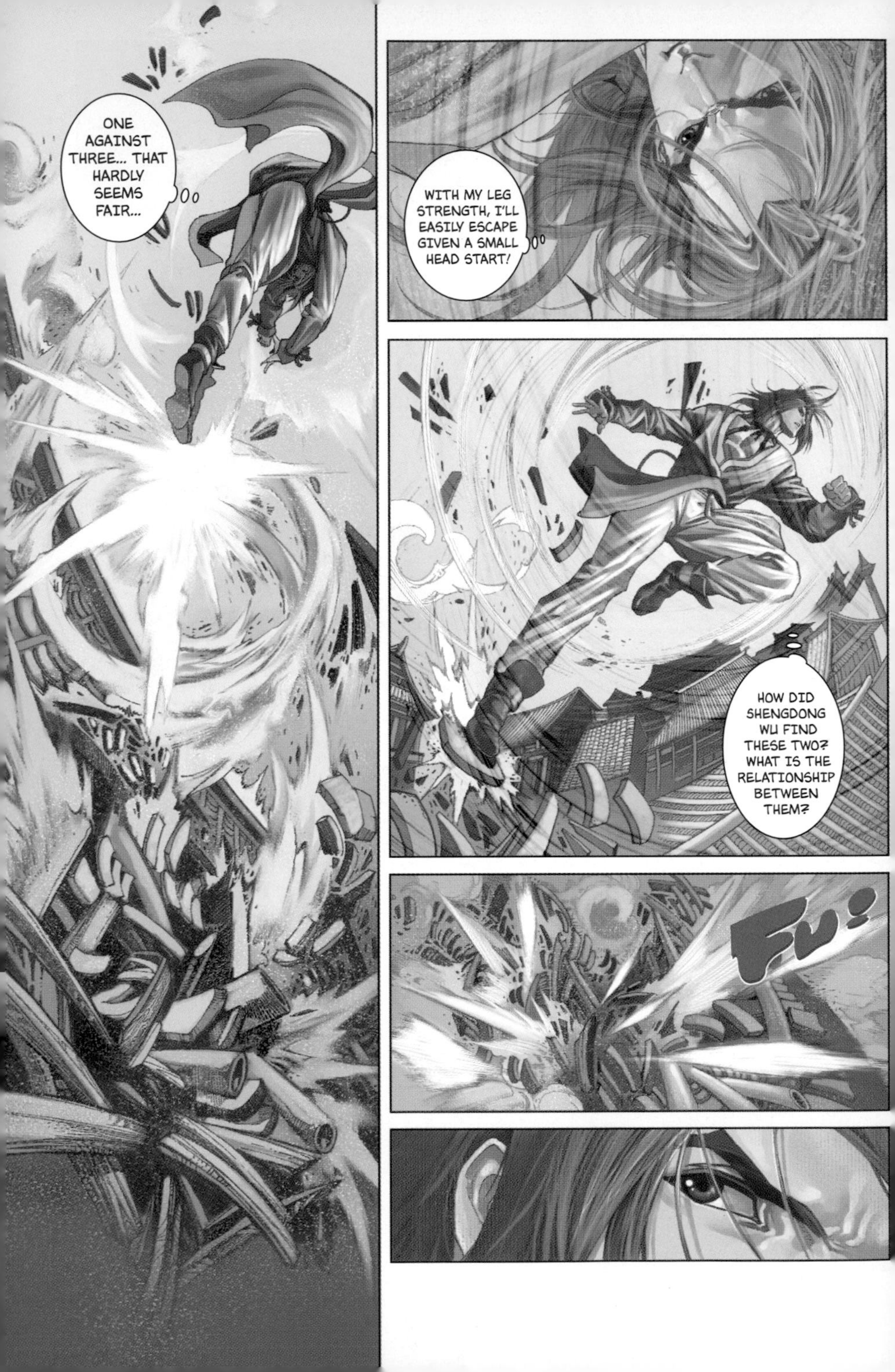
ONE AGAINST THREE... THAT HARDLY SEEMS FAIR...
WITH MY LEG STRENGTH, I'LL EASILY ESCAPE GIVEN A SMALL HEAD START!
HOW DID SHENGDONG WU FIND THESE TWO? WHAT IS THE RELATIONSHIP BETWEEN THEM?
FU!

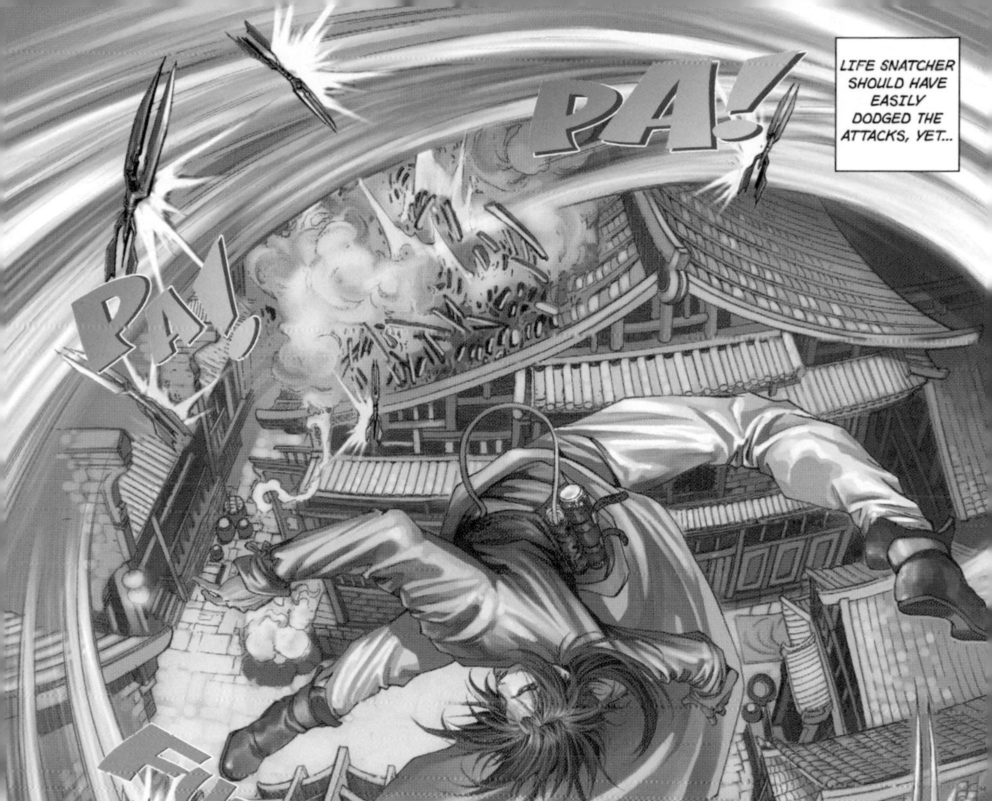
LIFE SNATCHER SHOULD HAVE EASILY DODGED THE ATTACKS, YET...
PA!
PA!
FU-
PA!
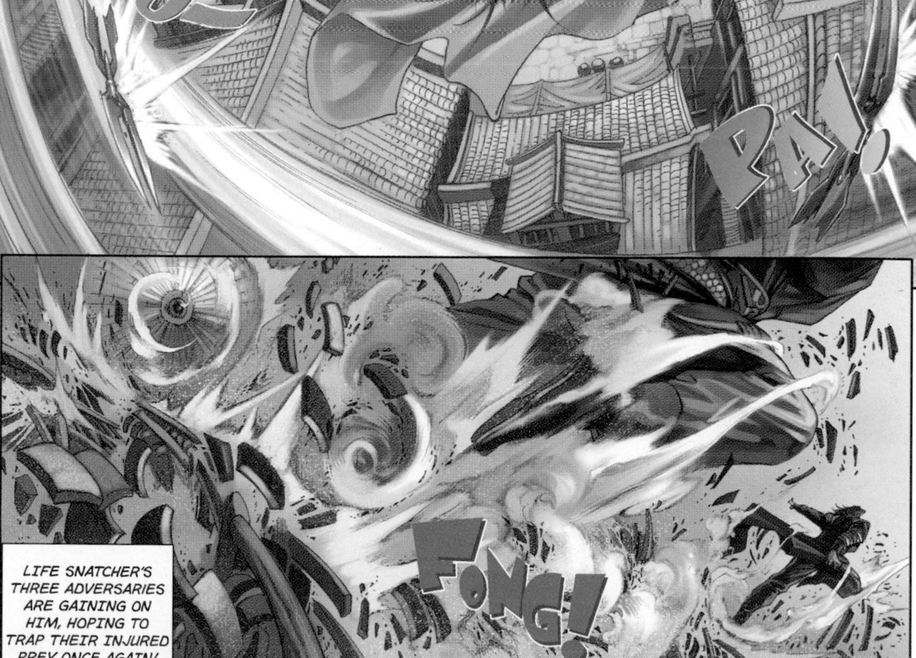
LIFE SNATCHER'S THREE ADVERSARIES ARE GAINING ON HIM, HOPING TO TRAP THEIR INJURED PREY ONCE AGAIN!
FONG!

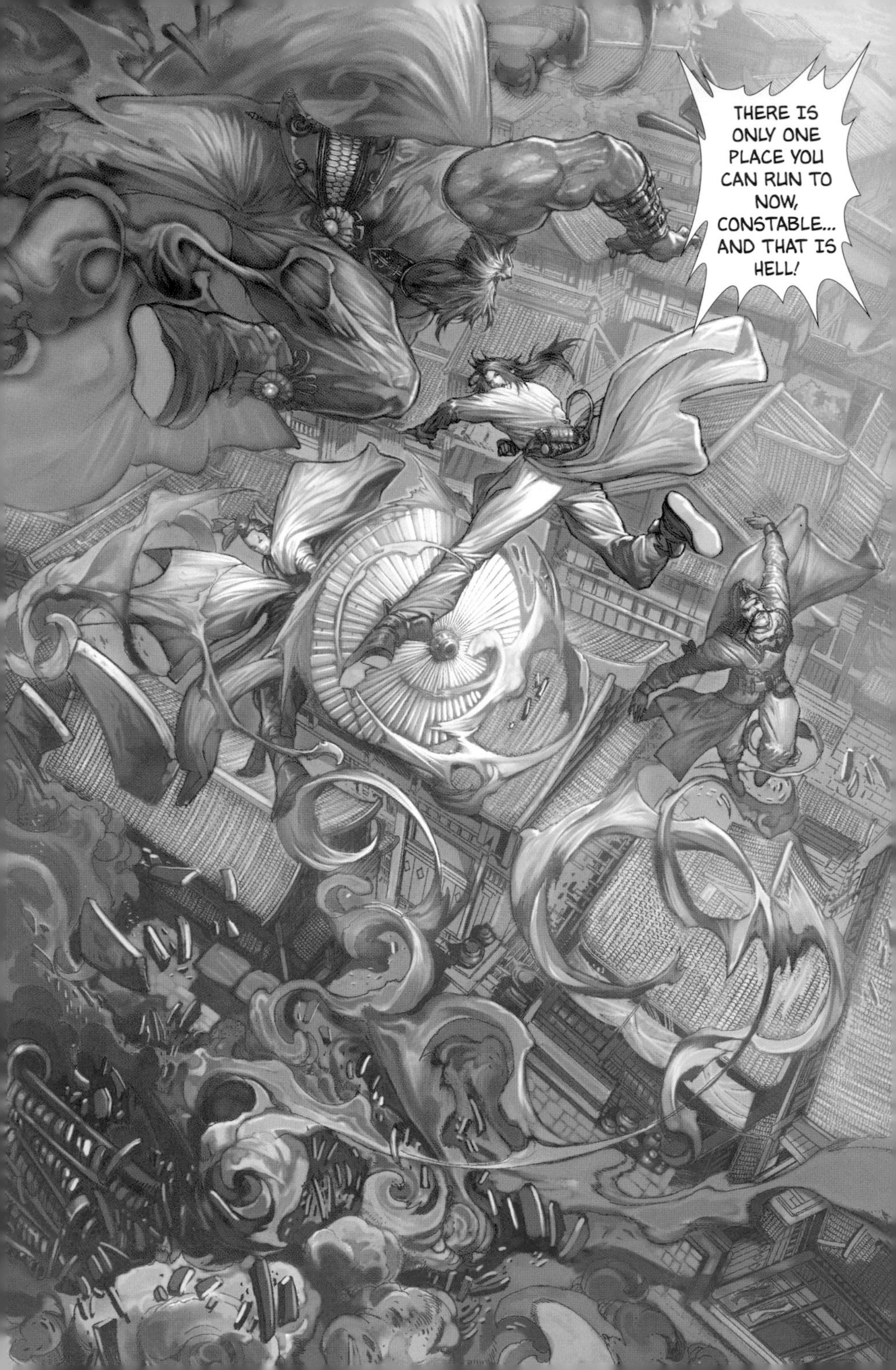
THERE IS ONLY ONE PLACE YOU CAN RUN TO NOW, CONSTABLE... AND THAT IS HELL!

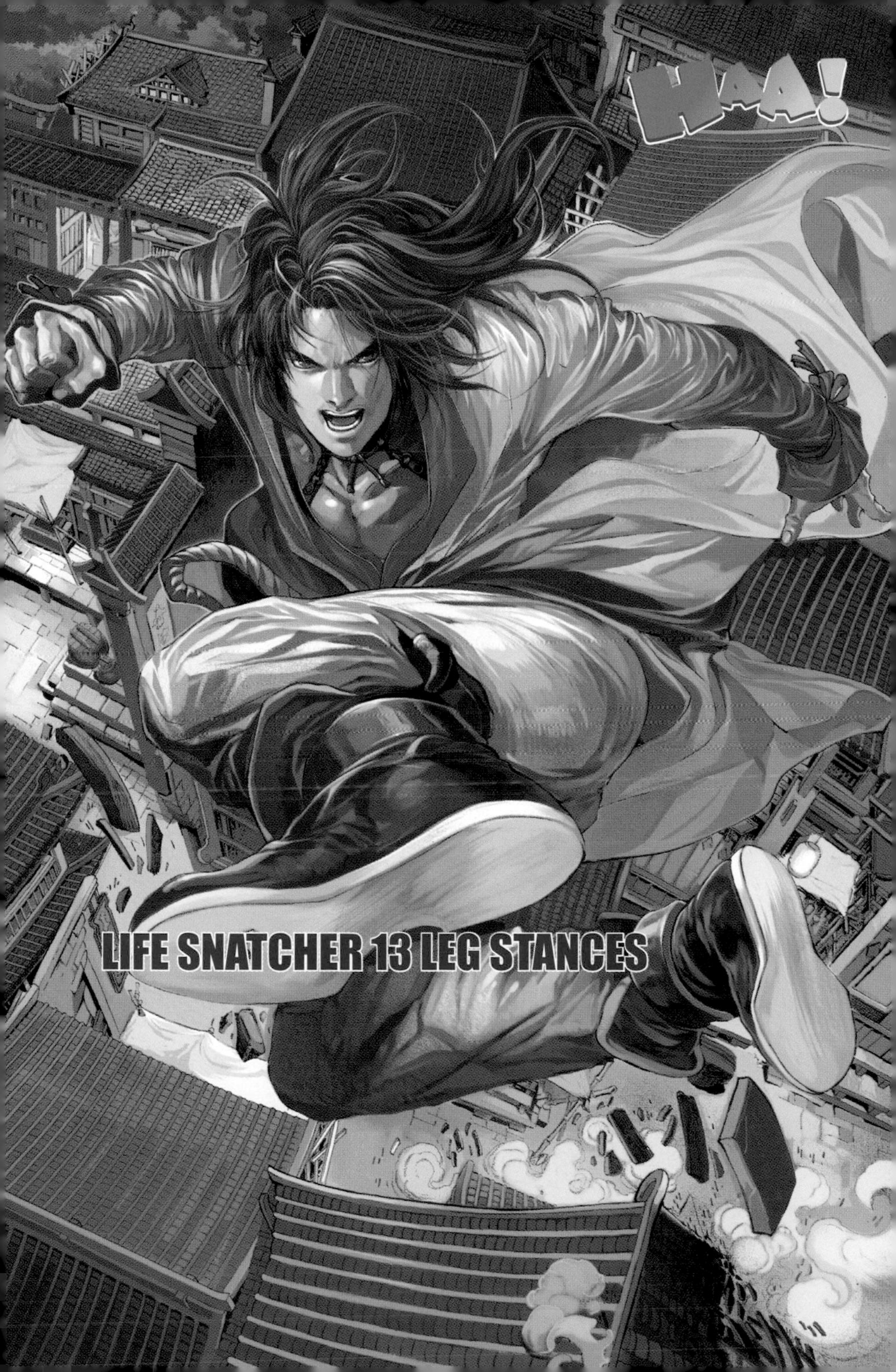
HAA!
LIFE SNATCHER 13 LEG STANCES

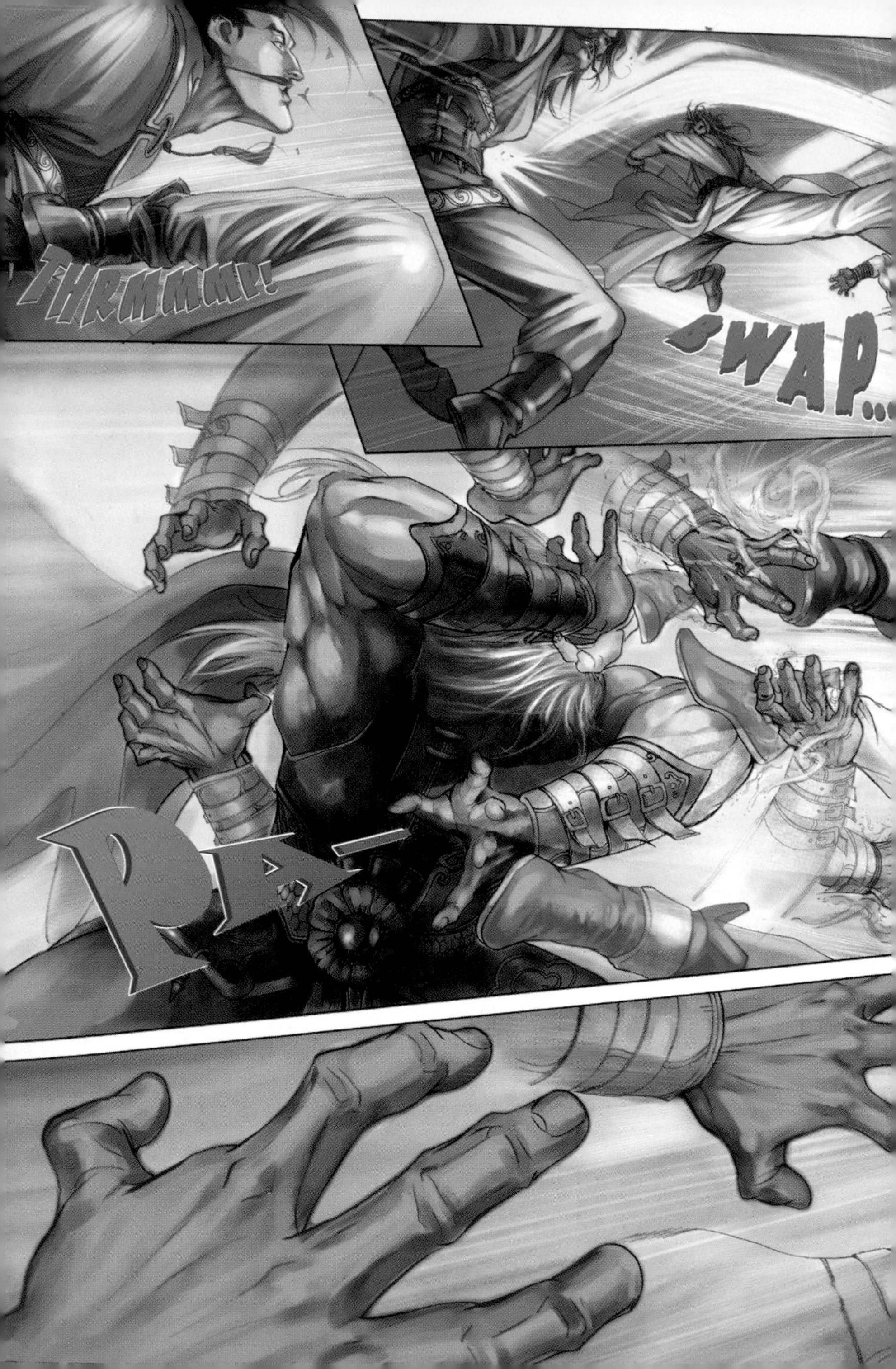
THRMMMMB!
SWAP...
PA-

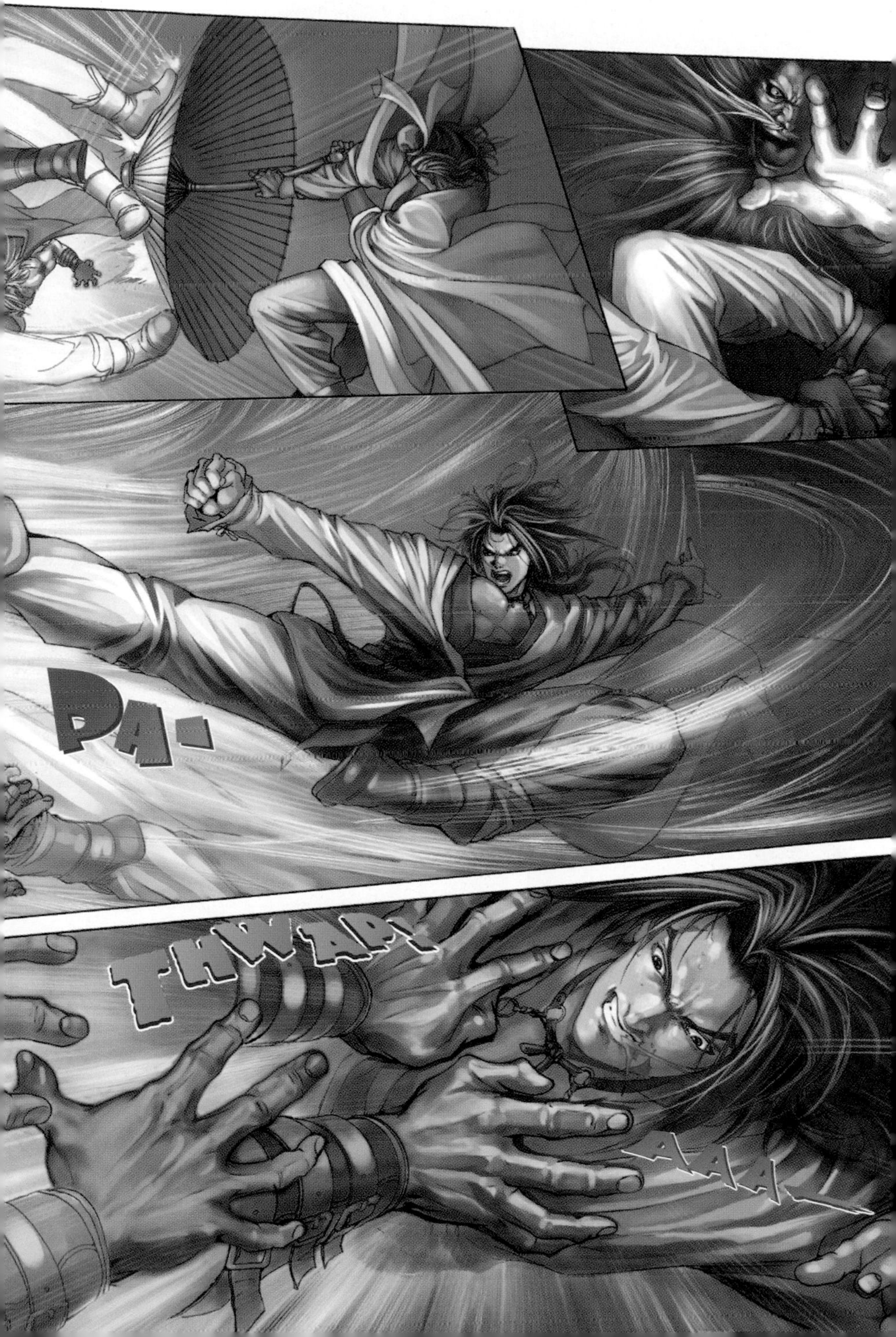
PA-
THWAP!
AAA

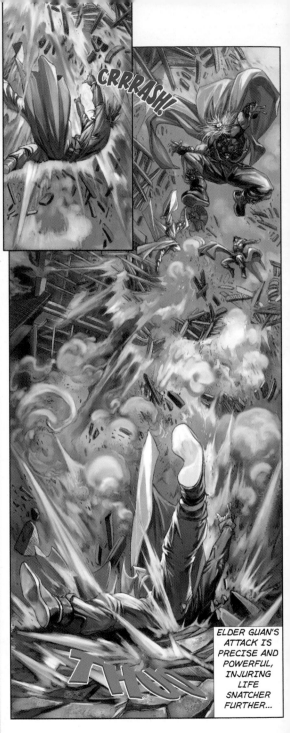

ELDER GUAN'S ATTACK IS PRECISE AND POWERFUL, INJURING LIFE SNATCHER FURTHER...

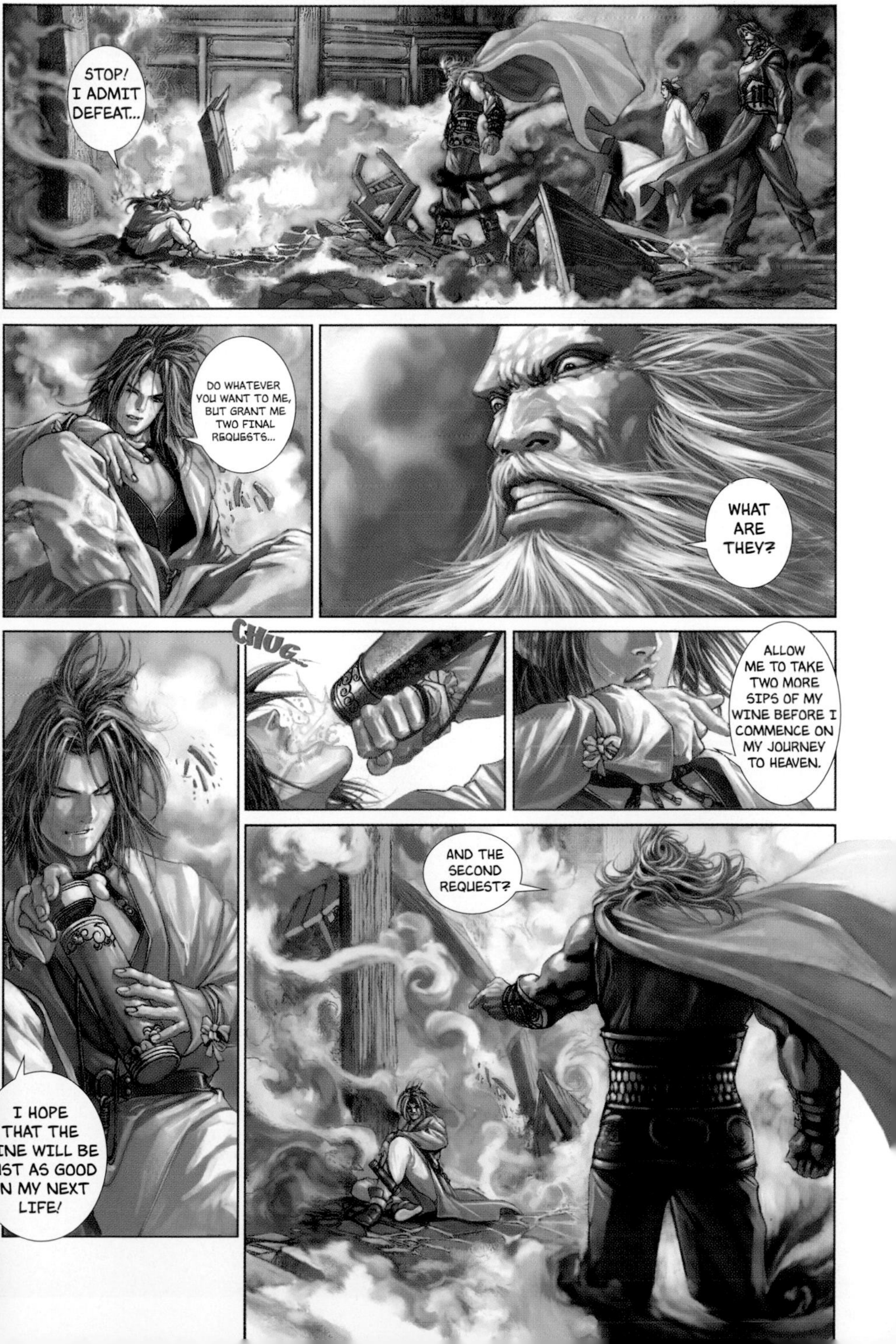
STOP! I ADMIT DEFEAT...
DO WHATEVER YOU WANT TO ME, BUT GRANT ME TWO FINAL REQUESTS...
WHAT ARE THEY?
CHUG...
ALLOW ME TO TAKE TWO MORE SIPS OF MY WINE BEFORE I COMMENCE ON MY JOURNEY TO HEAVEN.
I HOPE THAT THE INE WILL BE IST AS GOOD N MY NEXT LIFE!
AND THE SECOND REQUEST?

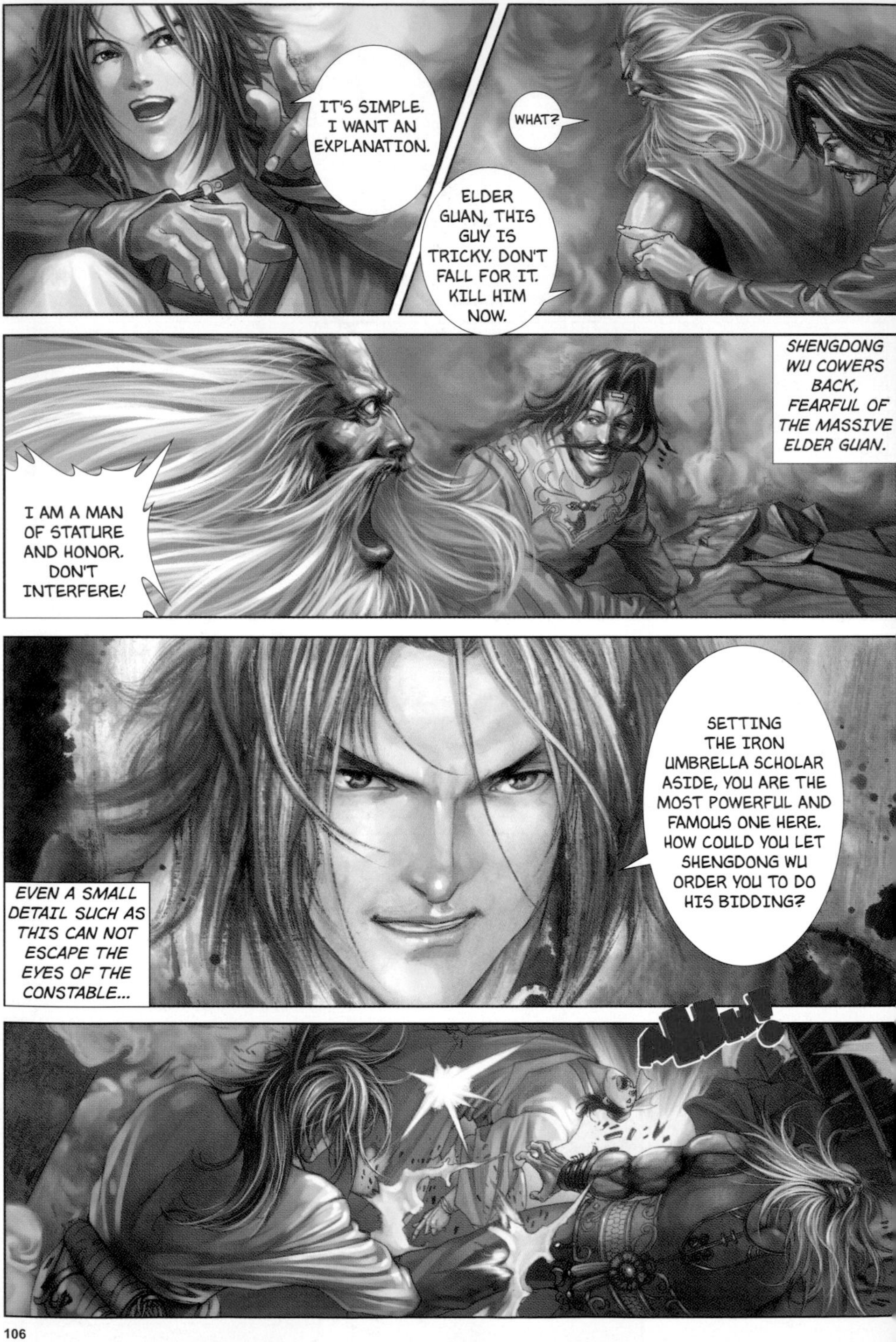
IT'S SIMPLE. I WANT AN EXPLANATION.
WHAT?
ELDER GUAN, THIS GUY IS TRICKY. DON'T FALL FOR IT. KILL HIM NOW.
SHENGDONG WU COWERS BACK, FEARFUL OF THE MASSIVE ELDER GUAN.
I AM A MAN OF STATURE AND HONOR. DON'T INTERFERE!
SETTING THE IRON UMBRELLA SCHOLAR ASIDE, YOU ARE THE MOST POWERFUL AND FAMOUS ONE HERE. HOW COULD YOU LET SHENGDONG WU ORDER YOU TO DO HIS BIDDING?
EVEN A SMALL DETAIL SUCH AS THIS CAN NOT ESCAPE THE EYES OF THE CONSTABLE...

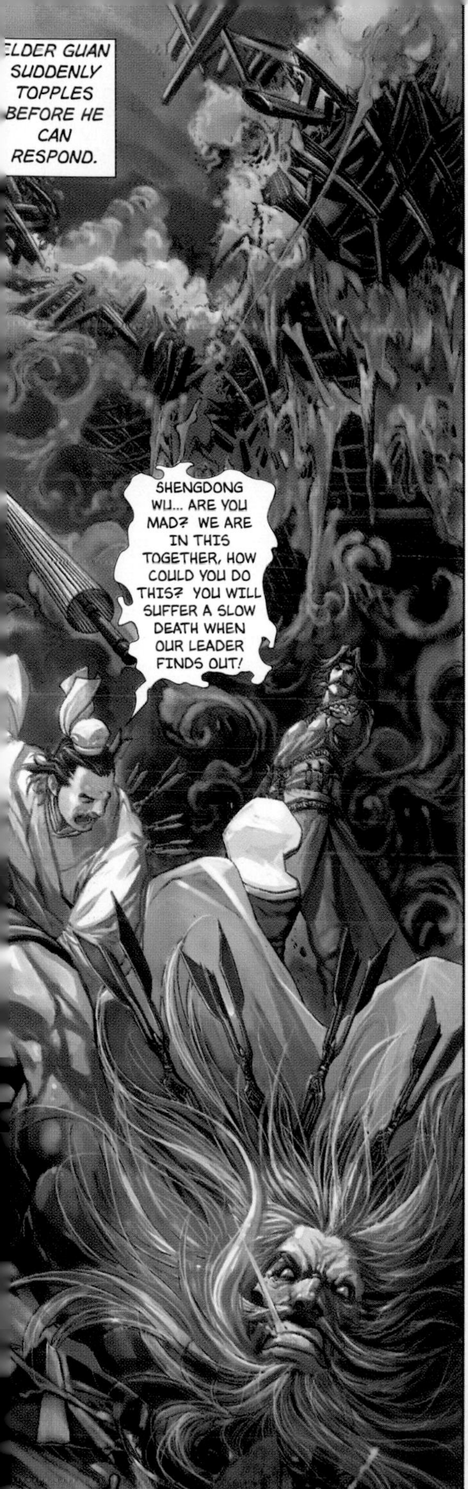
ELDER GUAN SUDDENLY TOPPLES BEFORE HE CAN RESPOND.
SHENGDONG WU... ARE YOU MAD? WE ARE IN THIS TOGETHER, HOW COULD YOU DO THIS? YOU WILL SUFFER A SLOW DEATH WHEN OUR LEADER FINDS OUT!

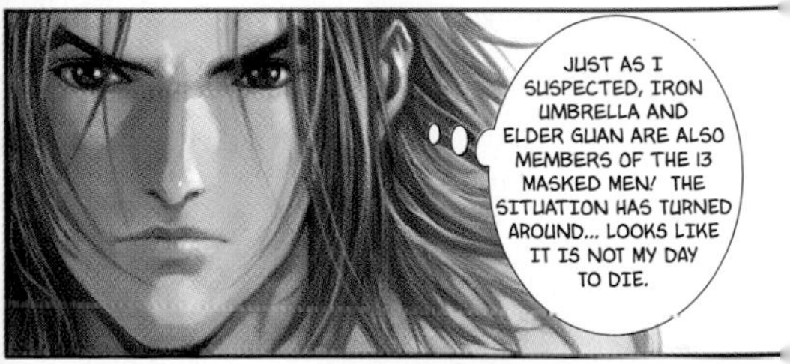
JUST AS I SUSPECTED, IRON UMBRELLA AND ELDER GUAN ARE ALSO MEMBERS OF THE 13 MASKED MEN! THE SITUATION HAS TURNED AROUND... LOOKS LIKE IT IS NOT MY DAY TO DIE.

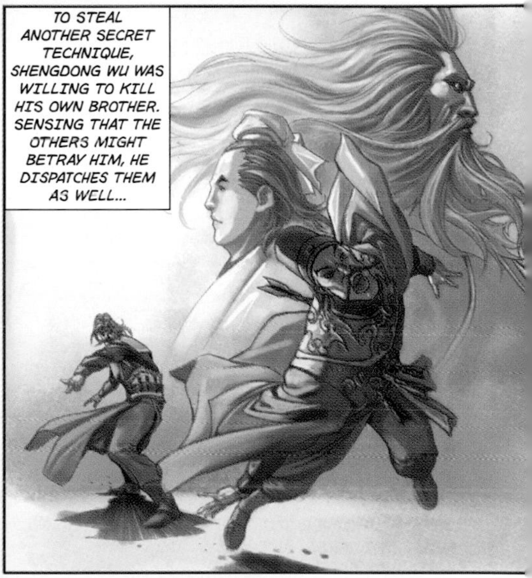
TO STEAL ANOTHER SECRET TECHNIQUE, SHENGDONG WU WAS WILLING TO KILL HIS OWN BROTHER. SENSING THAT THE OTHERS MIGHT BETRAY HIM, HE DISPATCHES THEM AS WELL...

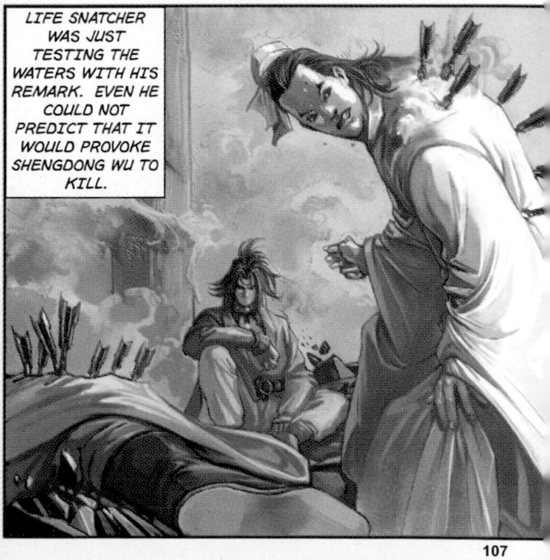
LIFE SNATCHER WAS JUST TESTING THE WATERS WITH HIS REMARK. EVEN HE COULD NOT PREDICT THAT IT WOULD PROVOKE SHENGDONG WU TO KILL.

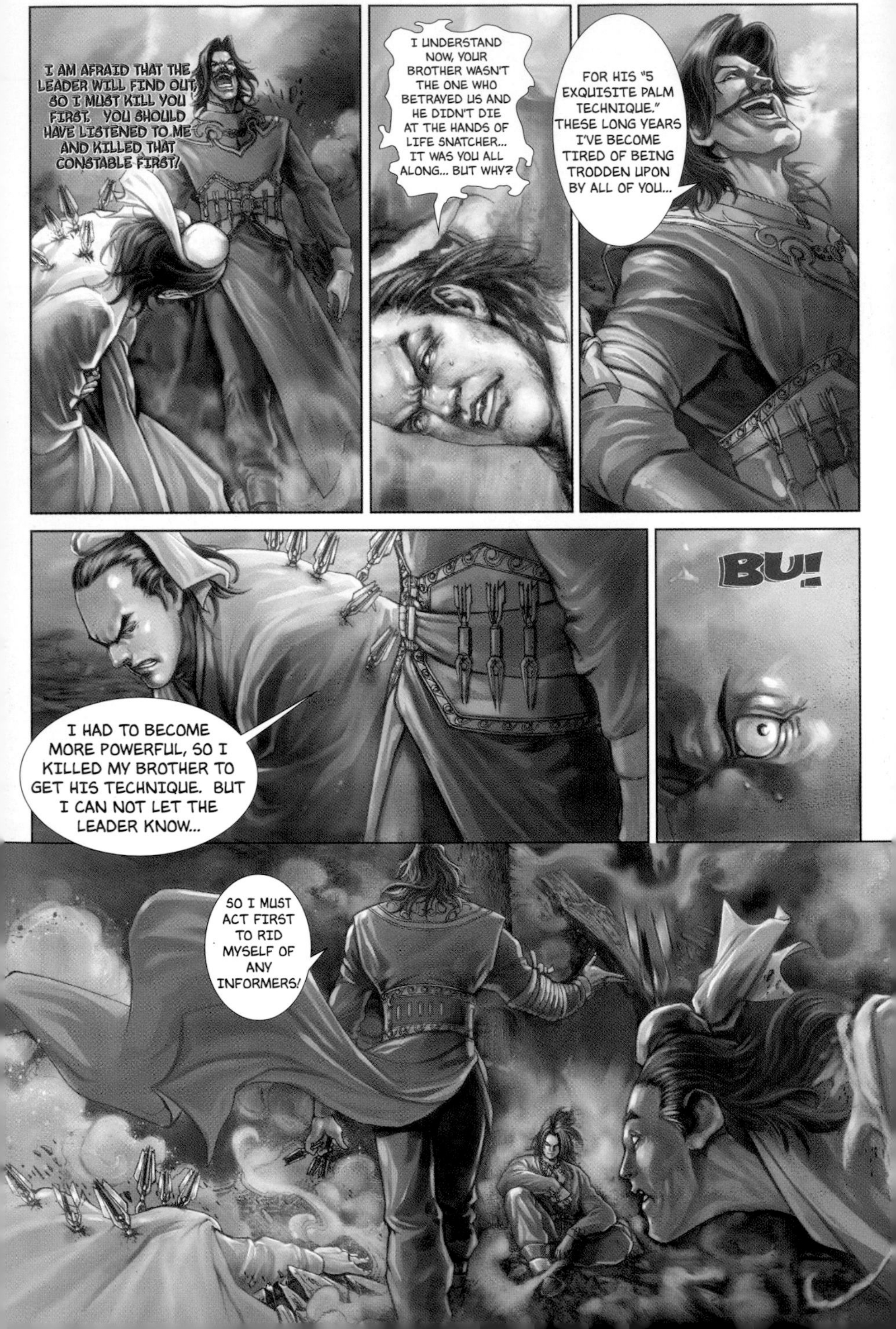
I AM AFRAID THAT THE LEADER WILL FIND OUT, SO I MUST KILL YOU FIRST. YOU SHOULD HAVE LISTENED TO ME AND KILLED THAT CONSTABLE FIRST!
I UNDERSTAND NOW, YOUR BROTHER WASN'T THE ONE WHO BETRAYED US AND HE DIDN'T DIE AT THE HANDS OF LIFE SNATCHER... IT WAS YOU ALL ALONG... BUT WHY?
FOR HIS "5 EXQUISITE PALM TECHNIQUE." THESE LONG YEARS I'VE BECOME TIRED OF BEING TRODDEN UPON BY ALL OF YOU...
I HAD TO BECOME MORE POWERFUL, SO I KILLED MY BROTHER TO GET HIS TECHNIQUE. BUT I CAN NOT LET THE LEADER KNOW...
BU!
SO I MUST ACT FIRST TO RID MYSELF OF ANY INFORMERS!

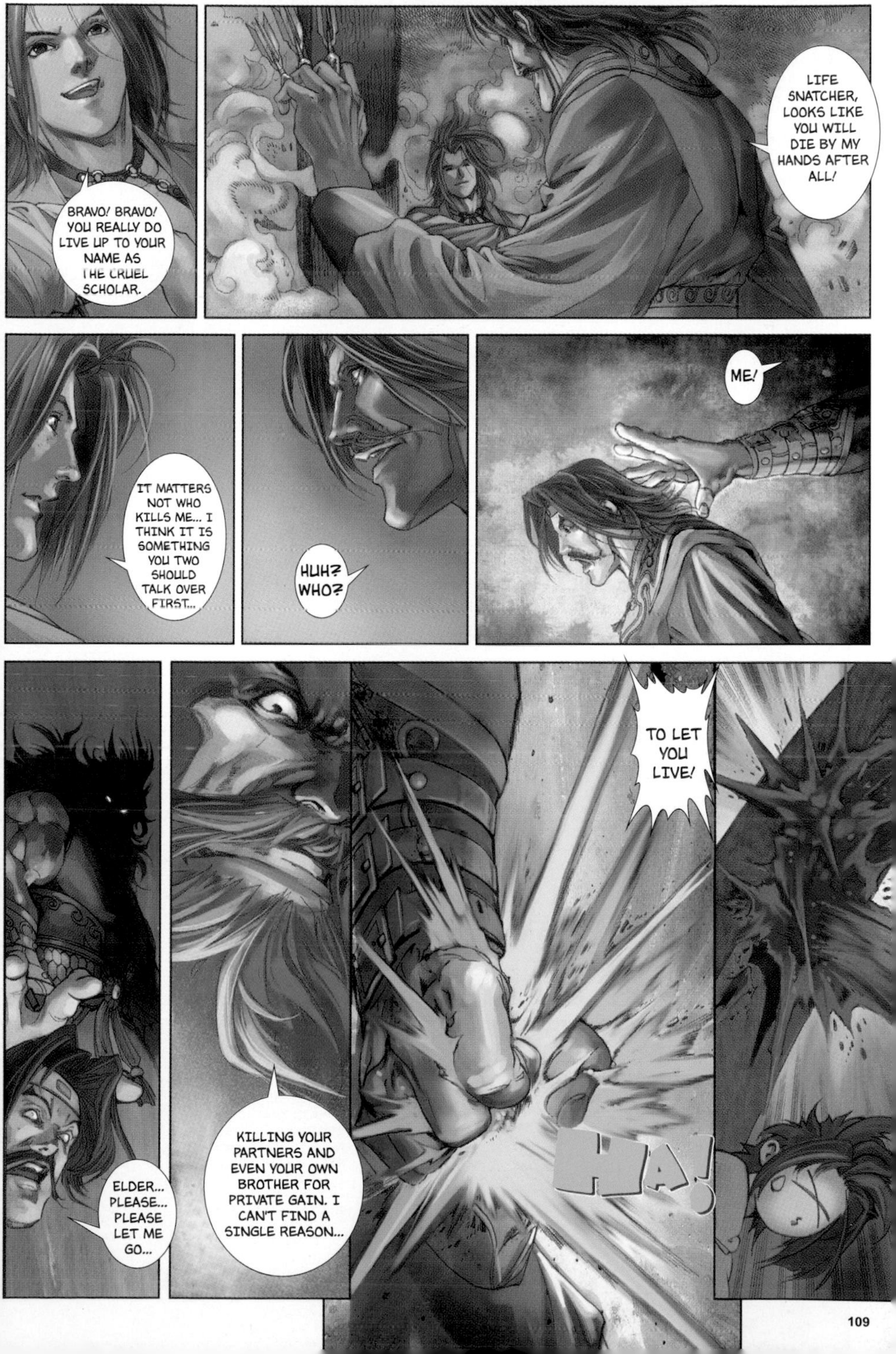
BRAVO! BRAVO! YOU REALLY DO LIVE UP TO YOUR NAME AS THE CRUEL SCHOLAR.
LIFE SNATCHER, LOOKS LIKE YOU WILL DIE BY MY HANDS AFTER ALL!
IT MATTERS NOT WHO KILLS ME... I THINK IT IS SOMETHING YOU TWO SHOULD TALK OVER FIRST...
HUH? WHO?
ME!
ELDER... PLEASE... PLEASE LET ME GO...
KILLING YOUR PARTNERS AND EVEN YOUR OWN BROTHER FOR PRIVATE GAIN. I CAN'T FIND A SINGLE REASON...
TO LET YOU LIVE!
HA!

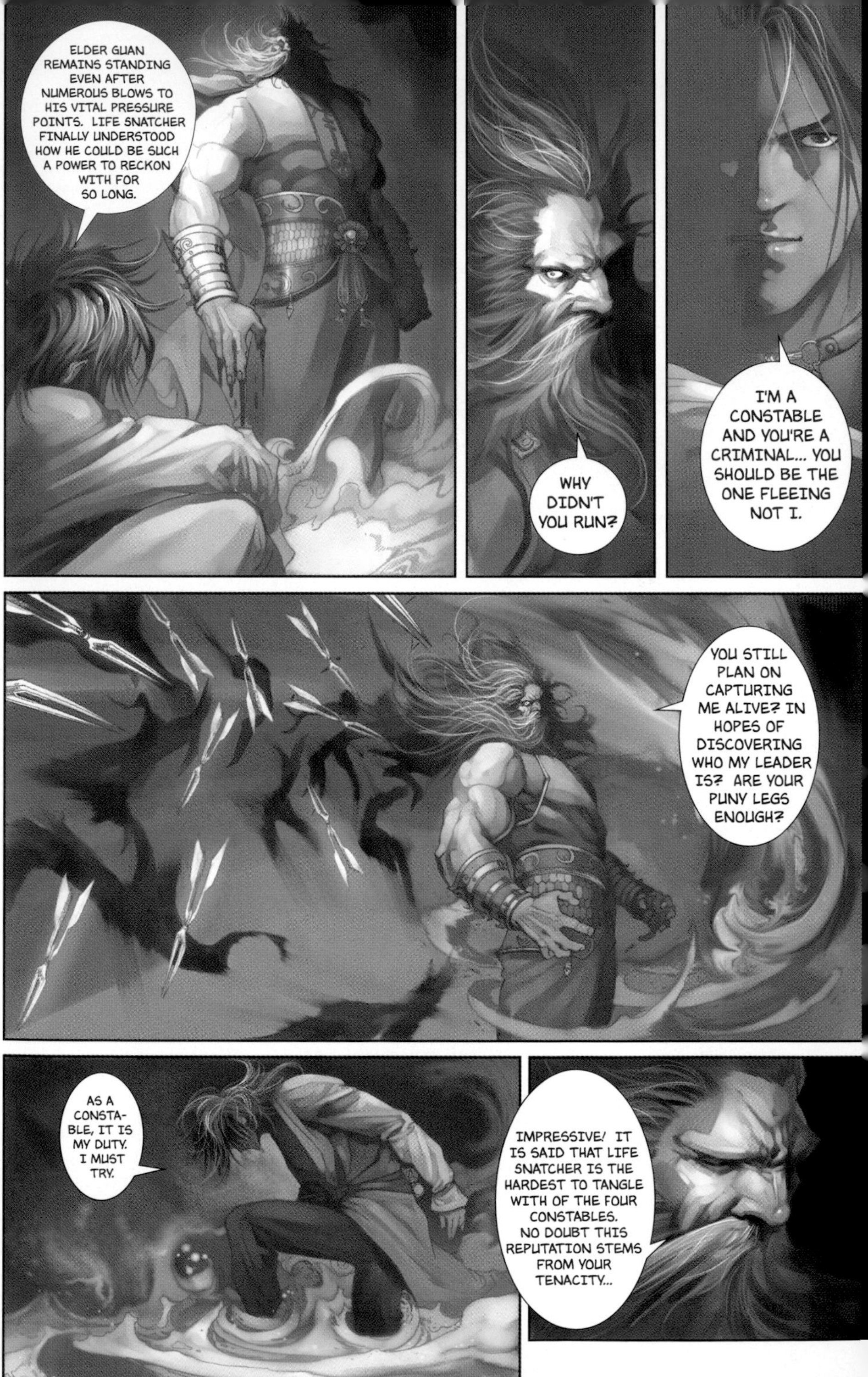
ELDER GUAN REMAINS STANDING EVEN AFTER NUMEROUS BLOWS TO HIS VITAL PRESSURE POINTS. LIFE SNATCHER FINALLY UNDERSTOOD HOW HE COULD BE SUCH A POWER TO RECKON WITH FOR SO LONG.
WHY DIDN'T YOU RUN?
I'M A CONSTABLE AND YOU'RE A CRIMINAL... YOU SHOULD BE THE ONE FLEEING NOT I.
YOU STILL PLAN ON CAPTURING ME ALIVE? IN HOPES OF DISCOVERING WHO MY LEADER IS? ARE YOUR PUNY LEGS ENOUGH?
AS A CONSTA-BLE, IT IS MY DUTY. I MUST TRY.
IMPRESSIVE! IT IS SAID THAT LIFE SNATCHER IS THE HARDEST TO TANGLE WITH OF THE FOUR CONSTABLES. NO DOUBT THIS REPUTATION STEMS FROM YOUR TENACITY...

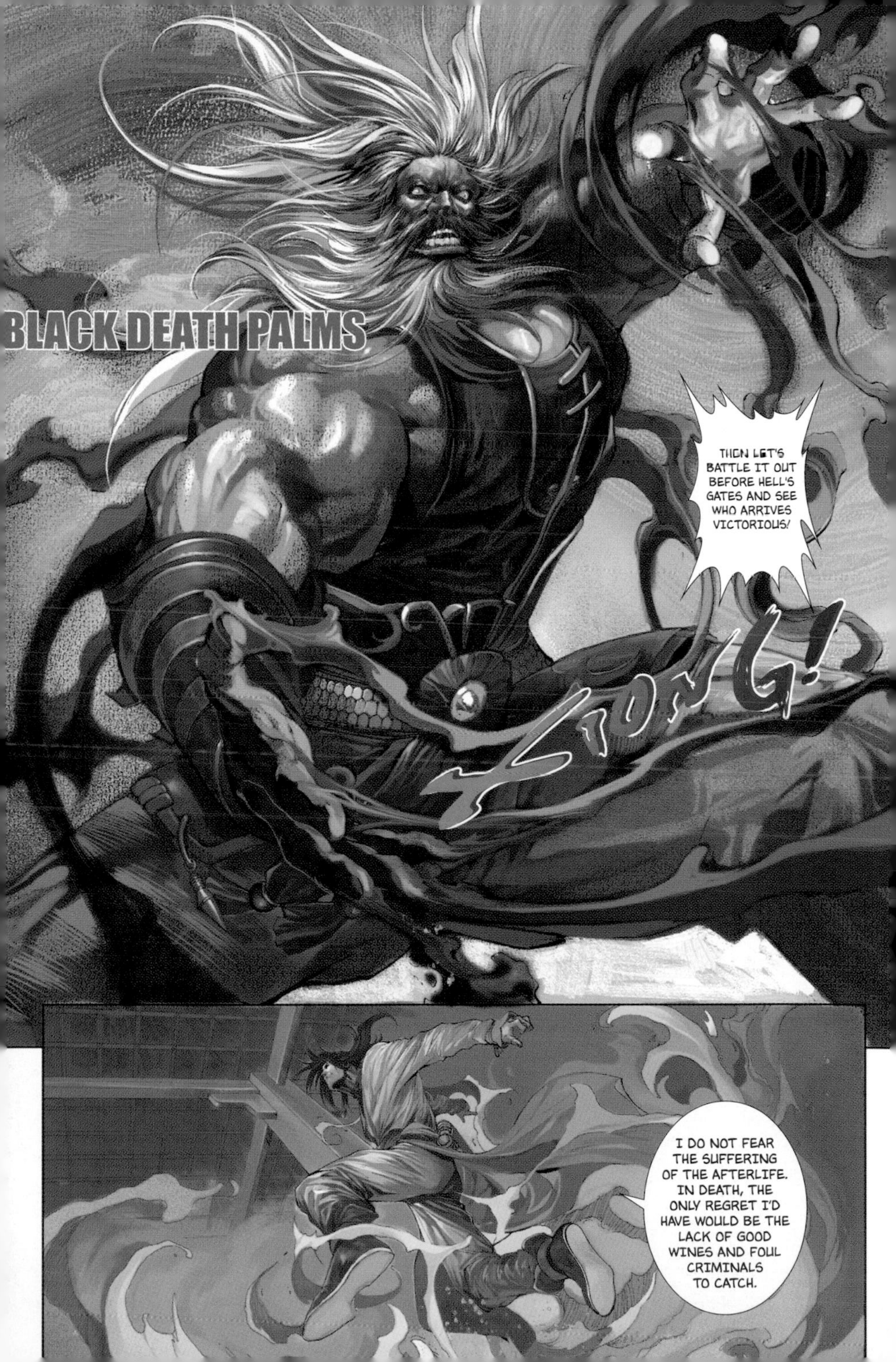
BLACK DEATH PALMS
THEN LET'S BATTLE IT OUT BEFORE HELL'S GATES AND SEE WHO ARRIVES VICTORIOUS!
SPONG!
I DO NOT FEAR THE SUFFERING OF THE AFTERLIFE. IN DEATH, THE ONLY REGRET I'D HAVE WOULD BE THE LACK OF GOOD WINES AND FOUL CRIMINALS TO CATCH.

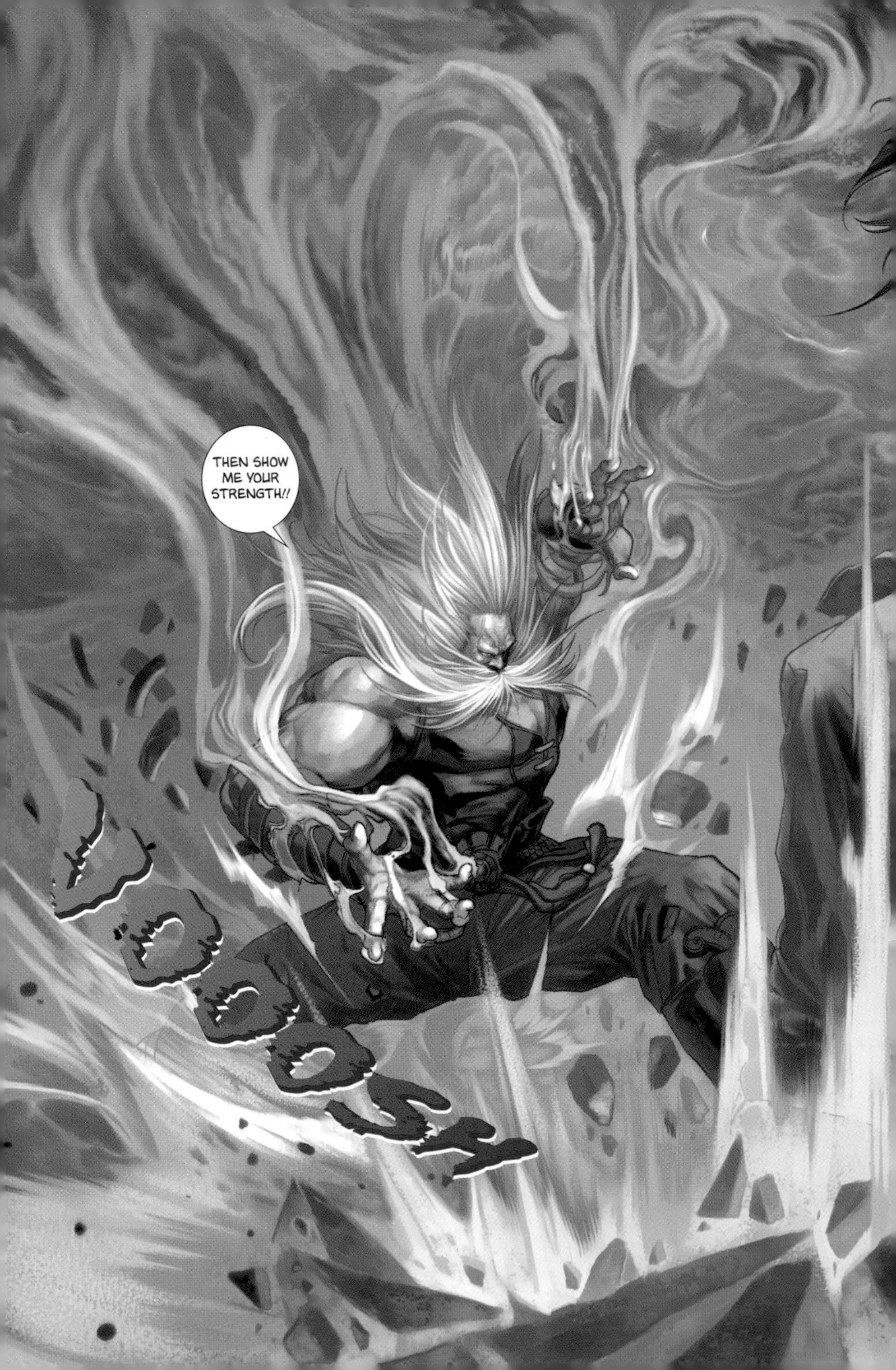
THEN SHOW ME YOUR STRENGTH!!

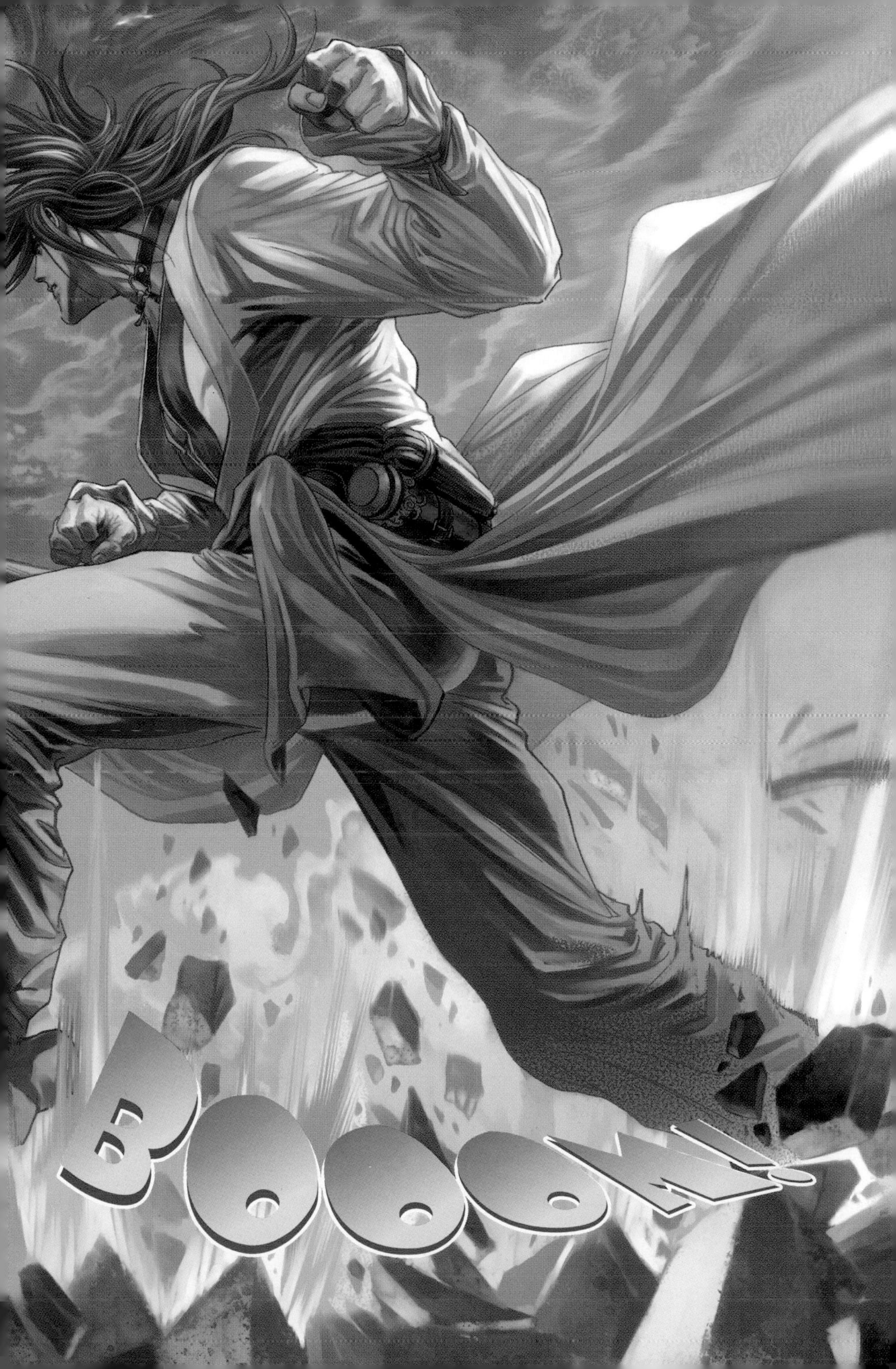
BOOOM!

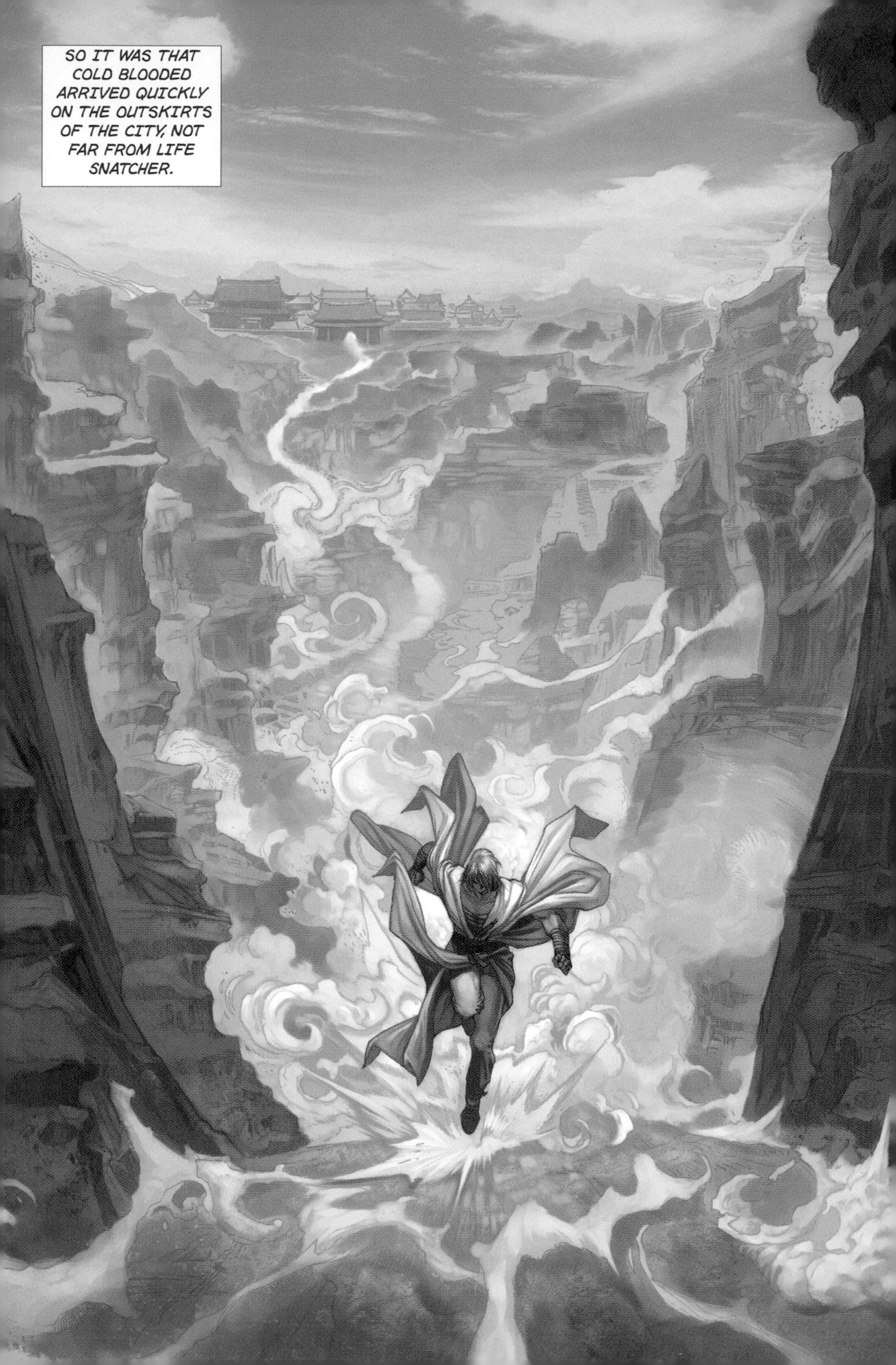
SO IT WAS THAT COLD BLOODED ARRIVED QUICKLY ON THE OUTSKIRTS OF THE CITY, NOT FAR FROM LIFE SNATCHER.

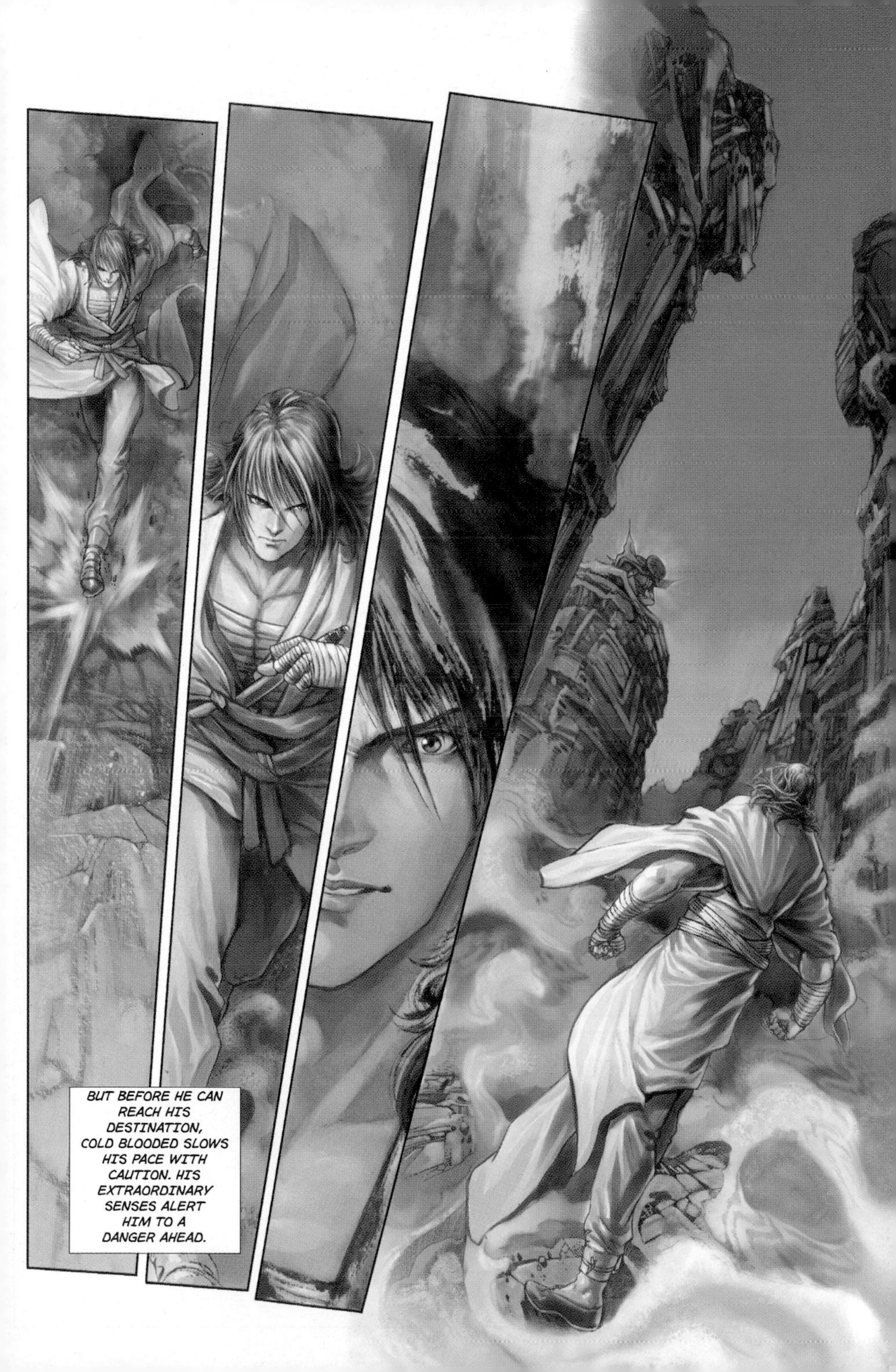
BUT BEFORE HE CAN REACH HIS DESTINATION, COLD BLOODED SLOWS HIS PACE WITH CAUTION. HIS EXTRAORDINARY SENSES ALERT HIM TO A DANGER AHEAD.

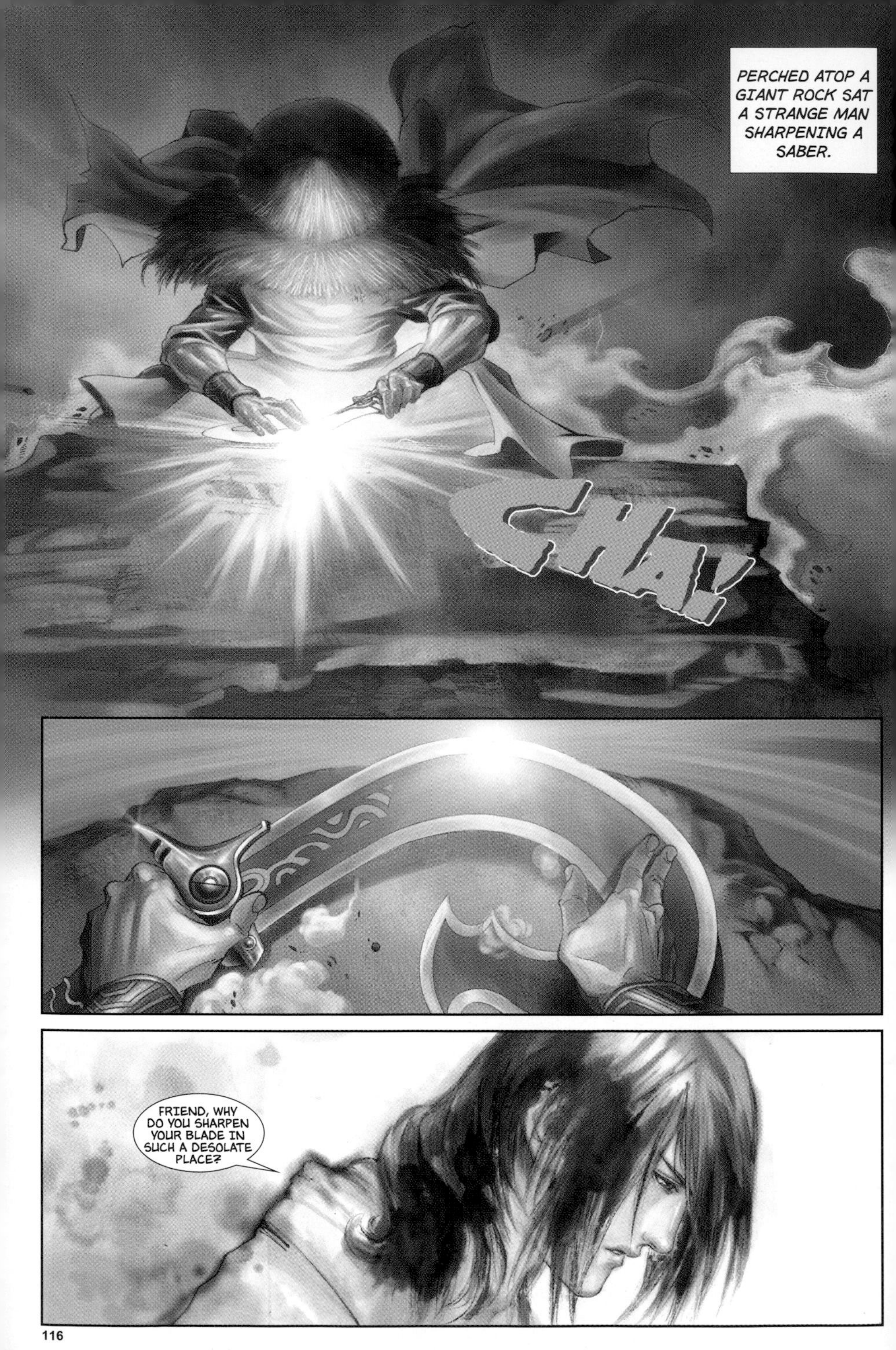
PERCHED ATOP A GIANT ROCK SAT A STRANGE MAN SHARPENING A SABER.
CHA!
FRIEND, WHY DO YOU SHARPEN YOUR BLADE IN SUCH A DESOLATE PLACE?

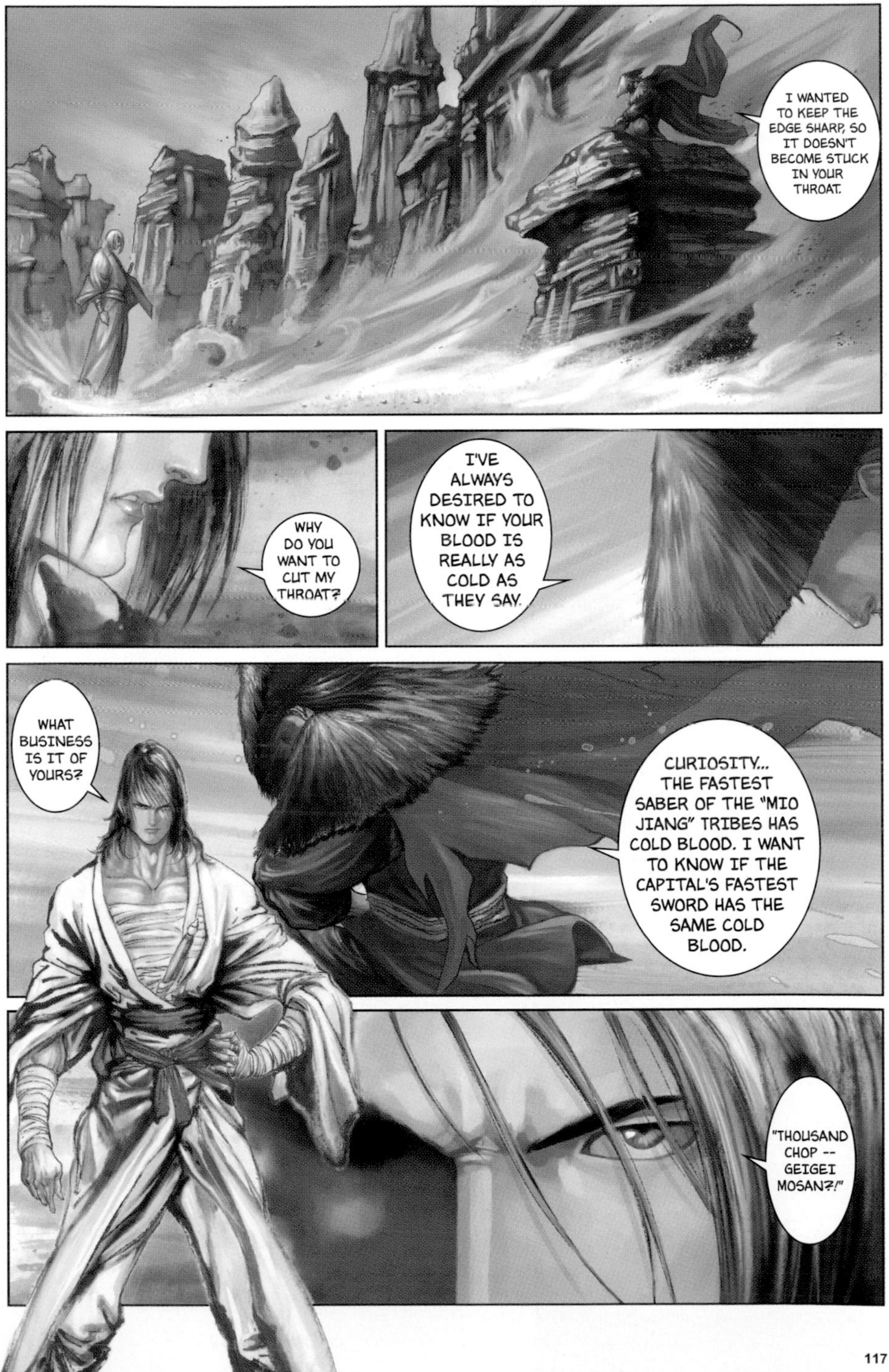
I WANTED TO KEEP THE EDGE SHARP, SO IT DOESN'T BECOME STUCK IN YOUR THROAT.
WHY DO YOU WANT TO CUT MY THROAT?
I'VE ALWAYS DESIRED TO KNOW IF YOUR BLOOD IS REALLY AS COLD AS THEY SAY.
WHAT BUSINESS IS IT OF YOURS?
CURIOSITY... THE FASTEST SABER OF THE "MIO JIANG" TRIBES HAS COLD BLOOD. I WANT TO KNOW IF THE CAPITAL'S FASTEST SWORD HAS THE SAME COLD BLOOD.
"THOUSAND CHOP -- GEIGEI MOSAN?!"

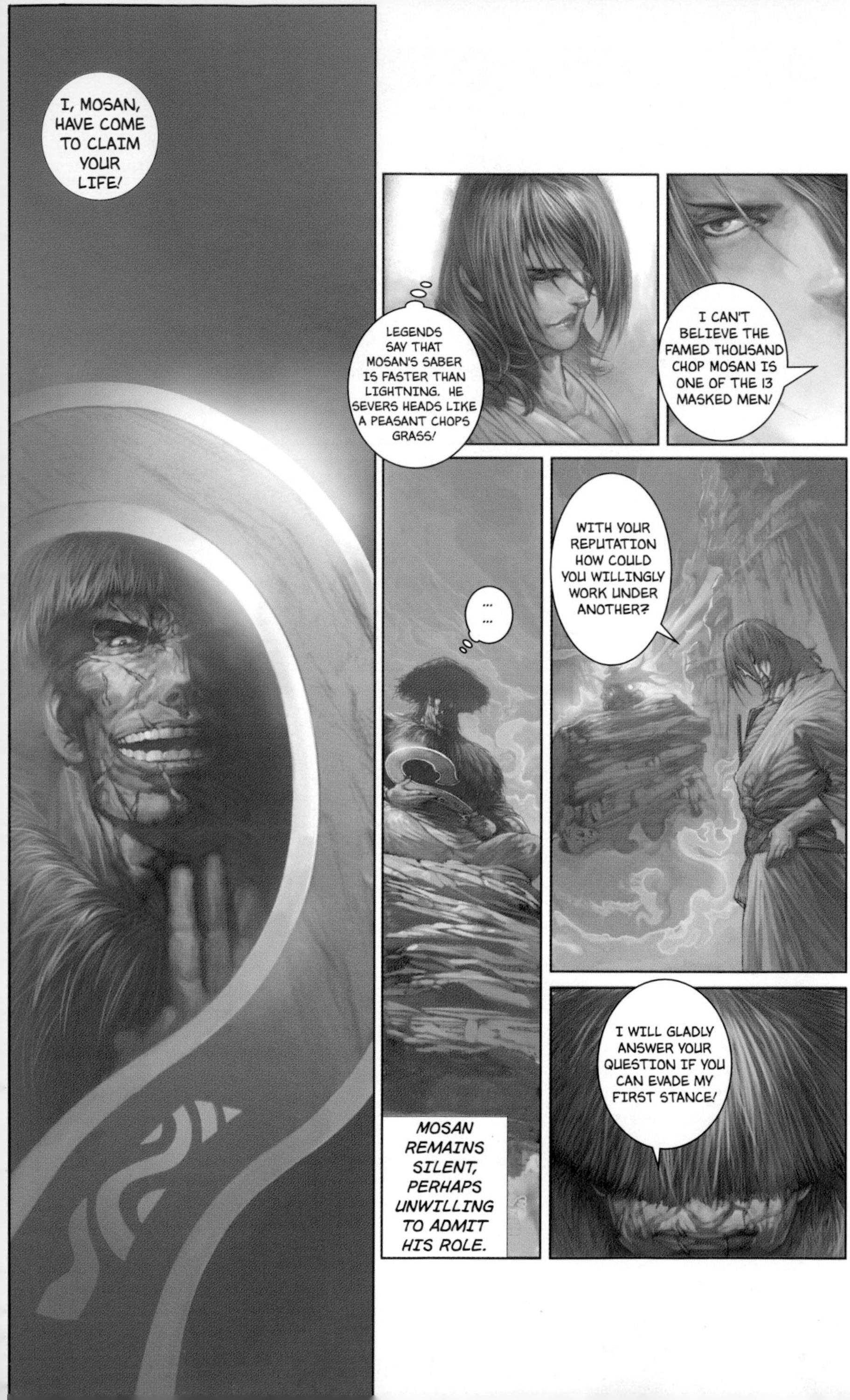
I, MOSAN, HAVE COME TO CLAIM YOUR LIFE!
LEGENDS SAY THAT MOSAN'S SABER IS FASTER THAN LIGHTNING. HE SEVERS HEADS LIKE A PEASANT CHOPS GRASS!
I CAN'T BELIEVE THE FAMED THOUSAND CHOP MOSAN IS ONE OF THE 13 MASKED MEN!
...
...
WITH YOUR REPUTATION HOW COULD YOU WILLINGLY WORK UNDER ANOTHER?
MOSAN REMAINS SILENT, PERHAPS UNWILLING TO ADMIT HIS ROLE.
I WILL GLADLY ANSWER YOUR QUESTION IF YOU CAN EVADE MY FIRST STANCE!

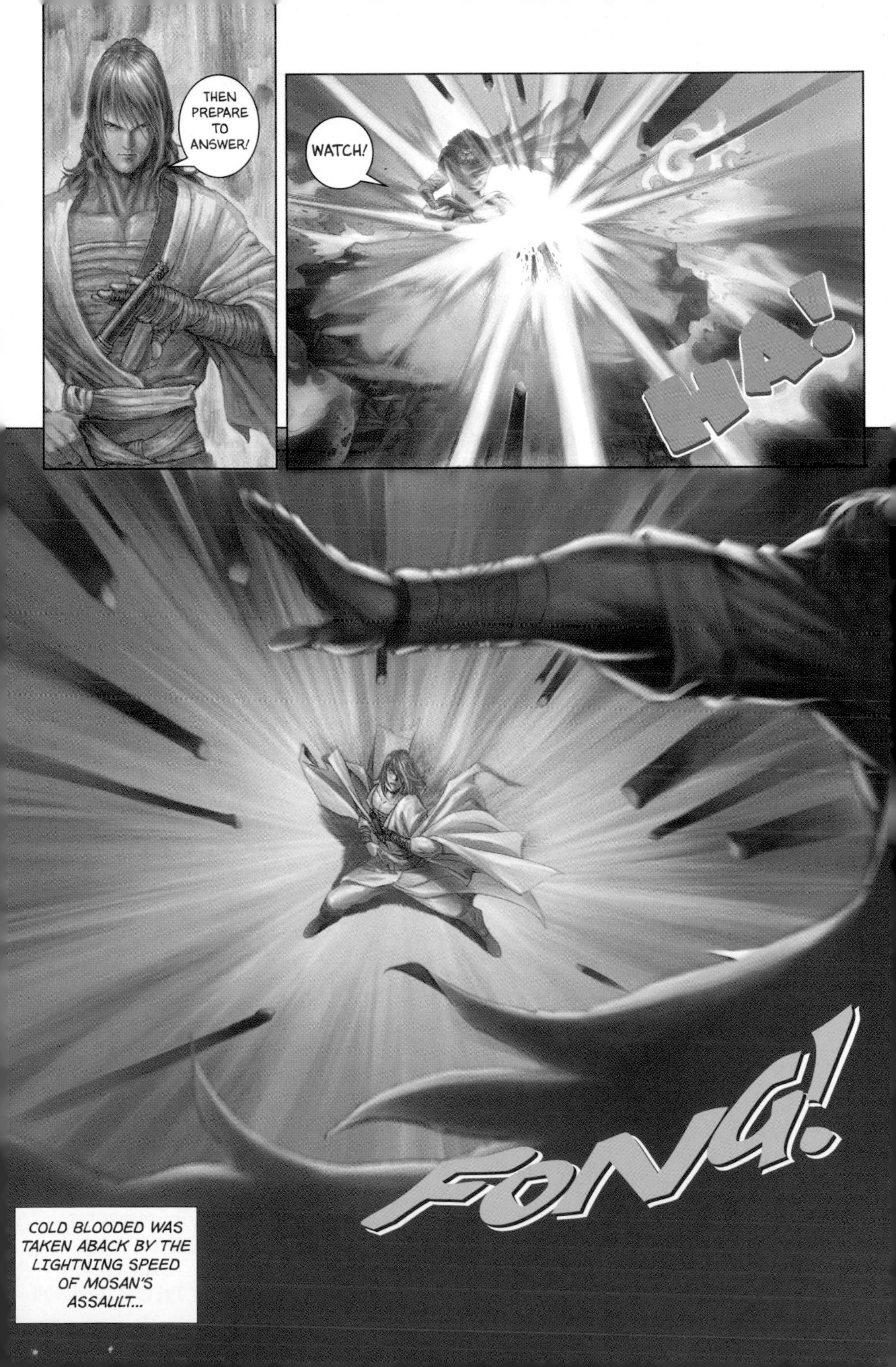
THEN PREPARE TO ANSWER!
WATCH!
HA!
FONG!
COLD BLOODED WAS TAKEN ABACK BY THE LIGHTNING SPEED OF MOSAN'S ASSAULT...

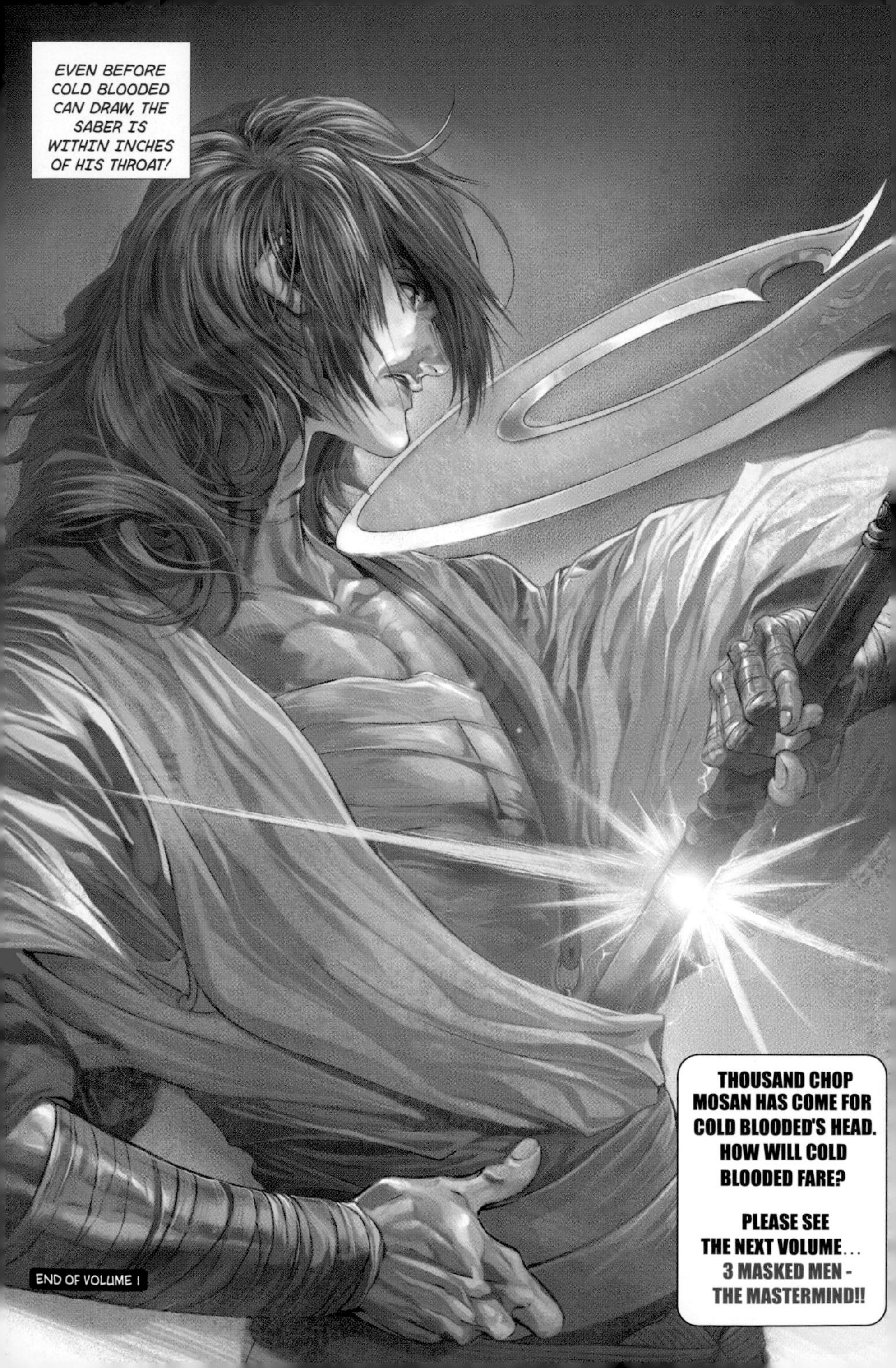
EVEN BEFORE COLD BLOODED CAN DRAW, THE SABER IS WITHIN INCHES OF HIS THROAT!
THOUSAND CHOP MOSAN HAS COME FOR COLD BLOODED'S HEAD. HOW WILL COLD BLOODED FARE?
PLEASE SEE THE NEXT VOLUME... 3 MASKED MEN - THE MASTERMIND!!
END OF VOLUME 1

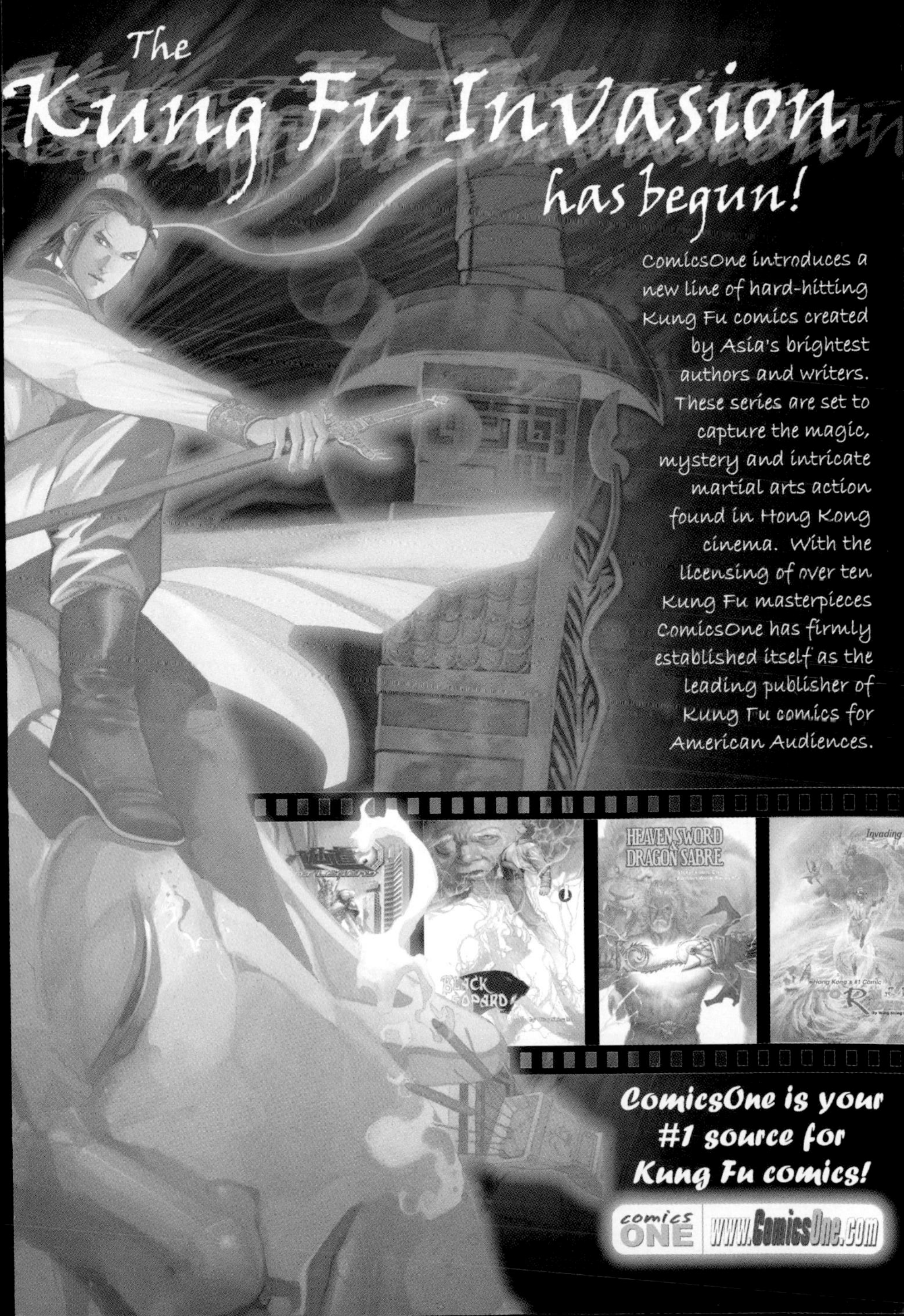
The Kung Fu Invasion has begun!
ComicsOne introduces a new line of hard-hitting Kung Fu comics created by Asia's brightest authors and writers. These series are set to capture the magic, mystery and intricate martial arts action found in Hong Kong cinema. With the licensing of over ten Kung Fu masterpieces ComicsOne has firmly established itself as the leading publisher of Kung Fu comics for American Audiences.
HEAVEN SWORD & DRAGON SABRE
ComicsOne is your #1 source for Kung Fu comics!
comics ONE
www.ComicsOne.com

# Weapons of the Gods

In Ancient China, Celestial Goddess was locked in battle with the Dark Spirit. She used five colored stones to create a magical weapon known as Heaven's Crystal. One hundred years later, Heaven's Crystal disappears. Now, evil forces are trying to use Tiger Soul to destroy the world. Our hero, Tian, must search for Heaven's Crystal; only its power can defeat the fearful might of Tiger Soul.

*Full Color Graphic Novel*

# SHAOLIN SOCCER

Young kung fu adept "Sing" is a honor-bound disciple of the legendary Shaolin Temple. His sole goal in life is to find a way to package the philosophy and physical teachings of his beloved Shaolin kung fu so that contemporary masses can learn, benefit and apply these doctrines to their daily life. When he hooks up with a former soccer champion - Golden Leg he quickly realizes that the world's most popular sport may just be the vehicle to spread Shaolin kung fu all over the globe. But first he must assemble a team worthy of the Shaolin name and learn how to play soccer himself. Yet his secular, out of shape former kung fu brothers are far from impressed with his idea. Shaolin Soccer is the hilarious comic book adaptation of Steven Chow's incredibly popular Hong Kong movie of the same name. Kung fu action and sidesplitting comedy are heading your way!

comics ONE | www.ComicsOne.com

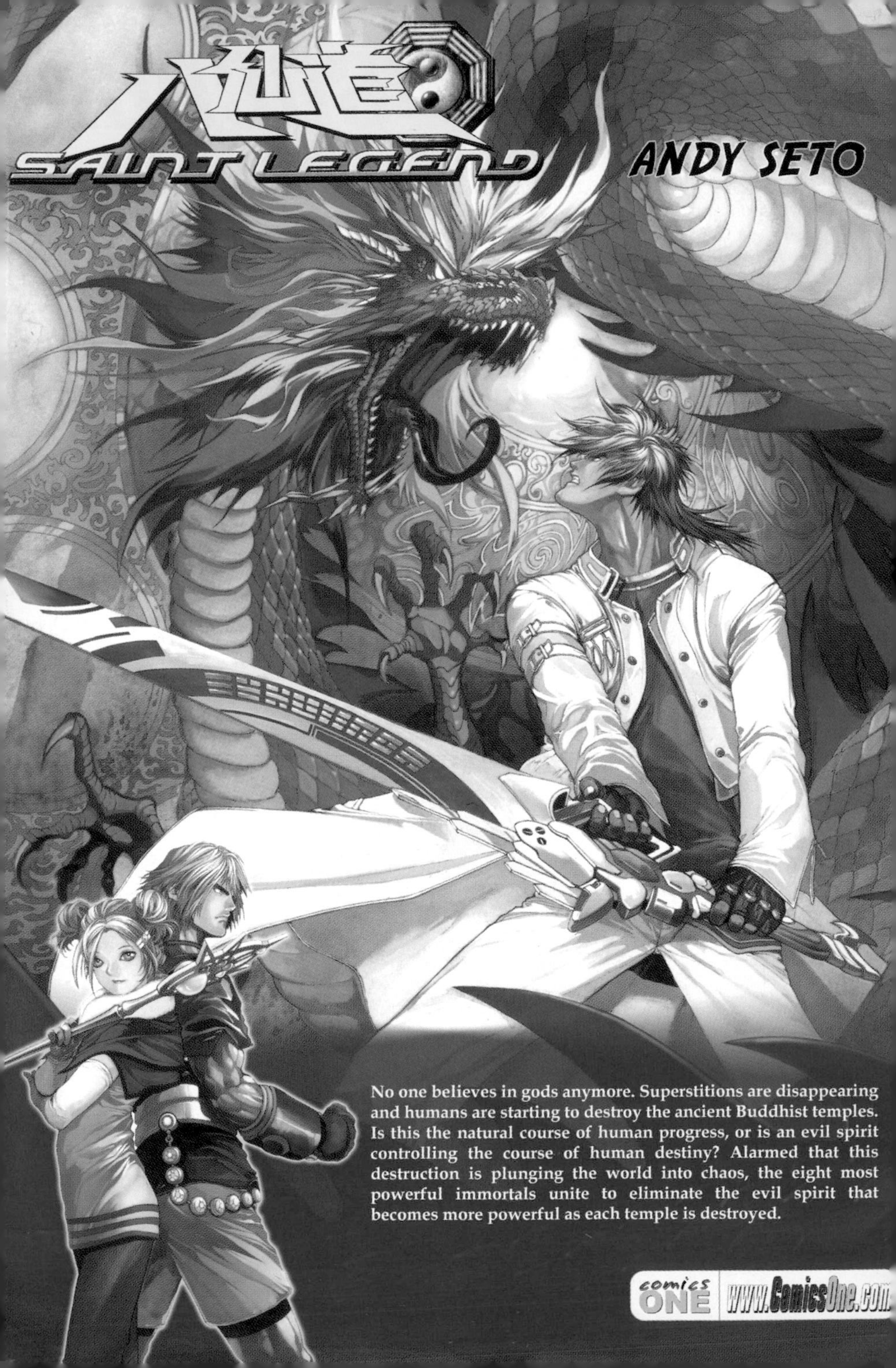
SAINT LEGEND
ANDY SETO
No one believes in gods anymore. Superstitions are disappearing and humans are starting to destroy the ancient Buddhist temples. Is this the natural course of human progress, or is an evil spirit controlling the course of human destiny? Alarmed that this destruction is plunging the world into chaos, the eight most powerful immortals unite to eliminate the evil spirit that becomes more powerful as each temple is destroyed.
comics ONE
www.ComicsOne.com